Hope for Families

My Hope for you is To
provide Hope for Families
wherever you are!

Margaret Sawin

1983

Hope for Families

Margaret M. Sawin

Library of Congress Catalog Card Number: 81-86265
ISBN: 0-8215-9902-X
123456789/98765432

Published by
William H. Sadlier, Inc.
11 Park Place
New York, NY 10007

Managing Editor: Gerald A. Johannsen
Project Editor: James T. Morgan
Art Director/Designer: Gail Schneider

Printed in the United States of America

Acknowledgements

"Cluster Poem" from *Christian Education in Family Clusters*, Mel Williams and Mary Ann Brittain, © 1982 Judson Press. Used by permission of Judson Press.

Cover Photo Credits

John Lei: bottom left
Mark Mittelman: center right
J. Gerard Smith: bottom right
Pat Walsh from J. Gerard Smith Associates: top
Lenore Weber from Omni-Photo Communications: center left

Hope for Families

Stories of Family Clusters in Diverse Settings

Edited by
Margaret M. Sawin

Sadlier

New York   Los Angeles   Chicago

Dedicated to leaders of
Family Clusters
around the world...

who have facilitated
families in their
growth processes;
thereby, growing
themselves.

Table of Contents

Foreword

The family is now in a most important transition. It could result in what is perhaps the greatest evolutionary leap since families began. Many people looking at this transition feel that the family is being destroyed. I believe the changes we see are the growth pangs for new possibilities compatible with our new knowledge of how people can be.

I believe that humanity as a whole is undergoing profound change. The main thrust of that change is that we are now able to look at the potentials of human beings, rather than concentrating only on, and emphasizing, the limitations. For so long, we have been looking at how we are *not*, instead of how we *are* and *can be*.

Until roughly 1955, the acceptable model of the family was very rigid and limited. Somewhat caricatured, the model could be described as follows.

Each woman was expected to find "Mr. Right" before she was twenty-three years old, become a mother, stay at home and raise children, and then sacrificially, and hopefully gracefully, fill out her days being a helping grandmother. She was expected to be giving, understanding and soft, and to be in charge of the emotional life of the family. Her role was to support her husband, further his career, and put her needs secondary to his, and to remain dependent on her man. In return, she was to be taken care of.

The young man was to find a "helpmate" before he was twenty-five years old who was expected to further his ambitions and be his unseen strength. He was to choose a way to make a living, work hard at the same job until retirement, save money for old age, and die prematurely thereafter. He was expected to be aggressive, fearless, a wise judge in all matters, and the total man of the house. He never really was expected to be counted in the emotional life of the family. His role was to be the financial provider and the behavior-shaper.

To fit the expectations of the acceptable model, the couple was to live happily ever after despite their experience of the relationship. It was a variation of "you made your bed, now lie in it." Some people could make that work.

Each young man and woman was expected to be mature enough to choose wisely at the tender ages between eighteen and twenty-five; thus, there was to be no mistake in their choice of a mate. If they later found that there was agony in the relationship, it became a matter of blame and failure on someone's part. And the courts upheld this through an adversary system.

"Endure your fate" was the rule. Not to do so would bring down the wrath of "What will people say?", and probably would result in one's becoming a social outcast, and almost certainly would bring psychological or premature physical death.

To be unmarried after age twenty-eight or thirty meant you were unacceptable. To be divorced meant you were a failure. To want a career, if you were a woman, meant you were unfeminine and turning your back on motherhood. If you were a man and experienced fear or sadness or cried, it meant you were unmasculine and weak. To want to have an exciting, stimulating life after marriage, whether you were the husband or the wife, meant you were deserting your family or, at best, were very unusual.

One mitigating circumstance that kept you peripherially in the social fold was if your mate died and you became a widow or widower. Then, you became a moderately acceptable fifth wheel.

These were all powerful restraints to keep some real human issues like pain, dissatisfaction, and loneliness from being revealed. They were, however, often seen in other forms—isolation, fear of rejection, resentment, self doubt, fear, alcoholism, drug use, violence, sickness, depression, and chronic dependency. Deprivation of the human spirit and a limitation in experiences of joyful living were seen as necessary to keep the status quo.

We cannot ignore the fact that individual human misery, interpersonal sterility, disappointment, and national and international calamities beset us on every side. Many of these outcomes can be related to the learning we had about how to be a person. This we learned in our families. It must be clear to anyone who pauses to observe that all adults are children grown big, carrying with them what they learned as children and acting on that learning as adults.

Now, we are beginning to see the potential of human beings, and we are slowly learning new ways to be more fully human. We are beginning to realize that having joy in our lives, feeling a connection with our Creator, and loving ourselves is the best way to change ourselves and our world in positive ways. The family is where this is learned.

New possibilities based on developing health and wellness started as a slow trickle in about 1954, and have been emerging slowly ever since. Now, twenty-seven years later, the consciousness about human beings has changed sufficiently so that we can begin to challenge our old limited ideas about people and families.

One result of this change of consciousness is that we are seeing new attitudes about what constitutes a family and new family forms. We are seeing one-parent families, blended families, co-parenting, extended families. It is important to recognize that where the people in any family see themselves as whole, the family can be a first-rate nurturing family, whether it has a traditional or new form. I believe the new family forms we are seeing represent the evolution of, not the destruction of, families. The potential for new vitality and joy within the family is very great. However, the sledding is not always easy. Pioneers do not always travel smooth roads, and intervention is sometimes necessary.

A logical point of intervention is to offer the families to be and the families currently developing some new possibilities for loving, sharing, and becoming more fully human.

Margaret Sawin presents in *Hope for Families* the Family Cluster Model, a model based on love, joy, and connection with the Source of our origin. It offers a positive point of intervention in families, a manifestation of, and a promising model for, showing families how to become more fully human.

Virginia M. Satir
Menlo Park, CA

Preface

The inspiration for this book came first from Lucinda Sangree and Ron Hunsicker, as they shared with me many insights and thoughts about Family Clusters. During these conversations, they persuaded me that there was a need for a compilation of stories about clusters.

The best way to find out about how clusters function is to go to persons who instigate and lead them! I appreciate the enthusiastic response the authors of this text expressed when invited to write chapters. They came from many different settings, but at heart all had interest in helping families to live their religious faith more fully. To the contributors of these case studies, I extend my heartfelt appreciation; for without their stories, there would be no book!

Likewise, the three respondents wrote out of their competencies and experiences and "responded" in full measure to the case studies. Virginia Satir, who has been a model of mine for many years, graciously consented to write the Foreword. To them I offer sincere appreciation.

Thousands of people have been trained for leadership of Family Clusters at many training events in the United States and abroad. My life as a traveling consultant is made joyous through the many friendships I have among those people. They have taken me into their homes, shared family living with me, and made traveling a source of tangible love and concern. For them, I give thanks.

The editors of Sadlier Publishing Company have provided insight, correction, and inspiration to keep at the book. These persons were Jim Morgan with whom I worked directly and Warner Hutchinson. To them I give thanks.

I continue to be blessed with loving "family" in the persons of Liz and Trevor Ewell; faithful friends who sustain and uphold me in all kinds of experiences; and by my brother—William Sawin—and sister—Anita Sawin MacKenzie. For them I give praise.

To those of you who read this volume, I hope the challenge of working with families will prod you to begin experimenting with ways families can grow and learn about faith living for such a time as this.

"The Word became a human being and lived among us (in a family). We saw his glory, full of grace and truth." (John 1:14, *Good News for Modern Man*)

Margaret M. Sawin
Rochester, N.Y.

The Family Cluster: Providing Hope for Families

Margaret M. Sawin

Hope for families—such nostalgic words! A decade ago we heard the family was dying, and it was popular to respond in negative fashion when questions were addressed about the fate of the family.

Today the emphasis has changed to one of admiration and respect for the family unit as it struggles to maintain its place in a fast changing society. The unit has few models from which to learn about survival without the presence of the extended family. It has no social advocate for teaching skills to live satisfactorily in relationship amidst constant change. The situation is like a oneway street; social institutions place more and more demands on the family, but no institution reciprocates by helping the family learn ways of coping and relating amidst the heavy demands.

The human potential movement of the sixties taught us how to use change as growth points for the individual. The present decade will be noted for using change as growth points within human systems, of which the family has the deepest impact. One way growth has taken place within families is through intentional, planned activities, such as found in family enrichment models.

The oldest and most extensively used of these models is the Family Cluster, developed in 1970. Since that time Family Clusters have spread around the world in churches of all sizes and denominations of all faiths. It has been utilized by some social work agencies and mental health units. The emphasis on systems has helped institutions to realize a new need for working with the complete family, as a unit.

This book is a compilation of case studies about Family Clusters from around the world. How they facilitated families in growth practices has provided "hope for families" as a norm for religious living.

What Is Enrichment?

"The basic meaning of the word 'enrichment' is to improve the quality of whatever is referred to," writes David Mace. It is "drawing from inside what is already there, latent and hitherto unappropriated, and allowing it to function. It is closely related to the concept of realizing potential. It may also be seen as achieving an optimal state of health."[1]

Because of this century's advances in technology and in the behavioral sciences, people have been afforded the leisure time and skills to better enrich their lives. It is also an expression of God at work in the betterment of people's lives, as a new era of history appears on the horizon.

The history of modern-day enrichment started with Abraham Maslow in the sixties when he researched and wrote about self-actualizing *individuals. Marriage* enrichment for couples emerged, as determined by the works of Father Gabriel Calvo in Spain and David and Vera Mace in the United States. *Parent-child* enrichment was brought into prominence in the seventies by Thomas Gordon with his book and program, *Parent Effectiveness Training. Family* enrichment, for the complete family unit, began in 1970 with the development of the Family Cluster Model by Margaret Sawin in Rochester, New York, and a similar model by Herbert Otto in California. A number of other models dealing with families have emerged in the past decade.

Family enrichment is based on the need to intervene preventively at a stage of family development when the members can be given insights, skills, and tools enabling them to deal successfully with their inter-personal relationships within the family circle. With the development of the Family Cluster the concept of support was added whereby families could be part of a sustaining group which would encourage mutuality. Because families face the stresses and pressures of a fast-paced society, they need to develop techniques and understanding in order to

- learn of problems in advance
- learn skills related to living together
- keep authentic intimacy
- celebrate life.

In contrast, most agencies which work with families in our society operate from the medical model of sickness. This model suggests that growth comes from pathology and crisis. Ironically, a family needs to become dysfunctional before it gets any help. Few agencies work from the enrichment model of wellness which advocates growth as a normal part of living and which can be intentionally planned.

In the case studies presented in this volume, the reader can see the evolving and positive process of enrichment within the Family Cluster Model. Not only do families grow and use tapped potential but they also acquire preventive skills to face minor crises and changes in day-to-day living.

What Is a Family Cluster?

"A Family Cluster is a group of four or five complete family units which contract to meet together periodically over an extended period of time for shared educational experiences related to their living in relationship within their families. A cluster provides mutual support, training in skills which facilitate the family living in relationship, and celebration of their life and beliefs together. A family unit is composed of any persons who live in relationship with one another, i.e. a nuclear family, a one-parent family, a couple without children, one or more persons who live in one household."[2] The group also becomes a place of caring and sharing between individuals, generations, and family units.

Basic Characteristics of a Family Cluster

There are five synthesizing concepts from basic disciplines of theory and research which provide undergirding to the model. The *foundation* of the model is using complete family units as the base for membership. Families bring their own energies to the cluster group which make for stability and vitality. Functioning families gain strengths from the way they interact with each other. Because the family system is an intricate network, it is greater than the sum of its members; it is exponential in its influence. Each family member brings to the cluster unique resources and each family unit can bring a sense of health and well-being.

The *strength* of the model is having a small group which develops support and gives feedback to family members. A prime way this takes place is through the contract or written agreement. By the contract

1 all members of each family commit themselves to be integral parts of the cluster for a prescribed length of time

2 the cluster group makes its covenant based on expectations, issues of time, decision-making, interactions, so that everyone—no matter what his/her age—agrees to the elements within the contract and signs it as a commitment.

Lucinda Sangree says that contracting is the "gem" of the Family Cluster model and helps determine the success of the involvement on the part of all family members.[3] What can happen when everyone is *not* involved in contracting is evident in several case studies. Often members in a cluster become close and provide a caring group, sometimes beyond the contracted time. This cohesiveness can become a "koinonia" type of sacred community[4] or what may be known as a "faith family." The latter is defined as a group of families which develop a way of living stemming from their faith styles and close support for each other.

The *outcome* of the cluster is change, followed by growth which can lead toward fulfillment or actualization, as Maslow puts it.[5] Because the family has the greatest influence on its members, growth needs to be fostered within the unit as well as within individuals. Between the family system and the members of it, there exists a constant influence and mutual reenforcement of growth patterns.

The cluster group can also become a system which lends its support to the growth/change process within the family and between family units. The family begins to change, to receive feedback from the group, and to move in the direction of growth important to its members. A cycle of intentional growth is started which is the kind of growth needed in a world of rapid social change. Families are encouraged to build on their strengths, dreams, and hopes as springboards to further growth.

A systems approach to growth makes for more potency in people than an individual approach. The authors of *No Single Thread* attest to this from working with families in a research setting.

> "... the systems approach was more apt to reveal the strengths of a family while the individual, 'composite' approach ... more often highlighted the family problems."[6]

The *method* of the process used is that of experiential education. Reflecting on one's experiences becomes the content or "meat" of the learning. The content/subject areas are determined by the families' interests, hopes, questions, concerns, and problems. This expression is enhanced through using creative techniques, i.e.,

- role play
- clay modeling
- relational exercises
- puppetry
- finger painting
- games and songs.

These are not only enjoyable to do but also germane to the expression of family interests. Children enjoy such activities, although many adults feel they are not learning while participating in such. This bias is particularly true of men and is illustrated in the London case study. Educational institutions put so much emphasis on cerebral learning that the introduction of experiential learning can be threatening to some people. The leaders of the cluster need to take time and effort to help a group reach conclusive thinking about such learning. Experiential education introduces learning from a cognitive standpoint as well as an affective one. Therefore, it utilizes all the learning capabilities within individuals which affect attitudes as well as ideas.

After participating in an experience, the group has reflective sharing. Usually the children "hang in" during these parts of the learning process. When the group moves into the didactic phases of analyzing and generalizing, young children will go to the play corner. From these discussions, future action can be determined by the older children, teenagers, and adults. Finally, helping a family to learn skills of implementation completes the cycle of experiential learning.

The *interpretation* of these experiences is accomplished through the medium of process theology in which lived experiences are interpreted theologically. The individuals and the families tell their own stories of faith from which theologizing is done. Scriptural truths are included to help interpret how people have dealt with human problems throughout history. Since all of life's experiences may have sacred interpretations, every occasion can become a setting for learning about one's life within a faith context.

These five areas of knowledge contribute to the philosophical foundations of the model:

1 family systems
2 group dynamics
3 potential for growth
4 experiential learning
5 process theology.

It is the synthesizing experiences of these five dynamics which give the model validity and allow for replication in diverse settings.

Case Study Implementation

The case studies which follow tell of the adaptability of the Family Cluster in diverse settings: churches of large and small denominations, a family service agency, a public school setting, with military families, in ecumenical settings, and among people of faith in Australia, England, and Canada. They point up the validity of the model as it has been replicated in various locations.

Three respondents were invited to reflect on the case studies and share how they saw:

1 families being affected by the cluster, and the cluster being affected by the families—written by Ronald Hunsicker

2 the cluster group process facilitating families as they struggle with group commitment—written by Lucinda Sangree

3 theological beliefs being expressed through the cluster experience—written by Robert Stamschror.

The case studies demonstrate the process of enrichment, "drawing from inside what is already there, latent and hitherto unappropriated, and allowing it to function."[7] This experience is not only true of Family Clusters, but also appears to be expressed in other models of family enrichment, as shared by Joyce Space in her "Review of the Research on Family Enrichment Programs":

> "It appears that many families in family enrichment programs are finding 'something' that contributes to their feeling more positive about their family and individual lives."[8]

The combination of family systems and individuals of various ages makes for a variety of responses. Add experiential learning and intentional theologizing to this mix, and positive growth can occur.

Often they bring new strength to a congregation because family growth was stimulated by a support group.

Goals of Family Clusters

From its inception, basic goals for the Family Cluster were established to serve as guidelines. They are listed as follows with brief examples from case studies of how each was achieved:

1 To provide an intergenerational group of family units where children can relate easily to adults and adults to children

This was shown in all the case studies. All had children, and many had adolescents. Clusters would be more balanced if single persons and senior adults were a part.

2 To provide a group which can grow in support and mutuality for its members

Most accounts indicated this goal had been reached. Several clusters continued informally after they had ended contractually. A few mentioned that they wanted to continue when the time limit was not as long as is suggested in the use of the model.

3 To provide a group where parents gain perspective about their own children through contact with other children and other adults' perceptions of their children; likewise, where children can gain perspective about their own parents through contact with other parents and other children's perceptions of their parents

A number of accounts suggested that this happened. Families wanted to know if others are "like us" but have few places where they can check it out gracefully. Family life is so privatized in our culture that this aspect needs to be intentionalized. Many people feel they are the only ones with certain kinds of problems.

4 To provide an opportunity for families to consider experiences seriously as they affect them as individuals, as family members, as group members, and as members of a faith community

This goal might be better implemented and probably is when leaders have more skills in fostering family discussions. When leaders reported groups doing this, it often lasted for just one session. Serious topics can be handled frequently for three to four sessions where cluster leaders have skills and knowledge in the areas of concern.

5 To provide a group wherein there is opportunity for families to model for each other aspects of their family systems in communication, decision-making, interrelating, problem-solving

This goal was met implicitly at times and is overtly stated in several studies. In cluster, children model from older children, as well as from adolescents and adults. Teenagers model from the adults, and adults model from each other. Where there are differing family lifestyles, it is important to have an opportunity to explore and to share these in a pluralistic society.

6 To provide a joint experience between generations where adults can share their concerns regarding the meaning of life's experiences for them during a time of rapid social change and redefinition of traditional values; children can deal realistically with their experiences, using the group as a gauge against which to check out the validity of their experiences

There did not seem to be much written evidence of this in the studies; it could be more intentional in the planning. Sometimes these concerns surface slowly and are more evident from outspoken adolescents. Often when adults say they want more biblical material, they mean they want confirmation of their values so as not to feel "lost." Most of us have not been taught to consider valuing within a pluralistic context where there are many ways of deciding a hierarchy of values.

7 To help families discover and develop their strengths through increased loving, caring, enjoying, and creating

This point was covered many times in the studies. Functional families naturally have many of these characteristics, and cluster gives the more hesitant families permission to try to achieve more depth in these areas.

8 To provide an opportunity for positive intervention into family systems so as to facilitate their living and growing together more productively

This seemed to occur when family members had great insight, or when a highly skilled leader guided it. It is most noticeable in the account from the Toronto Family Service agency.

Starting Clusters

How do Family Clusters get started? Most often it is initiated by a lay individual, usually a woman, who has a concern for bettering family life within a congregation or agency. There is a desire for change and a vision of how to obtain it. Many such persons attend a training event and then are ready to start. Many churches use it as an alternative to their traditional religious education programs. The use of the classroom approach with individuals in peer groupings is the traditional way of structured religious education. This model was copied from public schools and their style of teaching facts and skills. However, learning a religious lifestyle is *not* like learning to read, write and count. John Westerhoff proposes that the schooling-instruction model needs to be replaced "with a community of faith enculturation in which the community of faith is the context and interactions between generations are the means of education." For learning a faith life-style, he suggests a community/ socialization model have four ingredients:

1 a clear identity of the group
2 the intimacy of a small group
3 intergenerational contacts
4 role diversity and exchange.[9]

Churches need to decide their primary purpose of education and adapt the model which will best communicate that purpose. Also, the church must begin to conceptualize the systems approach in working with individuals in order to carry out an authentic family educational approach to religious nurturing.

Ritualizing in the Cluster

Ritualizing and celebrating have lost some of their impact in today's world, yet they are important to the stability and ongoing-ness of family life. Rituals often provide acknowledgement of the intangible realities that exist between human beings such as love, trust, faith, and goodness. Many persons no longer find meaning in the traditional forms of religious ritual and could benefit from developing new ones. Clusters often develop their own rituals of grace before meals, closure and farewell, affirmation and recognition of special events. The cluster stories tell of some of these rituals and the meanings given to them by individuals and families. The Raleigh, North Carolina Cluster even put some of its rituals into a poem! Families in the Air Force Cluster aroused the curiosity of others from rituals they developed.

Often, developing rituals in a cluster can have a carry-over to the family when they use them at home. Or some family rituals may be shared in the cluster, thus giving credence to the act of ritual-izing. Bossard and Boll wrote that "the overall conclusion that emerges from the assemblage of our material (families' reports of rituals) is that ritual is a relatively reliable index of family integra-tion."[10]

Training for Cluster Leadership

One strength which showed in the stories is that of reliable training given leaders which forms a strong focus from which to begin clusters. Learning cluster leadership skills in laboratory training allows potential leaders the opportunity to practice new skills with "real" families. The training format has been highly developed since 1972, and its authentic approach pays off in terms of how leaders learn and carry out their responsibility in a cluster. Much of the outcome of the group's process depends on the leader's

- personality characteristics
- previously learned skills
- working knowledge of the five areas of clustering
- ability to relate to a wide age range
- belief in the process.

A number of leaders have experienced also an advanced level of training after the initial one.

Training events are usually sponsored by an ongoing institution, i.e. local churches, judicatories, denominations, councils of churches, seminaries, or retreat centers. Most of the authors writing in this volume have had training at either a Family Cluster Laboratory or Workshop. Information regarding future training events is available from Family Clustering, Inc.[11]

Adaptation of the Model

Because the process mode of learning is based on the needs and wants of families involved in the cluster, it is an easy model to adapt to any type of family group. Most Family Clusters are held in church settings, partly because this is the one institution in our society which has the complete family within its clientele. Clusters have also been used in the following settings:

> diaconate training for Roman Catholic deacons
> pastoral training for Protestant seminarians
> clergy families

Jewish synagogues
family service agencies
canoe trips
camps and retreat centers
public schools which are inter-racially and inter-cultur-
ally mixed
branches of the military
expressions of holiday celebrations.

A number of the case studies have shown adaptations in time spans, size; and the Winnipeg story tells of having predominantly one-parent families.

Social change could also be accomplished through the cluster format. The nuclear unit of society is the family, and families provide the yeast for behavior within societal institutions. Families might undertake changes in their lifestyles, supported by the cluster. Healthy families could share their processes of well-being with dysfunctioning families who are beset with problems; thereby, teaching better ways of living within the family system. James Larson has written:

> "In the long run, it would seem that social change, those changes which affect the dynamics of human relationship, would be most effectively implemented when the interactional energy which exists within families be channeled for the ultimate good of society as well. We have only begun to realize the infinite possibilities available as we work together to identify and implement ways to see families fulfill their potentials as people makers and peacemakers."[12]

The London case study tells its connection with the Family Power-Social Change project of the World Council of Churches.[13] The Nova Scotia Cluster also participated in that project. Using families as a means of social change would be a new venture for our society and one which would affect family units, as well.

Conclusion

How families were affected by being in a cluster is told from evaluation reports in a number of stories. Each family is at a different stage of development, so each family receives differing attributes from being in a cluster. The uniqueness of each family helps each cluster to be a unique experience. There are surprises in every one! One cluster may have more meaning for one family then another, depending on many variables. To date, there has been no statistical evaluation of Family Clusters nor between various kinds of family enrichment models. That is an area yet to be researched.

The church could well consider a new mission for its life at the brink of the twenty-first century—that of helping families be strengthened to carry out their vital tasks as the "domestic church" or "the church which is within thy house."

> "In a family approach to religious nurturing, a model of New Testament belief is established which children observe and learn as the behavior of Christians. Adolescents are a normal part of the caring process as they participate in the behaviors of 'bondedness' and group responsibility. The adults are able to explore needed areas of change within a trust climate of freedom. The family, as a whole, can make choices and begin to intentionalize behaviors congruent with those choices. This results in productive, functional relating within the everyday life of the family when basic faith issues are explored and lived."
>
> "This can be the mission of the twentieth century congregation—to influence its families as human systems for living and growing abundantly in a world of future shock."[14]

Let us be on our way to provide *hope for families*.

Footnotes

1. David Mace. "Marriage and Family Enrichment—a New Field?" *The Family Coordinator*, July 1979, 28(3), pp. 404-419.

2. Margaret M. Sawin. *Family Enrichment With Family Clusters*. Valley Forge, Pa.: Judson Press, 1979, p. 27.

3. Lucinda Sangree. "Report and Evaluation of the Family Cluster Laboratory Process" (Written report, December 1974).

4. *koinonia*—a Greek word from the New Testament translation, meaning a mutual religious fellowship of giving and receiving which includes participation, impartation, and fellowship. From Gerhard Kittel (ed.) *Theological Dictionary of The New Testament*, vol. II, Grand Rapids, MI.: William B. Eerdmans Publishers, p. 798.

5. Abraham H. Maslow. *Toward A Psychology of Being*. Princeton, N.J.: D. Van Nostrand Company, Inc., 1962, p. 23.

6. Jerry M. Lewis, Robert W. Beavers, J.T. Gossett, and Virginia Austin Phillips. *No Single Thread: Psychological Health in Family Systems*. New York: Brunner/Mazel, Publishers, 1976, p. 204.

7. Mace, *op. cit.*

8. Joyce Space. "A Review of Research on Family Enrichment Programs." Unpublished manuscript for the Center for the Study of Helping Services, Graduate School of Education and Human Development. University of Rochester, Rochester, N.Y., 1980, p. 36.

9. John Westerhoff III. *Will Our Children Have Faith?* New York: A Crossroad Book, imprint of the Seabury Press, Inc., 1976, pp. 52-54.

10. James H. S. Bossard and Eleanor S. Boll. *Ritual in Family Living*. Philadelphia: University of Pennsylvania Press, 1950, p. 203.

11. Family Clustering, Inc.—P.O. Box 18074—Rochester, N.Y. 14618. Tel. (716) 244-0882 or 232-3530 (ans. serv.)

12. Jim Larson. "The Family and Social Change," *Family Life*, XXXIX: (4), July-Aug., 1979, pp. 12-13. (A publication of the American Institute of Family Relations, Los Angeles).

13. "Family Power, Social Change" produced by the Family Ministries Office of the World Council of Churches, Geneva, Switzerland, 1976.

14. Sawin, *op. cit.*, pp. 23-24.

Church-oriented Clusters

Most Family Clusters meet as an alternative to the traditional program of religious education and usually are under the sponsorship of a local congregation. There are three stories of clusters sponsored in this manner:

1 *A "Peace" of a Cluster* by Elaine Clymer
   A Mennonite cluster with its tradition of peace orientation.

2 *Reorganized Church of Jesus Christ of Latter Day Saints* by Carol and Joe Anway
   A cluster in a small denomination which is attempting to emphasize family life.

3 *Family Cluster in the Unitarian Church* by Joyce Space with Susan Maybeck
   A liberal church which has had Family Clusters many years.

A "Peace" of a Cluster

Elaine Clymer

Elkhart, Indiana

In February 1977, I received my first exposure to the Family Cluster idea during a weekend Workshop with Margaret Sawin in Elkhart, Indiana, where I live. I was excited to find a new method of forming intergenerational relationships in a church setting. A weekend seemed insufficient exposure, so I looked for additional training. My congregation, Belmont Mennonite Church, sponsored my attendance at a week-long Training Laboratory at New Windsor, Maryland the following summer. That week was a growing experience for me, as I learned how to organize a Family Cluster. When I returned, I hoped to use my new training within my congregation. Our church was already divided into "clusters." They were based on a model that did not necessarily include children but the task was to process congregational issues. However, my first opportunity to lead a Family Cluster was in another Mennonite congregation in Elkhart, the South Side Fellowship.

Sponsorship

I became acquainted with a woman from South Side Fellowship while we were working together on a community project. We began to share some of my experiences in Family Cluster training, plus my desire to lead a Family Cluster. She attended her church's Nurture Commission to discover if they would be interested in promoting Family Clusters within their congregation. She was also a part of a small group composed of five adult couples who had been meeting regularly once a week for more than a year. This group had an additional meeting usually once a month when they included their children for an evening of fun and games, but the group was beginning to feel that this was not enough contact with the children. I met one time with the adults to help them understand what Family Clustering was about, and they accepted the suggestion to have a Family Cluster experience. They asked me to lead their group in a six-week session around the theme of "Peace."

Leadership

I looked for someone to help me co-lead the group, since I had found how essential a co-leader is for effective leadership from my training. I found another woman from my congregation who had attended the same weekend Workshop with Margaret Sawin. Even though she had not attended the weeklong Training Laboratory, she consented to help me.

My co-leader, Letha Ressler, had experience in working with children through teaching in a nearby nursery school, as well as getting a degree in special education. She had chaired the Nurture Commission within our own congregation and had deep concerns about the education and the relationships children have with adults. She had been an effective leader in many other groups. Being outgoing, friendly, and assertive, these gifts helped her to be a good leader.

I had worked with children before, both elementary and secondary students. I had taught Summer Bible School, Sunday School and led various groups within the church. Both of us leaders liked music, but my co-leader did not enjoy leading songs. Neither of us played guitar which would have been helpful in informal singing; though one of the group members did play the guitar, so he helped us quite often.

My co-leader and I seemed to work well together, both in our planning sessions and in our group leadership. We were able to "look out" for each other and fill in when needed or remind each other when something was missed. Both of us were able to bring creative ideas and resources to our planning sessions.

We had a few problems as leaders. We each lacked experience in leading a Family Cluster and, therefore, were not always sure how to program effectively. However, this kind of experience comes only in doing the task. Occasionally, it would have been better to have had three leaders instead of two. I was sick for one session and could not attend; if we would have had a third leader, my co-leader would not have had to lead that session by herself.

Families

Here is an outline of each family constellation:

Family A	Family B	Family C	Family D	Family E
Father	Father	Father	Father	Father
Mother	Mother	Mother	Mother	Mother
Boy—7	Boy—1	Girl—12	Girl—9	Girl—3
Girl—3		Twins—9	Girl—7	Girl—less
		(Boy/girl)		than 1 year

The adults in the group were mostly in the 30-40 year-old range. Three of the five families had one or two children five years-old or younger. The other two families had school-age children up to about twelve-years-old. The children's ages ranged from about one-year to twelve-years of age. There were no adolescents. Since the nine-year-old twin boy was the only boy in his age group, he seemed to lack identity with the total group, although the adult men tried to help him feel included.

Two families had very young children; consequently, some of their time within the session was spent on child care and, at times, prevented them from becoming involved in the activities. The older children seemed to enjoy helping with the younger children. This may have happened because the children knew each other prior to the cluster experience. Also, it may have given them a sense of responsibility.

The families seemed basically well adjusted to each other with the normal amount of "give-and-take" which happens in most groups. The adults were exceptionally sensitive to the values of self-awareness, self-identity, and developing good relationships within and outside the family structure. Most of the adults were warm, outgoing, and willing to relate to people outside their immediate family structure. They were exceptionally aware of current theological and relational issues. Many were in professions which, I think, helped them to be open and caring. The group's make-up made it a very easy group with which to work. My co-leader and I felt fortunate to have such a good group with which to work for our initial experience in Family Clustering.

Contracting

Since the group was already in existence before we began, we did not have contracting with individual families other than a brief time during our meeting with the adults before the sessions began. There was already a commitment on their part to be there, since they decided as a group to do this. The contracting with the group as a whole was difficult. They did not seem to feel the need to state verbally the expectations they had previously used in their group process. We tried to encourage them to state their expectations about who was to be responsible for the children. One of the members queried about the need for doing this when it could be done as it always had been done before.

One of the advantages of working with a group that has been in prior existence is they have already worked through some basic expectations. One of the disadvantages is that it is easy to take too much for granted. Perhaps in this kind of situation, contracting is of more importance for the leaders' benefit so that they know the expectations of the group and the group can know what the leaders expect. We leaders might have taken more initiative to let the group know what we expected. An example of this was that we expected to be notified before each session if someone was not going to be there. The first time after this happened, we realized this should have been made clearer in our contracting.

Because the adults had been meeting as a group prior to the Family Cluster sessions, they had the advantage of knowing each other better than the children. We did not have to spend as much time getting acquainted as if the group was newly formed. Because the group knew each other fairly well, we could spend more time in personalizing the theme. However, because the group knew each other so well, some assumptions might have been made about past relationships that affected the present relationships. Also, the adults had to find new ways of relating to each other and to each other's children. This did not appear to be too difficult for most of them to do.

During the six weeks that we met, the group built good rapport, especially with the children. The children seemed to look forward and appreciate the cluster activities. They wanted to repeat certain activities, such as the "Scotland's Burning" song, done with dancing motions. Six weeks together was too short. The children seemed to sense this the most, because the adults planned to continue to meet together again after the Family Cluster sessions were finished. There was not a "conclusion" or ending in the same way clusters often feel when they will not be meeting again as a group.

When we began contracting, we agreed that Sunday evenings were the best time to meet. However, the sessions were to be kept brief (5:15 to 8:30 P.M.) because there were young children as well as school-age children needing to get up for school the next morning. The 5:15 P.M. starting time was chosen so we could eat a snack lunch together at the beginning.

The group agreed to meet in the basement of one of the cluster families' home. This basement was a large, open but narrow room and seemed ideally suited for cluster activities. There were already toys there with which the children could play, a piano, and a picnic table. The family accommodated us by rearranging the furniture each time we met so we would have more space. They also had some gymnastic mats so there was enough room for everyone to sit on the floor. The family agreed also to allow various articles and decorations to stay up on the walls from week to week so we could have a "cluster room" atmosphere.

The Learning Experience

We spent all six sessions on the theme of "peace." We focused on peace within the family as a way of looking at peace issues, since the leaders felt this would be more realistic for children than global peace issues. Also, adults tend often to intellectualize unrealistically such issues while glossing over their own family problems.

There were several activities the group greatly seemed to enjoy. One activity we did on the first evening was an echo-pantomime drama of the story of the Good Samaritan in which the leader acts and says a line, after which the rest of the group mirrors a response. Another activity which everyone seemed to enjoy was singing. We tried to include fun and action songs such as the "Butterfly Song" (in *In Song, Assembly Church*, Assembly Mennonite Church, Goshen, Ind., 1976.) and "Scotland's Burning" along with songs of love and peace—"Magic Penny" and "I've Got Peace Like a River." We used "Let There Be Peace on Earth" as our theme song.

The activity that seemed to be the most difficult to do was held at the last session. Each family was to make a banner from burlap and fabric scraps that would symbolize their family. For the two families with very young children, it meant that the parents did most of the work themselves. One of the older children became frustrated when her family could not finish in the alloted time of 45 minutes to one hour. But in spite of these problems the banners were very beautiful and creative. The families seemed proud of them. After the cluster sessions were completed, the group led the Sunday morning church service, so they could share their Family Clustering experiences. They all had their banners on display in front of the congregation!

Closure

At our last session, after the banners were made, we did a "Lemon Exercise" as a concluding experience. Each person was given a lemon and instructed to get acquainted with it. After each person felt he/she could identify the uniqueness of his/her lemon, he/she could name it. Then each person introduced his/her lemon to other people in the group. By this time most persons felt as if their lemons were themselves. Everyone then put their lemons back into the paper bag and sat in a circle with their eyes closed. We passed the lemons around the circle and as each lemon came past, the owners tried to identify their own. We let the little children peek! When everyone had his/her own lemon, we leaders tried to help the group think how the uniquenesses in lemons is similiar to the uniquenesses of people. After a time of sharing what each person felt they learned, we asked each person to share "themselves" in a concluding exercise and farewell. Everyone cut their lemon in half and squeezed out the juice to make lemonade. The children especially enjoyed squeezing, stirring and tasting our freshly made lemonade. We asked everyone to take a cup and a cookie (provided by the group) and share it with others in the group while expressing what they had learned to like about each person. We experienced a good time of sharing with our "Lemonade Communion." Many people said it was the best lemonade they ever tasted!

Evaluation

When we did our evaluation we discovered that some of the parents did not like one of the songs we had chosen as an action song. They felt that the song "Little Bunnie Foo-Foo" was not compatible with the peace theme. In the song a bunnie catches some mice and "bops" them on the head. At the time, the implications of the words did not occur to us!

One of the last steps in the cluster experience was an evaluation. Everyone, including pre-school children with parental help, was encouraged to participate. Following is a summary of the results of the survey:

—The concensus of opinion was that the Family Cluster experience was a positive one. We received much affirmation.
—Most families expressed a desire to try Family Clustering again.
—The families with school-age children were especially appreciative of the family activities.

In addition to the evaluation, I was present the Sunday morning the group presented their experiences to the congregation. Also, I did a few cluster-like activities with them to give them a taste of cluster life. This was an attempt to help the congregation learn more about Family Clustering.

In summary, I feel this experience was quite worthwhile both for the group and for us as leaders. If I were to do it again, I would like to contract with the group for at least eight sessions. I feel it would have been even more ideal to have ten or twelve sessions. I also would like to see more integenerational mix in the makeup of the group. It would have been nice to have had some older couples for "grandparents," as well as single persons. Much about the group was very good. The kinds of people made it an easy group with which to work. They were warm, outgoing people and accepting of new ideas and/or ways of doing things. I am willing to do it again!

Resources

Simon, Sidney et al. *Values Clarification.* New York: Hart Publishing Company, Inc., 1972.

Biographical Data

Elaine Clymer was a home economics teacher at Bethany Christian High School, a local Mennonite school in Elkhart and also taught a senior level "Interpersonal Relationships Class." Her husband, Jim, and their two children, Lisa and Jimmy, make up the Clymer family. She enjoys reading, sewing, gardening and talking with people.

Address:

5580 E. Pontiac Way
Fresno, CA 93727
(209) 292-8353

Reorganized Church of Jesus Christ of Latter Day Saints

**Carol Anway
Joe Anway**

Richmond, Missouri

Sponsorship

What an exciting experience it was to go to the Family Cluster Training Lab at Green Lake, Wisconsin. The week with the families and trainees was almost a magical experience in the kinds of relationships that emerged and developed in those few days. I wondered if the Family Cluster concept would work and be as effective in church congregations back home. It seemed imperative to find a ·place to try out the model presented at the Green Lake Lab and see if the concept could be translated into local terms that would bring equally rich rewards. The opportunity came more quickly than I had expected. Several families in a congregation of the Reorganized Church of Jesus Christ of Latter Day Saints (not Mormon), in Richmond, Missouri were anxious to do something that would enrich their family lives. After going through the proper administrative channels of our area administration, it was decided to share the Family Cluster Model in Richmond. The people were enthusiastic about participating. I was the only one who had received training, but my husband, Joe, had much experience in facilitating groups and was willing to help. We led the group while training other leaders through apprenticeship in the local setting.

Leaders

Four persons who expressed deep interest in participating as leaders were chosen to be part of the planning and evaluating team. My role was to help in training, to initiate planning, and to lead in evaluating. The other leaders in the planning team were to read the book, *Family Enrichment With Family Clusters*, by Margaret M. Sawin. These persons were all enthusiastic, personable, and had held positions of leadership in their local churches. They were also very interested in finding some way to enrich family life. The leadership mix was adult with three males and three females. Some of the preliminary planning was done by phone and correspondence. A calendar was developed indicating pre-cluster leadership planning sessions. Approximately a month and a half prior to the beginning of the cluster sessions the six leaders met for a general orientation session and a discussion of the philosophy of "clustering." Following the meeting, the team leaders were to share the message of Family Clustering with members of their congregation and to begin to identify those who would be interested in participating.

The team decided to start with a weekend retreat, followed by monthly meetings. Another meeting was held prior to the weekend cluster retreat. One of the difficulties involved in the planning process was that we lived a considerable distance (50 miles) from the other leaders. This made it rather difficult to get together as often as necessary for training and planning. The willingness of the other leaders to make personal preparation through assigned reading was very helpful. Planning for the weekend retreat of five sessions was done largely by the leadership team. The team worked out the objectives that were to be accomplished, the time frame, and the activities that were to be done. A leader was then assigned to each of the sessions.

Family Recruitment

Members of the congregation were informed about the impending cluster through announcements in the church bulletin and from the pulpit. Those who were interested gave their names to the Family Cluster representative. The four leaders in training also took responsibility to do some personal recruiting, while one leader made posters about it.

When families responded, they were asked to give a verbal agreement that they would attend the weekend retreat, as well as monthly meetings thereafter.

General Session Plans

The following information is included as a summary of the planning for the sessions:

Session I (Carol)   **Saturday Morning**

Objectives: To present an overview of what Family Cluster is about
To express expectations
To get acquainted and build trust
To work on group commitment (contract)

9:45-10:10	Gathering Activity-Nametags
10:10-10:25	Introduction of team members Family Huddle and each family introducing its greatest asset
10:25-10:40	Filmstrip of Family Cluster
10:45-11:05	Expectations—in small groups —presented to total group
11:05-11:20	Game—Parachute Play
11:20-11:50	Group Commitment
11:50-12:00	Closing

Session II (Betty) Early Saturday Afternoon

Objectives: To work together as a family
To learn a communication skill
To finish commitment

1:00-1:10	Group Singing
1:10-2:00	Family Collages
2:00-2:15	Game—Trust walk by pairs
2:15-2:35	Triads for listening
2:35-2:55	Family share in communication
2:55-3:00	Closing

Session III (Joe) Later Saturday Afternoon

Objectives: To emphasize the worth of each family member
To explore feelings
To consider how to respond to each other in the family

3:30-3:40 Cards hanging around neck—"I am special because ..." (sentence completed several times)

3:40-4:00 Filmstrip, *IALAC*, "I Am Loveable and Capable," Argus Communications, Niles, IL, 1974. Discussion.

4:00-4:10 Activity from *Family Enrichment Book*. Encouraging and Discouraging words.

4:10-4:40 Group discussion about encouraging and discouraging communication.

4:40-5:00 In family groups, sharing with each other what each felt was special about him/herself. Family members add to each others' lists by saying - "You are special because ...."

Session IV (LeRoy) Saturday Evening

Objectives: To worship together
To have fun together
To talk of ways our family can have fun together and with others

| 6:00-7:00 | Weiner roast |
| 7:00-7:45 | Campfire . . . |

      1 Fun songs; skits

      2 Short discussion shared on ways each family has fun together

      3 Concluding worship

Session V (Vic)   Sunday Noon

Objective: To work on decision-making as a family and as a cluster

               Activity on decision-making

               Cluster consensus on upcoming sessions

               Retreat closing

Lunch—Family-style service, with seating by place cards of family groups.

12:15-12:30	Decision-making activity.
12:30-1:00	Decision-making activity by family—remembering fun times and planning fun time for the coming month (while eating).
1:00-1:10	Summary of weekend.
1:10-1:25	Decision regarding future plans to meet as a cluster.
1:25-1:30	Closing circle using candles. "Hip, Hip, Hurray" closing. The members stood in a close circle, and large birthday candles were given to each person. A brief talk was given about ways we gain strength and "light" from each other. One of the candles was lit, and the song, "It Only Takes a Spark" started. The light was passed from individual to individual until every candle was lit. A brief prayer was offered. After the candles were extinguished, the members put their arms around each other and each gave a word expression of their feelings for the weekend. Then with three cheers, the group was concluded.
1:30-1:35	Written evaluation by all members of the cluster.

Description of Cluster Families

The cluster was composed of an interesting and diverse group. There was a good mix of ages, with nine families participating. There were six preschoolers, four children of elementary ages, eight teenagers, six adults of 20-30 years, seven adults of 30-40 years, two adults 40-50 years, and three adults over fifty. The composition of families was also very diverse. Two families brought preschoolers; two had elementary children; three had teenagers; one young family had no children; one was a retired couple, and one couple had college-age children, who were not present. One of the families was a single-parent family with a mother; she brought her own two teenagers as well as a niece and a nephew. Before the final session, we also discovered that the woman had plans to marry a man with three younger children. The cluster group voted to invite the man and his children to the final session which was a weekend slumber party. They came and seemed to adjust well to the cluster, in this situation.

The Cluster Contract

A group contract was developed in the closing forty minutes of the first two-hour session. On the weekend, the first session was to help the group gain an overview of what Family Cluster is about, to become acquainted and build trust, to express expectations, and to work on group commitment (contract). This process was begun by having a name tag-gathering activity which encouraged the participants to create a shape that expressed something about themselves and then to talk with others about the shape. After introducing the team members, each family went into a huddle to decide the family's greatest asset. The oldest child in each family introduced the family members and told what was that family's asset. As each family sat down the group gave a cheer for that family. The filmstrip, available for rental from Family Clustering, Inc., (P.O. Box 18074, Rochester, NY 14618) was used to help the families understand more about the Family Cluster concept. In small groups the participants wrote on newsprint what they expected from the Family Cluster experience. Then, these were shared with the whole group by having one person from each group present what their small group listed. These were taped to the wall.

After a few minutes of playing "New Games" with a parachute, the group met to work on a group commitment. The leader taped two sheets of newsprint to an easel and wrote the heading "OUR GROUP COMMITMENT." Some explanation was made by the leaders as to the need for group commitment, ways we were going to treat each other, and how we were to process our sessions. The leader had in mind, also, a few guidelines to give the group in case it was slow in getting started. They were also encouraged to include in the commitment that the items were open for negotiation at any future time. There was some resistance to the group commitment and questions as to whether there was really need for such a commitment. The leaders in training had sensed the importance of this and were supportive, while encouraging the group to continue the process of making a group commitment. This was accepted, and work on the contract continued. It was not completed in this particular session, but was left until later in the afternoon on this weekend retreat.

In the afternoon session a few minutes were spent in summarizing the group commitment, giving opportunity for further additions, having a group consensus to show acceptance of the commitment, and then ritualizing through signing by thumbprints.

Decisions of the Group

The schedule for meetings had been presented to the families before the cluster meetings and they were:

> Plans for a weekend retreat at the local church with sleeping at home on Saturday night;
>
> Dates for the five to seven remaining sessions would be decided by the whole group. This decision was made at the final gathering of the retreat which was a noon banquet meal held after worship on Sunday morning; each family was seated together.

The activities surrounding the Sunday meal were based on decision-making in the family. After a summary of the weekend, the group was given suggestions of possible ways to complete the rest of the sessions. They could meet once a week for several sessions, once a month for several sessions, or in the spring have another retreat which might be at a local campgrounds or in the home of the leaders fifty miles away. Or it could be a combination of those. The group decided to meet for four or five monthly sessions and to have a slumber party retreat six months later in the home of one of the leaders. The monthly sessions would be held in various homes of the cluster members.

Forces Building Group Process

Some of the forces which helped build the group process were: cheers and reinforcement to the individual family units; informal seating on a carpeted floor; creative activities that usually called for some media to be used; fun together; and a wide range of ages rather than too many young children only. It seemed like "the sky was the limit" in any kind of activity we wanted to have because of the wide range in ages. Good food was plentiful.

During the weekend event, a short presentation was made to the entire congregation on Sunday morning in the devotional church school period about Family Cluster, and several of the participants gave brief responses of their experiences thus far. Providing for good leadership and allowing for the process of decision-making so that the group became theirs, too, were strong points of commitment for the group. Their commitment was made even stronger by the realization that this was a closed group and that for a certain period of time it was one Family Cluster in which no one would be allowed to join without acceptance by the others except in the case of very unusual circumstances. However, this was a little difficult for the rest of the congregation to accept. But after they heard the participants rave about it, they wanted to join the group. This request was cared for by assuring these persons that other Family Cluster groups would be started in the congregation and community, and they would have an opportunity to be a part of new cluster groups.

The participants came reluctantly on Saturday morning of the weekend to the beginning session of the cluster. There were teenagers who really didn't want to be there, and skeptics expecting a long boring day of classes. By noon the group was beginning to loosen up and enjoy it, and by the time of the evening campfire and weiner roast the whole group seemed cohesive and supportive. Sunday morning included the brief presentation to the congregation and then a banquet lunch and session immediately followed worship. It was at the close of this session that the decisions were made regarding future meeting times and places. They were eager and enthusiastic about meeting and ready to volunteer their homes for meeting places.

The closing circle of that weekend was an experience of love, acceptance, and happiness at being together. This joy of being together seemed to permeate the monthly cluster meetings. The final weekend slumber party found a group of close friends who were looking forward to being together. The slides taken at previous meetings were shown, and it was a warm and fun reception as the group viewed themselves in various activities.

The Educational Process

The activities used continually supported communication between members of the families and also between members of the group. There was also an emphasis on decision-making as a group, as a family, and as an individual.

The group was given many opportunities to decide where and when to meet and asked for some input as to which activities would be desirable. There were also activities directed at guiding them through decision-making. Family skits were used in one session to facilitate discussion about what enters into family decisions; and discussion as to how each skit presented could have been handled in a variety of ways to solve problems and make the necessary decisions.

Communication skills were the focus in two sessions but encouraged in all the sessions. Communication was encouraged to take place in activities in which each family worked together by family groups, in activities that encouraged intergenerational, inter-family communication, and whole cluster sharing.

Enjoyment of each other seemed to be a major goal of our cluster meetings. We played games together, sang together, and ate together as well as doing the structured activities. Through evaluations that were obtained later from the cluster members there seemed to be no activity that was difficult for any of them.

The following lists some of the activities that were especially enjoyed by the group.

Exploring Our Homes

Goal: To discover feelings about our homes and share them in our family.

Time: 30 minutes

Materials: Tables covered with white paper, felt-tipped pens.

Procedure: Sitting in family groups, each person is to draw a floor plan of home. Smaller children may need some help from parents. Fantasy trip through the home—close eyes, leader guides them with the following: Your home. (*pause*) Enter the front door and walk through the house. (*pause*) Where is your favorite place in the home? (*pause*) Where is a place you don't like to go? (*pause*) If you want to get warm, where do you go? (*pause*) What do you like best about your home? (*pause*) Open eyes; talk together in each family about the questions that were asked.

Closure: Give the opportunity to the whole group for any expression of new things they have learned about each other, new feelings they had about themselves.

Valentine Cookies

Goal: To show love by preparing something special for another person.

Time: 30 minutes

Materials: Large heart-shaped sugar cookies (about 5 × 5 inches) already baked and frosted with plain pink powdered sugar frosting; baggies with small amount of white frosting in each (enough for one for every two people at least); red hots; silver decorative candies; the name of each person in the group on separate sheets of paper, basket or box to draw the names from.

Procedure: Seat the group around tables covered with paper. Give each person a frosted cookie (but ask them not to eat it!). Provide some frosting in baggies, red hots, silver decorative candies on each table. Cut apart the names of the persons in the groups; and put in basket for drawing. Ask each person to draw a name and to decorate the cookie expecially for the person whose name was drawn. Cut off a small piece in one corner of the baggie to squeeze out the frosting for decorating.

When everyone is finished, the cookies may then be presented or may be saved until later. These are good for refreshment or dessert time, served with punch. The important part is that the person presenting the cookie says something he or she likes about the other person. If there is plenty of time, this may be done one-by-one in front of the whole group or each one may find the person whose name they drew and all present at the same time.

Family Crests

Goal: To help the families make a lasting memento of the Family Cluster experience while making decisions and communicating about themselves.

Time: One and one-half to two hours

Materials: For each family: 1 sheet of newsprint, with a large crest outline drawn on it; 1 felt-tipped pen, 1 piece of cream-colored burlap—18 x 30 inches (put one-inch hems at top and bottom and zigzag raw edge), various colored pieces of felt, white glue, scissors, felt crest outline cut from brown felt.

To Make Crest Outline:

Make a large pattern outline similar to the one drawn at the right. The pattern should be in proportion to the size of the burlap backing. Pin the pattern on dark brown felt. Cut around the pattern. Remove the pattern. Put scissors in felt 1/2 inch from edge. Cut all the way around. Another 1/2 inch crest outline could also be cut from the piece. (See dotted lines on illustration.) Use the inside that is left over for scrap pieces as they make their symbols. Or some may want to use the center as their crest background rather than using only the crest outline.

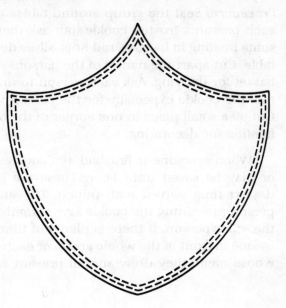

Procedure: Meet as a Whole Group. Give them an overview of the steps in this activity. Then ask them to close their eyes and ask them the following questions, pausing after each question to allow time for them to mentally picture their answer:

- What is the weather report of your family? (cloudy, sunny, stormy, etc.)
- What is one of the most fun times you have had together as a family?
- What has been one of the hardest times you have had as a family?
- If you could plan one thing to do together as a family, what would you like to do?
- What is the thing you like best about your family?

(You may have other questions which you would want to substitute for your group.)

Meet in Family Groups: Discuss together the various responses the members of the family had during the questions. Deal with one question at a time. Decide together what experience is most representative and draw a symbol in one of the parts of the crest to show that.

After the design is completed on paper, use the burlap and felt to create a permanent family crest based on the design created from their discussion of each question. Glue the crest outline onto the burlap. Cut symbols from the felt pieces and glue to the burlap. The family name may also go on the burlap.

Meet as a Whole Group: When everyone has finished, gather together. Sit in family groups and ask each family to show the crest the family created and explain it to the rest of the group. Use masking tape to hang the crests on the walls until time to go home.

Another activity which was really excellent in helping persons of all ages to interact was the making of kites in groups of six. We found that the oldest member of our group loved to make kites and he provided the equipment and helped the group create kites. They used colorful felt pens to decorate the heavy brown paper before completing the kites. What fun to see them airborne!

One of the group members was an amateur photographer and this person took slides of the group meetings. Viewing these slides together during our last session gave us a tremendous feeling of belonging.

Evaluation

It was difficult during the opening weekend retreat to have adequate time following each session for evaluation. We usually asked the team members in charge of the session to express how they felt it went. What were the strengths of the session? What could have been done to help it go better? Other team members and sometimes family participants helped in the evaluation process. Quick plans were made to give a specific direction to the next session, and a decision was made as to when the planning should occur in more depth.

An hour was used on Sunday morning for the leadership team to discuss each session of the weekend and to do some last minute planning to refine the closing session. Evaluation was made by the group using "happy faces or sad faces" and giving brief written responses.

During the ensuing months the team members continued to meet for the monthly planning sessions with a different person or couple who were in charge each time. Following each of the monthly sessions the team members gathered for a period of time to share in evaluating and planning ahead.

Midway during the monthly meetings, a written evaluation form was given to members to fill out with sentence answers to the following questions:

1 How would you define Family Cluster?
2 Why did you decide to attend Family Cluster?
3 In what way, if any, did your Family Cluster experiences affect your family relationships?
4 In what way did your Family Cluster experience affect your relationship with other members of the group?
5 What was your favorite cluster activity?

6 What does the Family Cluster experience offer a child and/or an adolescent?

7 What would be your reaction to an opportunity to participate in another Family Cluster?

8 Comment on the way the cluster was structured . . . Size, number of meetings, types of activities, etc.

Closing Session

This particular Family Cluster group closed six months later with a slumber party at one of the team leaders' homes where there was plenty of room both inside and out. Mattresses were brought in from a nearby campground, food was partially prepared, and job sheets posted for members to sign up to help with food preparations and cleanup.

Friday evening's schedule started off with a Mexican food fiesta (a specialty of the hostess) followed by singing, showing slides of previous Family Cluster activities, playing group games together and visiting during the rest of the evening. The families each chose their place to sleep, and mattresses were put out as each got sleepy. It was wall-to-wall bedrolls by two o'clock in the morning.

The next morning, after breakfast, it was time to make the family crests and share them together. Then groups were formed to make and fly kites. Horseback riding was also one of the treats of the weekend which seemed to be enjoyed most be the younger set, but the older set enjoyed watching and cheering them on.

Each family drew the name of another family and made a list of things they had come to love as well as strengths they saw in that family. They then prepared a special wish for that family. These were presented orally to the family as the rest of the families listened, followed by a special cheer for the chosen family. Each family went on its way at the close of the cluster commitment with hearts aglow and a desire to share these good times together with others in the congregation.

Plans have been made to start another Family Cluster group by two of the leaders trained in these sessions. There will also be times of "reunion" in getting together by the original cluster group.

Resources

Carol Anderson Anway and Fenn, R. Daniel. *Family Enrichment Book*. Herald Publishing House, Independence, MO. 1979.

Margaret M. Sawin. *Family Enrichment With Family Clusters*. Judson Press, Valley Forge, PA. 1979.

Biographical Data

Carol is employed by the Reorganized Church of Jesus Christ of Latter Day Saints in Independence, Missouri, as a staff executive in the Christian Education Office. She has a background in school teaching and school counseling. Joe is an instructor of business in the Kansas City Community Junior Colleges and is a minister in the RLDS Church. They are both working to develop skills in the areas of family and marriage enrichment and counseling. Joe and Carol have two sons and a daughter, all teenagers.

Address:

Rt. 1
Lee's Summit, MO 64063
Tel. (816) 566-2180

Family Cluster in the Unitarian Church

Joyce Space
Susan Maybeck

Rochester, New York

Sponsorship

One of the first churches to use the Family Cluster Model was the Unitarian Church of Rochester, N.Y. Both the minister and religious education director were interested in this model of programming for families and began them in 1971. The use of Family Clusters peaked in the early seventies, and then subsided until 1977.

Leadership

In 1976 my husband, Larry Space, and I went to a Family Cluster Training Lab at Five Oaks Conference Centre in Paris, Canada. That fall we began looking for a place to lead Family Clusters in Rochester. I contacted the minister's assistant at the Unitarian Church to see if they would be interested in sponsoring Family Clusters again; they were! Larry and I led two clusters there—one in the winter of 1977 and another in 1978. In 1979 Larry wanted to put his energies into other areas. Susan Maybeck had attended a 1978 Training Lab at the same Centre when I was a trainer. Being impressed with her skills and abilities, I asked Sue to co-lead a cluster with me. This case study is about the Family Cluster which she and I co-led on Wednesday evenings, 6:00-8:15 P.M., from February 14 to April 25, 1979.

As leaders, Sue and I worked with the pastor's assistant to help recruit families for the cluster. I spoke in the worship service, wrote blurbs for the church newsletter and showed the Family Cluster filmstrip (available from Family Clustering, Inc., P.O. Box 18074, Rochester, NY 14618) to interested persons. I had data collectors available at that meeting. Sue and I set the time and place for holding the cluster and with the minister and assistant we established leadership fees. We co-led in every sense of the word, with both of us visiting the homes of families and sharing the planning, preparing, setting-up, cleaning up, and evaluating.

The most important training Sue and I had was the Family Cluster leadership training at the Lab, but other types of training such as values clarification, family systems workshops, group process and leadership skills supplemented the basic training. Skills which enhanced our leadership were self-awareness, communication skills, a sense of what a "healthy" family is, and how family dynamics work. (In terms of the latter, we both feel we could use more study in this area.) Our traits of being organized, yet flexible within that organization, our past experiences with Family Clusters, as well as liking and being able to work with all age groups were important. My guitar playing added spirit to the singing.

Our teamwork was a very positive experience for both of us, as well as for the cluster. Sue and I started out by doing intentional team building where we shared with each other how we work, what our strengths and weaknesses were and what we wanted from the other. Then we reacted to what each other had said concerning those three areas. For example, I shared with Sue that my strength was having numerous resources and lot of experience with Family Clusters, but my weakness was pushing too hard and being impatient in planning because I would already have it in my head what I wanted to do. A carry-over of this might be that I would interrupt when she was leading.

Sue shared that she was skillful at reading groups, but she had not had experience leading a cluster before. She might tend to lean on me too much and, if I felt this, I should let her know. We found that we respected each other's skills, ideas, and experiences. We could talk to each other and keep communication flowing. Sue had a sense of how families work and I had a sense of what would work with families. Feedback from the cluster members indicated that seeing us work together was an important part of the experience.

Because of our trust in each other and our open communication, we had very few problems. One time Sue felt that I had taken her power away while she was doing the upfront leadership, and she had let me do it. What I had done was a pattern of mine which I had shared with Sue in our team building. Because we had talked over this prior to the cluster, it was easier for both of us to deal with the issue when it happened. Since Sue and I both tended to deal with certain issues in a way that sounds like a "critical Parent," we did avoid some issues that should have been talked about with the cluster. An on-going issue for us was when to intervene with families and when not to. In retrospect, we could have intervened and probably would have been helpful; we also know that sometimes we just have to follow our intuitions.

Ideally it would have been good to have had a male-female leadership team, but we also believe that our strength as a female leadership team was more important than a male-female team that might not have worked so well together.

Families

Our cluster initially had 24 participants plus two leaders. There were a total of nine individual family units which were divided into the following:

Family Units	Denomination
Young male, separated, no children	Unitarian
Nuclear family with a girl, 11; boy 9	Fant Mat (East Indian)
Blended family with a girl, 15; boy, 8	Catholic
Nuclear family with girls, 4 and 7; boy, 9	Presbyterian
Single, divorced mother with a girl, 10, boy, 6	Unitarian
Single female, middle-aged, never married	Unitarian
Single, divorced mother with boys, 11 and 15	Unitarian
Single male, separated, without custody of children	Unitarian
Single, divorced female with girl, 11	Unitarian

(I might add that we two leaders are Methodist and Baptist.)

Through leading clusters at the Unitarian Church for three years, I have found that single people and single parents sign up quickly, but not enough nuclear families are interested. Since I wanted a balance of different kinds of families, I limited the number of each type of family in the cluster. Sometimes I have had to go outside the Unitarian Church to recruit nuclear families. Other clusters I have experienced elsewhere were almost entirely two-parent families with two or three children. It appears that the Unitarian clusters are unique in that they have a variety of family types.

The make-up of a family, as well as the family system, contribute a great deal to what happens in a cluster. We were fortunate that, for the most part, the families in our cluster were very open and honest, had good communication skills, and treated children with respect. Therefore, they shared more quickly than some clusters might. There was a trust within the families, so each individual felt safe, accepted and free to try almost everything. Trust developed quickly in the cluster, so people also felt safe and free to try new experiences within the cluster.

We observed families where children were given a great deal of freedom. Other people did not know always how to deal with a child who disturbed others at times. This caused some discomfort among the cluster members. In families where one particular parent was considered to be the primary caretaker that parent wasn't always involved in the total cluster and didn't become acquainted with others. Sometimes adults can use the care of children as an excuse for not getting involved.

When parents had clear goals as to why they wanted to be in the cluster, the children seemed to be clear about why they were there and entered in fully. In families where the parent(s) was (were) ambivalent, the children were also ambivalent; and the whole family was not committed to the process. This caused uncertainty in the whole cluster as to what that family wanted from cluster and what their commitment would be. A family needs at least one member in that family who has positive power and is really "sold" on the cluster concepts. As a result, others will usually become committed.

If adults need to interact with other adults more than is provided for in cluster, they must be aware of this need and try to get it met in other ways. Family Cluster is for the total family, and often children want more attention from the parent(s) than some parents are willing to give. When parents are not aware of their own needs vs. their children's needs, or are unable to resolve this conflict, there is a struggle for attention; and this can reduce the impact of cluster.

Parents and adults who accepted children, listened to them, and understood their resistance to some things in cluster, had fewer hassles with the children. The children did not have to get into power struggles to try to be understood. They were free to become involved in the cluster instead of being driven by the need to fight opposing forces. In families where the parents listened less and controlled more, the children were in a struggle that prevented them from becoming as involved. The group missed knowing such a child and the parents as fully as they might have, and the parents and children missed being free enough to participate as fully as they might have.

Having single men and women in a Family Cluster added the dimension of some singles being comfortable and others being uncomfortable at the prospect of being paired with another single member of the opposite sex. This subtle, approach-avoidance issue underlay many activities and interactions, and it took careful planning on our part as leaders to work around it. We were somewhat aware of how each single felt so we could design accordingly. The married people felt freer to interact with all adults without any hidden agenda, and the single people could interact with the married people more freely. However, from the final written evaluation, we learned that at least one adult felt there had been a division between the married and unmarried adults. We wish this had been verbalized earlier so we could have dealt with it.

Contracting

Contracting started individually with each family during the home visits. At this time we asked each person separately if they would come to Family Cluster and be committed to attend each session. In most cases people answered yes eagerly. If there was reluctance (usually from children), we worded the question, "Would you be willing to join and attend every time even though you aren't too excited about the idea right now?" All did agree to that.

During the first session of cluster we talked about the group contract briefly and explained that the next time they would be letting us know how they wanted to operate as a group. In the second session we divided the cluster into two groups of adults, a group of teens and a group of children. The adults met on their own, Sue met with the teens, and I met with the children. We asked them to brainstorm their ideas on newsprint as to what they wanted from the cluster experience, how they wanted to function as a group, how they wanted to be treated, etc. Sue and I helped our groups by asking questions such as, "Are some people more important then others here? or, Is overyone equally important?" This led the children to say, for instance, that everyone should be listened to. The adults said they found the exercise difficult because they weren't sure of what they wanted to write about cluster, yet they liked the chance to work together and to begin to get to know each other. We put all the ideas on newsprint and hung them on the wall; a spokesperson from each group explained what their group had written. Sue and I then shared our expectations: starting and ending on time, staying in the cluster room (except to use the kitchenette or bathrooms), using "opt out" corner, a place with toys and supplies where people can go if they do not choose participate in a particular exercise, and encouraging everyone to try everything before opting out.

During the week Sue and I collated their ideas and listed them on one large piece of newsprint. When we met the third week, we asked the group to look over the newsprint to see if anyone wanted to add anything or had questions about an item. Then we had a ceremonial signing of the contract by using chocolate pudding. Each person put a print of his or her hand, thumb, foot or nose on the contract to say symbolically he or she would honor it. Ideas from the cluster participants which were not contract type material (e.g. at least two but not more than three pot luck dinners) were listed on a separate sheet, so we could incorporate their ideas into our planning.

We didn't have any problems with people accepting and signing the contract, except for one family which was ambivalent about its commitment to the cluster. They were absent the night the group signed, and finally dropped out. (They did sign the contract the fourth session, but the commitment was lacking.) The problem arose when other members questioned the value of signing a contract if it couldn't be enforced. This wasn't handled as effectively as we would have liked. Sue and I can see in retrospect how we might have handled it differently; initially, we should have sensed that from the home visit that particular family didn't seem committed. We might have shared our concern about their ambivalence and explored further about their commitment before they ever started cluster. Since we did not do that, we were at a loss as to how to handle their sporadic attendance without sounding like "critical Parents"; we did little except to call them to let them know cluster plans for the coming week and to verify if they planned to attend. In the adult session we had time to share our frustrations and concerns about how we might have handled this problem; others were aware of our feelings, and they had a chance to verbalize their feelings.

Group Process

For several reasons this group became cohesive faster than some other clusters. Some of the people had been in a Family Cluster before or were familiar with the Family Cluster concept, so they knew what to expect. Their expectations were high, and they were willing to work within their families and within the cluster. The pre-session activities were structured to help the group process, so people were involved quickly with each other during each session. The families were fairly open at the beginning and shared readily. Children were accepted as "persons" right away, so they felt free to participate and share. We leaders modeled the kinds of communication that would promote a group cohesiveness. I shared with the group my concern over my mother's cancer and impending surgery. This opened up a sharing from others who had personal concerns. One person shared a poem, and soon others were bringing in poems or readings, either of a fun or a serious nature. A pot luck dinner on the fifth week was the peak time for the cluster. An especially close feeling prevailed that evening. In the eighth session, while children were doing arts and crafts in another room, an adult session helped build further cohesiveness. This session provided an opportunity to clear the air of a lot of underlying issues that weren't actually disrupting the cluster program, yet were there and were noticed.

Our inability as leaders to deal with a few issues involving personal dynamics which were getting in the way of the cluster did somewhat deter the group process, but the cluster had so many strengths that these issues didn't impede as much as they might have with another group. The relationship of one single woman with another single woman and her children was never quite clear to that family, to the cluster, or to us leaders. The single woman was a close friend of the family and had been at the family's home when we made the home visit. It appeared that she assumed she would work with that family when families worked together on activities, but the children sometimes resented her presence and wanted to work only with their mother. For the family and the friend this was a source of conflict which Sue or I should have handled more directly by offering to work with them on that issue while others worked on the structured activity for the evening. We saw this in retrospect and checked it out with the two women if that would have been helpful. They agreed that it might have been.

Absences often can weaken a group's cohesiveness. It was not an issue except for the one family mentioned previously. There were absences, but they were typical ones of many clusters—illness, trips, etc.

In general, we saw the group move through the three recognized stages of group life—inclusion, control, and affection. Almost everyone moved through the stage of inclusion fairly soon, with the exception of the ambivalent family. We aren't sure that they ever felt included because they missed so much of the group process that lent itself to that stage. The control stage was never a vital issue in the life of this Family Cluster. Ideas were shared and listened to, but in the end it was up to the leaders to do as they saw best with the information we had received from the individuals in the cluster. The members were included from the beginning and felt this inclusion. We leaders knew our role, were clear about it, had power in a positive way, and had the participants share in a positive way. We feel this lent itself to creating an atmosphere where the control issue was minimal. There was a lot of caring among the adults and between some adults and children. We think this was because of the atmosphere of trust and openness that was felt. The children did not overtly show as much affection among themselves as was shown among the adults and between adults and children. However, they did feel affection for the cluster as a whole. Warmth and caring were present and felt by participants.

Educational Process

We started the cluster with "getting-to-know-you" type activities, but then proceeded to build in communication skill activities for four sessions which would meet objectives of both areas. During the fourth session, intra-family work was shared as to what each person appreciated about each other person in the family; they used the previous communication skills to relay these appreciations to each other. The fifth session was the pot luck dinner and a family talent show. The overall theme for the cluster was communication within the family, using areas such as decision-making, handling conflict, affirming, and having fun.

The most well-received activity was one in which the family planned a vacation together to anywhere in the world, for any length of time, and money was no object. Families found that it was plain fun to fantasize together and learn what each other would like to do. Also, they found that by fantasizing, they came up with ideas they might be able to try some day. They found that by listening to everyone's ideas, they had more ideas of their own and felt closer together because everyone had a say in the plans. It helped one family see the importance of trying to make some of their dreams come true. One person responded negatively to the idea because she found it hard to pretend with something that was so unrealistic. Some children found it difficult to see their parents pretending this way because they were so used to the parents' plans being "real." That helped the parents realize how important it can be to pretend more with their children.

Other activities that played an important part in this cluster were the pre-session activities; the pot luck dinners; the song, "Alice's Camel"; the adult discussion session; as well as singing, caring and sharing time which brought us closer together. One important activity was an adult-child meal time when each child could choose an adult to be his or her meal partner for the next cluster. The adult-child pair planned together what they would each contribute to the meal. There were more adults than children, so the experience was less positive for the "not-chosen" adults. We had some older children eat with two adults, but we would need to try to find another way of doing the activity in the future so that people didn't have a "left out" feeling. Possibly having the children meet with us privately and decide which adult(s) would be with each child; then pairing people might eliminate the "being-chosen-last" feeling.

Another activity received with mixed review involved the role play where children played the adults and adults played the children in family conflict situations. Some children found it hard to play adults and others reveled in the role. It helped some parents to see how a child perceived his or her own parents as the child played a parental role. Adults found it fun to try life from the perspective of a child. The role play led to a discussion of how to handle certain problems, but the discussion happened to revolve around two-parent families; so, the one-parent families felt left out of it.

When you have single people in a cluster, one issue which is always difficult is how to arrange activities for them when the experiences for the evening are specifically for families of two or more people. Sometimes we would make changes in the basic instructions for the single people, but even then, they didn't always want to do the activity and would prefer to just watch. Sometimes they would be invited to work on their own activity alongside another family.

Our second session had an activity which combined getting acquainted with communication skills through a double circle with the inner circle facing the outer circle. People answered questions about themselves for one minute with the partner listening only; then they reversed so the other person talked; then the inner circle would move on to a new partner. Most people enjoyed the activity because the questions were safe but interesting; and they liked learning a lot about others in a short time. Some children found it more difficult because they felt they had to talk even when it was sometimes uncomfortable to talk to someone they didn't know too well. But they did it—no one quit!

Sharing-and-caring time had too much talking for some children, but overall it was seen as a time of closeness for everyone. The younger children would go to the opt out corner while adults talked. The middle-aged children felt they were too old to be in the play corner but were bored with all the sharing. Sometimes their impatience reminded us to move on.

We had open communication throughout the cluster as ideas and feedback were shared continuously; we used a graffiti sheet in a middle session which had the titles of "Things I like about Family Cluster are . . .," "Things I don't like about Family Cluster are . . .," and "In Family Cluster I wish we would . . . ." They wrote on these as they arrived. During sharing-and-caring time we asked if anyone wanted to say more or to ask about anything written there. This helped everyone sort out feelings about cluster and helped us leaders to see where to go next. Our final evaluation was a written one which each person filled in during the last session. There were a few surprises on the evaluations that we wished had been verbalized during the cluster sessions, but mostly the evaluations were positive and reflected what we saw as the overall experiences of each person there.

In our last session we enjoyed a pot luck dinner, filled out the evaluation forms, planned a reunion picnic, and had a strength bombardment exercise (each person receives affirmation and strength from the others in the group). A person's name was called one at a time, and the other people verbalized what they liked about that person. I wrote the phrases down on a piece of paper and handed the paper to each person. Hearing many positive affirmations helped us end on a high note.

The reunion picnic was a success, and everyone attended. I have seen different families occasionally during the year and they still talk about what a positive experience cluster was. One nine-year-old boy just asked me if there would be a cluster in the city again this winter because he wanted to be in one. The families talked about how nice it would be to get together again.

Resources

I have been collecting resources for Family Clusters during the last five years and have edited the Family Cluster newsletter, "The Purple Turtle" for three years. In this process I have accumulated so much material that I cannot pinpoint any one book that I used more than anything else. What I did find extremely helpful was attending a workshop on Values Clarification, led by Sid Simon, as well as using exercises from Virginia Satir's *Peoplemaking* (Palo Alto, CA: Science and Behavior Books, Inc., 1972). If I had to suggest particular resources to a new person starting clusters, I would recommend:

Back issues of "The Purple Turtle"

Agard, Bonnie. *Family Cluster Resources*. Chicago: Evangelical Covenant Church, 1977.

Benson, Jeanette, and Hilyard, Jack. *Becoming Family*. Winona, MN: St. Mary's College Press, 1979.

For information regarding prices for all three recommended resources, write to Family Clustering, Inc., P.O. Box 18074, Rochester, New York 14618.

Biographical Data

Joyce Space is a wife and mother, and an Ed.D. candidate at the University of Rochester. She is a former teacher and a Peace Corps volunteer. Presently she is a counselor in an elementary school. She has participated in and led Family Clusters for seven years and has been a trainer for four years.

Address:

11 Littlebrook Drive,
Pittsford, New York 14534
(716)248-2736

Susan Maybeck is an ordained American Baptist minister and has been a leader and participant in small groups and workshops for eight years. Presently she is an associate minister in Washington, D.C. She is also a wife and mother.

Address:

1216 N. Frederick St.,
Arlington, VA 22205
(703)525-3278

Clusters in Church School

A few Family Clusters have been initiated to take place during the traditional church school time. Here are two stories showing this mode:

1 *The Story of a Church School Class* by Mary Ann Brittain and Mel Williams
A cluster held in a Baptist church which is affiliated with both northern and southern denominations.

2 *A Family Cluster Experience in a United Methodist Church* by Cynthia Bonnet
A cluster in a church which has a tradition of growth groupings in its congregation.

The Story of a Church School Class

Mary Ann Brittain
Mel Williams

Raleigh, North Carolina

This cluster grew out of an expressed need for more community—more closeness—at Pullen Memorial Baptist Church in Raleigh, North Carolina. While adults generally found church school classes to be stimulating and worship services satisfying, people continued to make such remarks as these: "Something is missing here," "We don't know each other," "I want my children to know other adults in this church." One person said with some frustration, "This church is like a great big birthday cake—it looks delicious, but I just can't seem to get to it. I can't reach it."

How could we develop ways for people to get to the "cake?" How could we help families know each other and build a stronger, more caring church community? During the early 1970s, we tried the usual things: monthly fellowship gatherings in homes, informal outings, an unstructured retreat. None answered the need satisfactorily: they were enjoyable, but did not particularly build community. The investment of the participants was minimal.

While we were looking for a method to catch people's imagination and energy, two things happened: the church's Board of Christian Education appointed an ad hoc committee on Family Life; Mel Williams, Associate Minister of the church, and Mary Ann Brittain, an active lay person, began seeking training in family ministry. It was with the Laurel Ridge Family Enrichment Training Program* that Williams and Brittain discovered a model and resources.

---

*An eight-day intensive training event for Family Enrichment leaders, held annually since 1974 at Laurel Ridge Moravian Camp in Western N. C., sponsored by the Moravian Church Board of Christian Education, the N. C. Baptist Hospital School of Pastoral Care, Family Service of Charlotte, Lutheran Family Services of N. C., and the Elon Children's Home (United Church of Christ).

The Laurel Ridge training introduced the Family Cluster concept developed by Margaret Sawin, offered group process skills, taught design experiences to teach families and offered practical ways to enhance family strengths, communication skills, and self-esteem. The method seemed to be a way to help people "get to the cake" by incorporating into one cluster nuclear families, single parents with children, and single persons.

In the fall of 1975, the Family Life Committee sponsored the first of what have since become annual family retreats. People came back excited from the retreat and with a feeling of having been connected to each other. The central focus of this weekend experience (Friday supper through Sunday lunch) was the clustering of four to six family units into one extended family group. Much careful planning went into this retreat and those that have been held subsequently. Goals are set each year toward building family strengths, strengthening communication and self-esteem, and having fun together. Brittain and Williams designed and led the "program" sections of the early retreats, while Family Life Committee members led worship and recreation.

Because of the positive response to the retreats, early in 1977 the Family Life Committee offered a six-week Lenten Family Cluster experience. More than one hundred people signed up as families to meet in homes on consecutive Sunday evenings, beginning each session with a simple meal. The Family Life Committee recruited two leaders for each cluster of five or six families, selecting people with group leadership skills or previous experience in leading intergenerational groups.

The response of the congregation was so favorable that these Lenten Family Clusters have now become an annual event in the church calendar year. In addition to the community building, the Lenten clusters offer families an opportunity to contemplate Lenten themes—sacrifice, obedience, discipline,—in a context of daily experience. The Family Cluster format encourages further discussion in individual family units by providing a structure.

A Family Cluster Church School Class

The Lenten family groups generated an even greater interest in the cluster model. In response to this interest, Brittain and Williams outlined a proposal to the Board of Christian Education for a Family Cluster church school class which would meet on Sunday mornings for four months. The goals were 1) to offer families an opportunity for in-depth relationships across family and generational lines, and 2) to increase awareness that each family is a part of the family of God. The proposal was accepted, and Brittain and Williams became leaders of the new project. They actively recruited families, asking for a four-month commitment. Every family was asked to attend the class each Sunday morning from nine to ten-thirty, being absent only in the event of an emergency.

The project was intended to involve a mixture of family sizes, varieties, and age groups. We wanted families consisting of single persons and single parents as well as nuclear families. Letters were mailed in early August to prospects, with a description of the proposed class. Within three weeks, nineteen individuals (nine family units) had responded positively, and we began the process of informally interviewing each family. The purpose was twofold—to allow leaders to assess each family's personal situation (individual needs, family patterns, roles, etc.) and to further explain the cluster class concept, soliciting any questions and concerns. We asked:

"Do you understand what we will be trying to do?"

"Are you willing to leave your regular church school classes to give this a try?"

Beginnings

On a Sunday morning in September 1977, nineteen people walked into the homelike atmosphere of the church parlor for the first session. There were two nuclear families, one single parent family, five single person families which included divorced, never-married, and widowed persons, and one sibling group family with a house-parent from the nearby Children's Home. The youngest person was seven; the oldest, fifty-nine. From the beginning, this diverse blend of families was surprisingly compatible. The two nuclear families—a total of seven people—already knew each other well. Most of the people liked and trusted the leaders and came with the anticipation of an exciting adventure at church. The need for friendship from the divorcees and the sibling family brought out the caring resources of the group.

The first session was designed for getting acquainted and for building a contract with each other. The leaders presented these goals for the four months on newsprint:

1 To build an extended family group
2 To explore our family religious history
3 To learn what the Bible teaches about family relation-ships
4 To observe religious occasions together (Thanksgiving, Advent, Christmas)
5 To have fun together.

Members of the group expressed agreement with the goals by writing their initials on the sheet of newsprint. In order to solicit the members' expectations, a blank sheet of newsprint was put up with the heading "Things I would like to see happen in our cluster." Suggestions from the group were written on the sheet—camp together; have Thanksgiving dinner together; play the game "Magic Ball"; carol at Christmas.

Housekeeping items concluded the contracting session. A newsprint sheet was unveiled with the following information:

Time and Place of Each Meeting:	Sunday, 9:00-10:30 A.M. in the church parlor
Duration of the Group:	Four months (through the Advent season, when the group will have an option to continue for the rest of the church year).
Attendance Commitment:	Everyone should be present for all sessions if possible. If anyone has to be absent, that person should let the group know in advance.
Breakfast:	Assigned responsibility for the shared breakfast.

On the following Sunday the group gathered around the breakfast table. The leaders had chosen "Faith" as the theme for this session. After reading appropriate scripture, singing a blessing, and "table talking" during the meal (approximately fifteen minutes), the tables were cleared and put away. Suddenly, a "surprise" visitor entered wearing full rain gear—yellow slicker, rain hat, and hip boots.

"Hi!" he said. "I'm Noah."

Noah was actually one of the men in the cluster who had slipped out and returned in the role by prearrangement with the leaders. First he told the story of the flood and then allowed the cluster members to interview him. Questions came thick and fast. "Did your neighbors laugh at you?" "How long did it take to build the Ark?"

Noah's story of faith led cluster members to make their own family shields of faith. The extemporaneous drama and the ensuing discussion and activity actually set in motion a form and climate for the rest of the year—a lively, dramatic, experiential approach to Christian Education.

The Format of Each Session

From the first few sessions, a weekly ritual began to emerge which became a format to be followed the rest of the year.

1 *Group Builder and/or Energizer*—a variety of "get-on-board" exercises to help everyone get awakened and present for the group session.

2 *The Scripture*—a reading from the Bible which presented the theme of the session and was read when persons were seated at the breakfast table. Scripture readers changed each week and included the children.

3 *The Blessing*—a sung blessing chosen from a number of available musical blessings.

4 *The Breakfast*—a simple meal brought and shared by each family unit around one large table.

5 *Table Talk*—a discussion at the table, initiated by the leaders, which centered around a topic related to the theme of the session.

6 *Transition*—a brief break, during which chairs and tables were removed. Also, it was a good time to initiate some other energizing activity, depending upon the energy level of the group.

7 *The Learning Experience*—the "meat" of the session. It involved the participants in the learning theme-goal-event of the morning.

8 *Closure*—a family circle with prayers or a song which closed the session and gave opportunity to say goodby. (This was preceded by instructions and/or assignments for the next week's session.)

Using this structure, the leaders then began to develop a curriculum to help build a faith community around the seasons of the church year.

The Educational Process

In adapting the Family Cluster Model to a church school set-ting, a decision was made to shift away from the previously used retreat model which focused specifically on family development issues, toward a focus on biblical material. The leaders hoped that family strengths and communication would develop as a by prod-uct of the process.

For many adults, during the years of growing up often we heard talk of "family devotions" as a way to nurture faith within families. In the experience of most individuals, this method never seemed to work; nevertheless, people ended up feeling guilty for not doing it. In devising a curriculum for the cluster, the leaders searched for a way to promote faith development in families without the old pious expectations. Is it possible to unite faith and fun while devel-oping some authentic religious rituals? After a few months in the cluster, the morning Scripture lessons around the table, the sung blessings, the acting out of Bible stories, and the "eyes wide open" prayer used at each closing became natural Sunday rituals. Permis-sion was given therefore, to *practice* a devotional life as a family unit.

The content of the sessions was determined by the needs of the cluster, as it developed an intentional group life, as well as the liturgical year. After the initial group-building sessions, the focus turned to the theme of faith development—in families, in individu-als, in biblical people of faith. The lessons proceeded from Septem-ber to Advent, then to Lent and Pentecost, completing a nine month cycle.

In all sessions there was a strong level of participation by the group members. The children were especially eager to be involved in the learning activities. Participants seemed to gain more from the sessions which involved them personally. For example, on All-Saints day each person was given a name tag upon entering the room—"Saint Fred" or "Saint Connie." The leaders emphasized that in the early Church everyone was called "saint," meaning a believer in Jesus Christ. The sessions developed around saints we have known and the qualities of people we know as saints. The conclusion was a new awareness of one's self as a saint—a believer.

During Advent the cluster read the stories of the birth of Jesus and then made birth announcements. At Epiphany everyone wore crowns (from the local Burger King), sang "We Twenty Kings of Orient Are," and then made gifts to take to the infant Jesus. One child made a megaphone out of paper, and said, "The baby Jesus would grow up to teach and preach and he needs to be heard."

During Lent the story of Jesus' temptation was used as a way to focus upon what each person valued most (Is what is most important to Jesus also most important to me?) In a session on responsibility in early spring the cluster met out of doors, and each member brought a pet. The purpose was to increase each person's awareness of the needs of the pets as a part of individual responsibility for God's creation. Cluster members were asked to imagine that they *were* their pet, and from that experience to be more sensitive to what they needed to do for their pet.

The final session at church was a celebration of Pentecost—a re-creating of the Acts 2 account of the day of Pentecost, complete with a live dove from the local museum. The discussion moved then to ways people experience the Spirit of God.

The Sense of Groupness in the Cluster

An effective group must attend to three basic needs of its members: *task* needs (complete the assigned session, meet the goals for the lesson), *individual* needs, and *maintenance* needs (all that is done to help the group function smoothly as a group). The strongly structured sessions enabled the task need to be met adequately. Both children and adults easily joined in the weekly format.

Because of previous friendships that existed among four families, there was a camaraderie and caring from the beginning. These "core people" were basically outgoing and were committed to the cluster concept; therefore, they readily welcomed the newer people and quickly built relationships. Some people came with rather urgent personal needs such as one woman had recently separated from her husband, while another joined the family after prolonged hospitalization). The acceptance they found brought some healing, or a place at least to just "be." In structuring the learning experiences the leaders intentionally allowed time for directed interaction among members, for various community-building exercises, and for scriptural lessons focusing on friendship. Not to be overlooked were the hugs and backrubs that happened spontaneously and regularly. Permission to touch brought permission for more closeness in the group. Outside activities—a camping weekend in the mountains and Thanksgiving dinner—together helped to solidify the group also.

However, as is true in most groups, some people were more involved than others. The people who were friends prior to the cluster became the emotional core, while the single adults tended to be less "in the middle of things." They found the group to be pleasant but probably needed more peer support or therapy at that time rather than a lively cluster class. These personal concerns did not affect the group's life negatively, but may have caused particular individuals to invest less energy in the group. Some of them opted to leave the cluster at the end of the initial four-month commitment. Other families took their places immediately. One family had consistent difficulty with regular attendance. This kept them from being involved in the group as "the regulars."

During the year the group moved through several noticeable phases. At first everyone was delighted with the whole experience. There was a perceptible drop in interest at the end of the four months, but then a gradual rebuilding and stabilizing took place through the spring. Characteristic throughout the year was a steady and continual caring for each other as members assumed the role of "minister" to others in the cluster.

Another important stimulant was the awareness that membership in the cluster class did not have to be static. Early plans had anticipated a "closed group" with no possibility for drop-in visitors. However, within a few months, the group moved beyond this expected exclusiveness, and eventually grandparents, relatives, and friends visited regularly. While there was a rather intense closeness among members, a ready sense of openness to others had developed as well. The principle we discovered is that a healthy family (cluster) is an open family (cluster).

Likewise, as several members made decisions to leave the cluster, there was a satisfactory letting go, made possible by time spent in giving appreciations to the leaving person and saying goodbys. At the end of the first four months we said goodby to the sibling family group and to two of the single persons. At the same time, we welcomed two new single persons and another child from the Children's Home.

The Closure of the Cluster Class

Over the nine month period an intense, loving, lively community developed in the class. To prepare the group for the ending, the leaders announced, six weeks in advance, a closure weekend at Laurel Ridge in the mountains of North Carolina. Initial reaction to the group's ending was mixed. There was some puzzlement (Why do we have to end such a good thing?) and anger (We're losing the best experience at church we've ever had!). "Why," one member persisted, "do we have to stop when we've spent all this time developing this great group?" The leaders' task was particularly difficult during this time; although we had grown too and benefited greatly from our participation in the group, we had already made commitments to other projects for the coming year.

At the closure retreat the leaders faced the task of facilitating the grief process as well as giving reasons for the closure. We said we must end so we could spend our energy facilitating this kind of experience for other groups. We said we thought it was important for each person to take the gained enrichment back to other church school classes or groups. We said we would prefer that potential leaders from this group use their time and energy to begin new clusters for other people.

During the weekend gradually the group worked through the resistance, ending the cluster around a breakfast table set, almost surrealistically, on top of a mountain. We read Isaiah 55, "You shall go out with joy ... and the mountains and the hills shall break forth into singing. ... " In a twenty-minute period, we re-enacted a typical cluster session—gathering, Scripture, blessing, eating, learning, praying, singing. We wept and thanked God for this amazing year!

The mountain-top breakfast was just one of the weekend's experiential exercises designed to help us remember, celebrate, grieve, and move on from the year we had shared together. Another of these exercises resulted in the group poem which follows. With this, each person was asked to write one or two lines reflecting their feelings about the cluster. Then, they were to fold the paper over, so that only one line was visible to the next person making a contribution. When everyone had written a line or two, the paper was unfolded and the poem read in its entirety. The tribute was as follows:

Cluster Poem

There once was a great cluster
Who gave each other all they could muster;
Each one can face life's fears
With these memories to guard him all those years.
Activities over—all songs have been sung
Best part of all—you've made me feel young,
Beginnings, endings—so must it be
But memories cherished will live for all time.
Begin! The rest is easy! But what about "End,"
The middle keeps us moving and ties us to friends.
I like breakfast in our cluster
And Mary Ann when she flusters;
I like finding out where we've been
I like finding out what we've done;
What seemed to be a harbor between the fishers' voyage
I discover the cluster is the source of power
Like the wind to a kite
Like gas to a car
Like being at home at last
And fourteen suns
Shine God's smile on me.

Group Evaluation

Overall, the evaluation of the year was positive from the class members. The collaborative cluster poem gathers up some of the end-of-the-year feelings. A simple evaluation questionnaire brought mostly positive feedback. Perhaps, of greater value, are the statements below, made three years later after the euphoria and enchantment of the experience had faded. We asked this question of several former cluster members: "What difference, if any, has being in the 1977-78 church school Family Cluster class made in your life?"

"It generated a new source of support for me which I needed badly. It pulled together for me a method for integrating daily experiences with religious concepts. It set up a mechanism for discussing religion in my family."

"I still feel a sense of belonging to that group of people even though we don't meet. It increased my sense of commitment to the church. I have a different sense of bonding than I did before. It just really enriched my life."

"I made many friends who are still friends."

"I got real insight into people I hadn't known before and I enjoyed the close fellowship in a worshipping atmosphere. I learned from the children."

The following comments were from two of the children. One is now age ten; the other, twelve:

"I made lots of new friends and making friends is important."

"It's given me insight to the different types of Sunday Schools that there could be. I learned a lot more about the Bible because you remember more when you're having fun while learning."

Leader Evaluation

As leaders, we felt elated with the year's experience insofar as the group's development was concerned. Upon observing that there were children talking to adults who were not their parents and sitting in other adults' laps one person said, "This group is so flexible you can't tell who the real parents are." On the negative side, probably we failed to develop adequate leadership among others within the group. We so thoroughly enjoyed leading that it was hard to give up the leadership role to others. There was heavy dependence on the two of us for creating the agenda and leading, but we may have aided in creating that dependency.

We found much personal benefit in using our imaginations to devise the learning activities. The weekly process of creating kept motivation and energy high and gave us conviction about what we were doing. The weekly curriculum has since been developed into a manuscript, published as *Christian Education in Family Clusters*, Valley Forge, PA. Judson Press, 1982.

The Bible was our major source book. We used few other books in the actual guiding of the cluster class, although we are well aware that we stand on the shoulders of such people as Herbert Otto (whose family enrichment workshops we attended), Virginia Satir *(Peoplemaking*, Palo Alto, CA: Science and Behavior Books, Inc., 1972), and Margaret Sawin (*Family Enrichment With Family Clusters*, Valley Force, PA: Judson Press 1979).

Biographical Data

Mel Williams, a graduate of Wake Forest University and Yale Divinity School, served ten years as Associate Minister at Pullen Memorial Baptist Church in Raleigh, North Carolina. Since February, 1980, he has been minister of the Oakhurst Baptist Church in Decatur, Georgia. He has led numerous personal growth and family enrichment events in the southeastern United States.

Address:

Oakhurst Baptist Church
222 East Lake Drive
Decatur, Georgia 30030
Phone: Office (404) 378-3677
        Home (404) 284-5218

Mary Ann Brittain, a graduate of Wake Forest University and the University of North Carolina at Chapel Hill, is currently Curator of Education at the North Carolina State Museum of Natural History. For four years she was chairperson of the Pullen Church Family Life Committee and has had vast experience as a workshop and conference leader in the field of family enrichment and child care.

Address:

3305 Clark Avenue
Raleigh, North Carolina 27607
Phone Office (919) 733-7450
      Home (919) 828-7023

A Family Cluster Experience in a United Methodist Church Cynthia Bonnett

Pittsburgh, PA

It finally happend! The first Family Cluster of the McKnight United Methodist Church was formed. A "CLUSTER IN SESSION" sign was taped to the social room doors. It was a private affair. However, singing, laughter, and other sounds echoed from the open windows. As the families left that day, dressed casually in jeans, sweaters, and slacks, they seemed to show a sense of pride and accomplishment—somewhat like a first grader returning home from school on the first day. Some of his thoughts might have been: What will it be like? Will I like my teacher? Will I want to go back? The cluster members' faces suggested it had been a good experience. The father of a family of six commented, "Hey, we had a good time!" Another middle-aged father was singing a little tune about "being a cluster." What was the reason for the happy faces? What made Family Clustering something special? How did it get started?

Beginning

Family Clustering at the McKnight United Methodist Church had its origin with the pastor. He was familiar with Herbert Otto's Family Cluster Model and had been acquainted with Margaret Sawin's work. In August 1977, the pastor's family participated in a Family Cluster Training workshop as a demonstration family at Kirkridge Retreat Center in Pennsylvania. That proved to be a positive and stimulating experience of what the pastor hoped could be provided at his own church. He kept in touch with Dr. Sawin and learned that in 1978 a Laboratory Training School in Western Pensylvania to train leaders for Family Clusters would occur.

The pastor discussed the possibility of Family Clustering with the Council on Ministries. (The group in the United Methodist Church which develops and implements programs.) The Council agreed to sponsor two persons to attend the Lab School, pay their tuition, and help with other expenses. The persons in training represented the church and were expected to provide leadership for Family Clusters.

Nine months later, two other persons received Family Cluster training at a Workshop in Rochester. Again the Council on Ministries paid their tutition and helped with expenses, with the understanding that leadership would be provided for the local church.

There were other events that preceded the formation of the first Family Cluster in the McKnight United Methodist Church. Members and friends of the church had had the opportunity to participate in a variety of other groups. These included Marriage Enrichment, Systematic Training for Effective Parenting, and an Interpersonal Communication Lab. There was a climate for small group work and discussion. People had overcome the fear of being put on the spot and saying more than one might be comfortable, in sharing. A "comfort level" for open communication existed and participants learned various ways of exchanging meaningful experiences. As a result of these activities, couples discovered many common themes emerging in their relationships.

Family Clustering represented a new and exciting option to the people of the church in the fall of 1978. The cluster would meet Sunday mornings from 8:30 to 10:30 in the social room, while regularly scheduled classes met in the church school. The clusters in the fall of 1978 and 1979 were led by a team of two women who had received Lab School training. The third Family Cluster, which met in the winter of 1980, was led by two persons who attended a four-day Training Workshop. This case study will be about that Family Cluster experience.

Leadership

The leadership team for the Winter Cluster of 1980 was composed of Katie and Henry. Henry is a middle-aged salesman with a wife and three teenagers. Katie is a young mother with a husband and two pre-school children. Henry and Katie would describe themselves as "people" persons, meaning they like people and enjoy working with them. Henry brought to the leadership team experience in working with people in church ministries, business, civic groups, and community projects. Katie had taught in elementary schools in a variety of settings for five years and worked as Children's Co-ordinator of the Church School since the birth of her children. She enjoys writing and creating new programs.

Both Henry and Katie considered themselves sensitive to the needs of others. Also, they discovered the importance of being aware of each other's needs as a vital part of good planning. They recognized their individual leadership abilities and accepted the challenge of working together as a team. Katie once remarked, "This is one of the first activities with which I've been involved in a leadership capacity that I didn't try to dominate and control. I tend to assume a lot of responsibility for things and thus insure them getting done my way. However, planning for cluster is different. I really want it to be a team effort."

The initial planning started two months prior to the beginning of cluster. Written articles and announcements appeared in the church newspapers and bulletins. Interested families were asked to contact the leadership team or the pastor. Six families expressed interest, and appointments were made to visit each family at home with all family members present.

Contracting with Families

Henry and Katie developed a system when they visited each family. He read a chart that defined a Family Cluster and its purpose. Using another chart, Katie discussed the kinds of activities that might occur at cluster, asking family members to comment on personal favorites. She remembered visiting one family where the father expressed serious interest in "clay modeling." The teenage daughter and eleven-year-old son had raised eyebrows which suggested, "That's news to me!" After each family had a chance to ask questions and share some feelings or reactions, Henry brought out the bridge chart. The theme for the Winter Cluster was "Building Bridges." The family had to decide if each member wanted to participate, knowing in advance that the cluster would meet for ten consecutive Sunday mornings beginning Janaury 6, 1980, from 8:30 to 10:30 A.M. If the entire family was interested, each member would write his or her name on a cut-out paper stone and paste it on the bridge. The stress was upon the individual person and their unique importance to the cluster. Every member of the family was also asked to complete a Family Cluster data collector sheet. It contained information about personal preferences and opinion questions. These were completed at the leisure of the family and mailed to the leadership team.

Once all of the families had contracted to participate in the cluster, Katie and Henry could begin to concentrate on their team planning. Knowing the families was essential to Katie and Henry, so they prepared a chart that included every person's name, age and ersponses to the personal preference questions. The composition of the cluster looked like this:

Family—F
Father (Gerry)
Mother (Lynn)
Daughter (Suzy—3 yrs.)

Family—I
Father (John)
Mother (Sarah)
Son (Jeff—14 yrs.)
Daughter (Lisa—11 yrs.)
Son (Jason—6 yrs.)

Family—A
Widow (Grandmother) (Mary)

Family—L
Father (Larry)
Mother (Carol)
Daughter (Julie—9 yrs.)
Daughter (Jenny—6 yrs.)

Family—M
Father (Rick)
Mother (Kathy)
Son (Brian—15 yrs.)
Daughter (Carol—12 yrs.)
Son (Mat—10 yrs.)

Family—Y
Father (Joe)
Mother (Marian)
Son (Eric—4 yrs.)

Three of the participating families, the F, M, and I's were intact nuclear families. Families L and Y were blended families. On Katie and Henry's first visit to the L family, the girls openly discussed the death of their father and fondly remembered asking Larry to be their dad and marry their mom. In family Y, both the father and mother had remarried. Her four-year-old son lived with them, but his children did not. One of Joe's initial questions concerned his daughters' attending cluster. Katie and Henry agreed that since they did not live in the same house wih the family, they should not participate.

There was considerable range in the number of years couples had been married. Mary had been widowed after twenty-seven years of marriage. Parents in Families M and I had been married about seventeen years; Family F, seven years; and Families L and Y less than two years.

There was a variety of family systems noticeable upon visits to the homes, and this needed to be considered in planning and administrating the cluster sessions. The younger children definitely knew how to get the attention of their parents and were generally focal points. Sometimes their needs appeared to become automatic priorities and in other cases were given degrees of attention. The comfort level of the parents correlated directly to the behavior of their children. In several families, children felt free to ask questions and to express their feelings. In other families, the children were quiet and more reserved. These factors would eventually influence the cluster.

Planning

Several planning sessions were needed to put the initial cluster session together and the cluster room in readiness. Henry and Katie had to get used to working together, which meant listening to each other's ideas and trying to agree on mutually exciting ones. The smiles and joy were obvious when their thoughts jelled or when one thought served as the catalyst for a new possibility. A level of faith was present in agreeing to try something about which one person had mixed feelings, but that was part of the give and take of being a team. As the plans developed, responsibilities were evenly shared, and Katie and Henry soon learned who preferred certain tasks.

Finding a block of time for planning was essential. To work effectively, they needed to be in touch with each other's moods and openly communicate frustrations. They chose to begin each planning session with a written evaluation of the previous cluster. It was important to know the emotional high and low points and things to avoid doing again. Once they were clear on what had occurred during the previous cluster, they could begin to prepare for the next session. Katie found that reading resource books and writing ideas on note cards was very helpful prior to planning sessions. It did not take long before Katie and Henry realized they had to be careful not to over-plan the sessions with too many activities.

A general schedule was followed for most cluster sessions:

8:30—9:00	Breakfast
9:00—9:15	Songs and warm-up
9:15—10:15	Educational experiences, games, and other happenings
10:15—10:20	Clean-up
10:20—10:30	Closing

The Cluster as a Group

Many of the forces which helped to build the group came from the consistency of certain parts of the schedule. They felt "groupness" as they came together every Sunday morning for breakfast. At first, families would sit together and watch out for one another, but gradually, they moved apart and felt free to choose with whom they wanted to sit from the group. It was especially interesting to watch the three- and four-year olds. Suzy became quite independent and seemed to thrive on making her own decisions. The parents of younger children seemed more relaxed as they felt free to sit with other adults and engage in conversation. Mary, a grandmother whose grandchildren lived a distance from the local area, enjoyed helping the children and tried to make them feel comfortable as well as important.

The families rotated preparing scrambled eggs for breakfast and would arrive half an hour early to insure the eggs and coffee being ready for 8:30. Creativity abounded as cheese, ham, and other delicious items were added to the eggs. Usually the women did the cooking, but there were lots of jobs for fathers and children such as setting the tables, getting the chairs, and arranging the serving table. No one was too young to help! One family offered to come early to help Mary, who would otherwise be alone as she prepared breakfast. The "Johnny Appleseed Grace" was sung each week which could be started easily by any adult or child.

The First Sessions

Following breakfast, everyone gathered on the large rug in the room for warm-up and songs. At first, families sat together as units, but gradually new friendships developed, and there was a blending of people. The L Family's children, in particular, enjoyed other people and would hold hands, put their arms around someone, or sit on a friend's lap.

Some of the songs the cluster sang had motions, and the inhibitions were obvious at first. A few teens and adults found it difficult to behave in such a "child-like" way. Were they wondering what people would think of them? What did they think of themselves? Favorite songs of the cluster were "Peanut Butter and Jelly," "Six Little Ducks," "Alice's Camel," "Bingo," "Father Abraham," and "The Cluster Song."

The first time we played Farmer in the Dell, the adults seemed to view it as a game for children. However, by the last week, Rick, the father of three, seemed excited to be chosen the farmer. His attitude, in turn, heavily influenced his teenagers and enabled them to relax and actively join the game. It seemed that the teens were trying to model adult behavior and were only as open as their parents or other significant adults might be.

After the cluster seemed "warmed up" and "loosened up," they discussed the objectives for the day. A cluster schedule was printed on newsprint and posted on a bulletin board each week. At first Katie and Henry discussed the schedule, but, after a few weeks, let the people read it on their own.

The educational activities, games, and projects were all derived from the theme "Building Bridges." It was an open theme that could be taken in any direction. Katie and Henry hoped to connect each person in the cluster to his own feelings. to the feelings and thoughts of members of his family, and to the feelings, thoughts, and actions of other people in different families.

The first activity involved each family creating their house and the vehicle in which they rode to cluster. Construction paper, scissors, paste, markers, and crayons were used. Katie and Henry had allowed ten to fifteen minutes for this project, but soon found everyone needed more time. A pipe cleaner was needed for a basketball hoop, tissues were needed for curtains, and more time was needed to create the detail the families wanted to express.

Katie had drawn a road map of the area on a large paper tacked to the wall: this was the focal point for sharing the houses and cars. Each family located the street where they lived and pasted their home on the map. Then, using yarn, they showed us how they drove to cluster and left a path of yarn with their car pasted on it at some point. Some families had lots of hills to travel over and might have difficulty on cold, icy mornings. Creating the map gave everyone an opportunity to see the distances people would travel to the place they came together for cluster sessions. From the various homes came many different feelings, values, abilities, backgrounds, systems, expectations, and dreams. Family Cluster would try to get in touch with some of those areas.

The Cluster Contract

For the cluster group to operate efficiently, it needed a contract to indicate the rules, expectations, and system that would provide a framework for the interactions. Families were asked to be prepared to discuss the content of the contract and to share their thoughts the second session of the following week.

"Building Bridges through Communication in Our Families" was the theme of the second week. The families were asked to think about the project they had done the previous week of making houses and cars. How did the family decide what to make? How did they communicate their ideas as a family?

Each person was asked to go to one of the tables containing pieces of cardboard, clay and toothpicks. On the cardboard, each one was to create a representation using clay and toothpicks of how his or her family communicated. About ten minutes later they took their creations over to the rug and sat in a large circle. The families then took turns going to the "fishbowl/center" with each member sharing with his or her family what he or she had made.

Some of the questions they were asked to consider in their sharing were: How were decisions made? Who made most of the decisions? Did anyone feel frustrated? How was the frustration handled?

This activity was something some families seemed open to doing, and the children indicated they had some experience in sharing their thoughts and feelings with other members of the family. However, other families seemed to show the strain of coming together to discuss their creations. Discomfort and anxiety prevailed. One boy had taken a hunk of clay and broken tooth picks in little pieces, which he then jabbed in his clay. His face was serious, and he did not want to share. Katie and Henry sensed the discomfort and suggested that the families might like to find opportunities at home during the coming week to discuss further how they communicated.

In the time that remained, the cluster contract was to be completed. The families had been working hard on their communication activity, played a game, and probably felt a little drained to start something else. Katie and Henry, realizing they had overplanned, suggested and wrote most of the contract. Families having previous cluster experience voiced their thoughts the most. How should the contract be signed?

The leaders had chosen to let the cluster decide the method for signing the contract. Three teams which had formed for playing a game were asked to determine a team suggestion for signing the contract. The three suggestions were presented and voted upon. Most people wanted to use the idea they had thought of, and no one method was collectively accepted. Larry, who was generally quiet, said, "Let's have anarchy!" So, Katie and Henry proposed that everyone be given the opportunity to sign the contract in their own way. This was unanimously approved; it would occur following the warm-up of Session Three.

Wow! Way too much had been planned for the second week. The leaders needed to consider this carefully in future planning and find time to restructure or to eliminate plans as needed during a cluster session. Katie and Henry decided their main objective for Session Three would be to complete the contract, to have it signed and to celebrate.

Since the third cluster was also the occasion of the NFL's Super Bowl, the leaders planned a Super Cluster Bowl complete with streamers, goal posts and teams. The local football team was to play in the Super Bowl, and everyone was encouraged to wear team colors.

After breakfast, the first order of business was signing the contract. Paints, potatoes, carrots, markers, and pens were used as each person signed his symbol. There were footprints, handprints, profiles, faces, and other creative representations. Everyone helped clean-up the materials and the Super Cluster Bowl began.

The whistle blew! Sarah and Mary were appointed team captains and asked to take turns selecting team members. Punt, pass, and kick competition ensued. New athletic ability was discovered! Lynn smiled proudly as she threw the ball the length of the field; and Joe commented, "We've got real jocks on our team!" Even eleven-year-old Lisa felt the need to prove she was a female who could perform punting, passing and kicking as well as any male. When the final whistle blew, the competition was over, winners announced, and cluster had its closing.

Meaningful Activities

Succeeding clusters dealt with talents, trust, frustrations, values, and self-esteem. A variety of activities and games were used, but, the following seemed to be the most meaningful to the majority of cluster members.

"Body Tracings with Inside Information"involved finding someone to trace your body on a large sheet of paper and then cutting out pictures or words from magazines that would identify what was important to each person. These were pasted inside. Each one thought about the size and shape of their body, knowing someone else would be touching and realizing the size too. Especially Mary was delighted that day because six-year-old Jenny wanted to work with her. Jenny's drawing abilities were not as sophisticated as some; but, her interest, enthusiasm, and caring were genuine.

Soon the cluster had a gallery of unique individuals' drawings taped to the walls. The following week, a "gallery tour"enabled each person to share personally and to describe what the inside pictures and words meant. Special interests, talents, and feelings were individually owned and proudly displayed. There was more to this cluster group than some had imagined. People seemed to feel special.

The "Decision Walk" forced everyone to make some clear-cut decisions in certain areas. Henry took charge and asked everyone to sit in the middle of the rug. He then asked each person to decide if he was a city person or a country person and go to the city or country-designated side of the rug. Then each separate group discussed why each person made his choice. Other decisions included these categories: a thinker or a doer, an on-time person or a late person, a leader or a follower, a cat or a dog. Some of the teenagers and children said they wanted to sit in the middle because they were not sure which they preferred; it's hard to acknowledge that sometimes it is difficult to make decisions.

Making valentines was another activity the cluster needed extra time to complete. Each person drew a name and then proceeded to make a valentine to give him or her. The valentines ranged from plain and simple to fancy, lacey, and elegant. Some of the adults commented, "I haven't made one of these things since I was a kid." Doilies, lace, construction paper, paste, scissors, and markers were used. Katie was pleased as she watched three-year-old Suzy present fourteen-year-old Jeff with the valentine she had made for him. He stooped down to make eye contact and expressed his delight at her special efforts for him. She responded with a hug and a kiss on his cheek. It appeared she had won his heart! Expressing affection does not have to cost anything; in fact, it can be priceless. That morning members of the cluster realized how much they valued each other and enjoyed expressing it.

Concluding Cluster Session

The final cluster activity was one of affirmation with the intent to build self-esteem. It was called "Pot Filling." The younger children made colorful flowers from construction paper which were taped to pipe cleaners that had been placed in clay. The pieces of clay were lodged in plastic cups that became flower pots. Leaves with names were attached to the pipe cleaner stems. Each person in the cluster had a flower pot. While the children had been working, the adults had been writing affirmative statements to everyone in the cluster on separate sheets of paper. The messages were folded and placed in the appropriate cups. Based on Virginia Satir's idea of "pot" or self-worth, the special statements hopefully would contribute to each person's self-esteem and be something to take home as a reminder of his or her special self.

The final cluster also included the opportunity for members of each family to share some dreams they had for their family. The families met separately and wrote their ideas on a special "dream card" that was to be taken home. Katie and Henry were gratified to see families really listening to each other and hopefully valuing what was said. It was exciting to identify dreams and to think about their possibilities for fulfillment.

The final cluster concluded with the usual closing, but somehow it had added significance because it would be the last time this group of people would be together as a cluster. Everyone stood in a circle as a cluster song was sung. Then they held hands for the Cluster Prayer.

> "Thank you God for our Family Cluster.
> Thank you for the chance to be together.
> In particular, thank you for . . . (They went
> around the circle saying everyone's
> name out loud)
> We are special people."

Evaluation

Prior to the final closing, cluster members were asked to complete this evaluation.

1 How did you feel?
   Enthusiastic   Neutral   Disappointed

2 How did the participants seem?
   Involved   Somewhat Involved   Uninvolved

3 How strong was the group cohesiveness?
   Solid   Moderate   Non-Existent

4 How facilitative was the leaders' behavior?
   Very   Somewhat   Not at all

5 Amount of Intergenerational interaction was . . .
   High   Moderate   Low

6 Family members' awareness of each other seemed to . . .
   Increase   Stay the same   Decrease

7 The opportunity to increase one's sense of self-worth existed . . .
   Always   Sometimes   Never

High points and things which were liked:

Family equality
Sharing times
Meeting new people
Quiet moments of reflection
Super Cluster Bowl
Pot Filling
Body Tracings
Breakfast together
Making houses
Discussion of feelings
Playing games
Children's comments
Fishbowl talks

Low points and things which were not liked:

Singing juvenile songs
Not enough processing of group direction
Too many games
Super Cluster Bowl
Not enough time to share

Things which helped the family:

All members had a chance to express themselves with others listening attentively
Co-operative family tasks
Hearing other families discuss their feelings
Seeing how other families act toward each other
Learning that other families have similar problems
Sharing feelings and group discussions
Setting aside time to be together.

Leadership suggestions for Katie and Henry:

Try to integrate towards goals better
Be less concerned if group gets off pre-arranged schedule
Be more assertive in maintaining schedule; start on time
Allow more time for some activities.

Katie and Henry considered their first cluster experience to be positive and successful. Their objective of providing opportunities for relating each person to his or her own feelings, to the feelings and thoughts of other members of the family, and to the feelings, thoughts, and actions of other people in different families had been met. The openness, honesty, sincerity and awareness of persons in the cluster had enabled many special moments to occur. However, poor cluster attendance seriously affected the cluster's ability to grow as a group and develop closeness. Chicken pox, the flu, other illnesses, travel, and unexpected events had contributed to the entire cluster being together only four sessions. This made planning and building on previous experiences difficult. Despite these factors, the leaders believe that the Winter Family Cluster of 1980 at the McKnight United Methodist Church was an opportunity for growth and enrichment.

As people in Family Clusters continue to get in touch with themselves and others, they will grow in their ability to experience the richness and fullness of living in relationship to others.

Resources

Agard, Bonnie. *Family Cluster Resources*. Chicago: The Evangelical Covenant Church of America, 1977.

Elkins, Dr. Dov Peretz. *Teaching People to Love Themselves*. Rochester: Growth Associates, 1977.

Waschow, Louise. *Experiential Exercises for Family Clusters*. 416 Pine St., Mill Valley, California (privately distributed).

Biographical Data

Ms. Bonnett obtained a B.S. in Elementary Education from Penn State; taught in rural mountain schools of Virginia 3 years and in suburban Pittsburgh 2 years. She has been married to a bank trust officer and mother of two pre-school children; past volunteer for the local Y.W.C.A.'s Racial Justice Task Force; Children's Co-Ordinator McKnight United Methodist Church; author of the "Church Family Experience" program for local church. She is presently attending Pittsburgh Theological Seminary.

Address:

402 Park Place
Pittsburgh, Pennsylvania 15237
(412) 364-1037

Ecumenical Family Clusters

Clusters in an ecumenical setting take more planning but are rich in diversity and sharing of religious traditions:

1 *An Ecumenical Family Cluster* by Agnes Burroughs, Ruth Baxter, Doyle Prier, and Lorraine Prier
A cluster in a fast-growing suburb of Halifax where three denominations share a common building.

2 *Shalom Family Cluster* by Sam Matthews
A cluster made up of families who attempted to create an intentional Christian community.

An Ecumenical Family Cluster

Agnes Burroughs
Ruth Baxter
Doyle Prier
Lorraine Prier

Nova Scotia, Canada

In the fall of 1975 two churches in Lower Sackville of Nova Scotia, Canada, St. Jean Vianney Roman Catholic Church, and Knox Disciples-United Church of Canada, sought to respond to the needs of people who need each other with an experience called Family Cluster.

Today, the Family Cluster program continues through the cooperation of St. John Vianney Roman Catholic parish and the church campus congregations of St. Timothy's Disciples-United Church and Saint Elizabeth Seton. The Church Campus is a facility shared by the Roman Catholics and Disciples-United Church of Canada.

The thrust that the church has taken in Sackville has been greatly influenced by the decisions of the Government of Nova Scotia as a community developer. In its decisions, the Government allotted one large tract of land in the Nova Scotia Housing development for "church purposes." This parcel of land, in the centre of the developed area, is the site of the Church Campus building.

Five denominations met and shared their concepts of a common facility. Finally there remained three—Roman Catholic, Disciples of Christ, and United Church of Canada—who shared in the construction of a multi-purpose building. This building houses a central worship area which congregations use for their separate worship services. At other times the same area is used for various purposes; religious, social, educational, recreational and community. It also has a permanent sanctuary, offices, meeting rooms, kitchen and a nursery.

The community was a growing one that seemed to "mushroom" over a short period of time. Up to 1960, the community was predominately rural, with a population of about 5,000. Through the Nova Scotia Housing Commission, much of the land was used for a cooperative housing project, so in 1980 the population grew to about 50,000.

The community is composed of families from across the world who are often far from the support of parents, grandparents, aunts and uncles. Although the population is stabilizing, there was a time when the families were very transient with an average stay of three years. Because of the rapid growth of the community, services such as schools, recreational facilities and counseling centers were inadequate. In the struggle to obtain services, efforts were made both in the direction of crisis intervention and of positive family life education.

Initiating the Concept

Due to the many commitments of the families and the difficulties involved in the scheduling of evening clusters, it was decided to invite families to a weekend cluster experience. At first it was a pilot program to see if it would respond to the needs of the people involved. The experience was such a positive one that weekend clusters have been held for the past five years.

For the first year it was thought that families should attend just one cluster weekend; however, in the years that followed this changed as families expressed the desire to attend several of the events. Over the past five years more than six hundred persons have participated in clusters.

Leadership

The persons who initiated the concept were Sister Agnes Burroughs and Vern MacAdam of the Roman Catholic congregation, Rev. Doyle Prier and Mrs. Lori Prier of the Disciples-United congregation. Because of their involvement in the community and their ministry to families, the group saw the need for a program such as Family Cluster. To enable themselves to be skilled leaders, Doyle, Lori and Sister Agnes attended a Family Cluster Training Laboratory in the summer of 1975 at the Atlantic Christian Training Centre in Tatamagouche, N.S., a facility of the United Church of Canada. Vern MacAdam served on the staff of the Lab. While at the Training Lab these four from Sackville decided that they would begin the cluster program on an ecumenical basis in the Sackville area. With the guidance of Don Reid, Director of the Atlantic Christian Training Centre, this became a reality.

The group of four persons who formed the original leadership were self-chosen, in effect. They saw the need for family life education with a preventative focus. They saw the Family Cluster Model an effective way of meeting this need; thus, creating the principal leadership for a number of years. After the first year, Vern had to discontinue the leadership role because of his heavy commitments elsewhere, but he has contuined to help in other ways. In July 1978, Lori and Doyle moved away.

The second group of leaders has emerged from the families attending the clusters. Encouraged by the original leaders and recognizing the value of cluster events for the community, two couples joined Sister Agnes in the leadership of cluster events: Ruth and Denny Baxter, representing the Disciples-United congregation and Diane and Don Walker representing the Roman Catholic congregation. In turn, they encouraged two couples to join them: Ron and Marian Weagle and Bernie and Emily Coffin who represented the two congregations, respectively.

The role of the leaders is varied. Up to the present time they are involved in and are responsible for every aspect of the cluster event:

1 Preparation of the event (includes setting dates, arranging for accommodations and meals, finalizing cost, and so on.)

2 Gathering of the families (including recruitment, screening, home visiting, agenda gathering, presenting the preliminary sessions.)

3 Design, implementation and evaluation of the program. This is done, using the human relations process of designing as outlined in *Family Enrichment With Family Clusters* by Margaret M. Sawin.

Also, the role of the leaders is to facilitate the group. They gather data from the families through an agenda-gathering process named "Stepping Stones" (see Appendix). This data gives direction to the weekend. The leaders then design an experiential-reflective process which provides an atmosphere in which the participants may grow. Sensitive to the hidden and unspoken concerns of the group, they enable the group members to articulate their anxieties. In their enabling role, the leaders remain part of the group, participating in the activities, reflection and sharing.

Each leader has brought different skills and experiences to the leadership. Following are some that were found helpful in carrying out leadership tasks:

> Openness to people and willingness to learn; a trust in people to carry out their agreement; an enjoyment of younger people; fun-loving; specific communication skills (active listening, "I-statements," conflict resolution); educational training; a facilitative-type of leadership; the sharing of power through contracting and agenda setting; understanding and facilitating of interpersonal processes between all ages; music; creativeness; experience in various kinds of growth groups; faith in God and in people; joy; involvement in community groups; caring; and a willingness to share.

Complementary Aspect

Team members became acquainted with each other's gifts, strengths, and weaknesses. Each member of the team complemented the other. A team approach was used in every aspect of the cluster event. Responsibilities were shared. There was a rotation of leader roles and participant-observer roles among the team members in each session. Observations were shared in an evaluation session of the leaders.

Basic Assumptions and Objectives

The original group of leaders spent many hours thrashing out its beliefs regarding persons and relationships. Assumptions were clarified regarding theological, educational and philosophical stances. A common ground was found on which all could agree and commit themselves. Some of the basic assumptions and objectives were :

- the heart of the religious education program is in the home, in the family;
- the source of a person's beliefs and values comes from the individual's human experience;
- the total life of the child is the arena of religious education;
- what one believes is reflected in the manner in which one deals with the joys, sorrows, problems, crises and concerns of daily life;
- reflection on beliefs should suggest ways life's issues are to be approached;
- the Family Cluster is an educational model through which families might grow;
- the Family Cluster is not therapy; it is not problem-oriented;
- the Family Cluster tries to create the possibility (opportunity) of looking at new ways of doing things as a family and as a member of a family;
- Family Cluster is for all families who want to build on their strengths and to grow together.

Objectives of a Family Cluster:

- to provide an opportunity for all ages (children, parents, grandparents) to share together fun, joy, singing, discussion, learning games, etc.;
- to provide a support group of all ages so that children can learn from the adults and adults from the children;
- to provide a learning place so that the family can plan, discuss and reflect upon ways to meet their needs in today's society;
- to provide an opportunity for the family to reflect upon its beliefs and values;
- to celebrate beliefs and life together;
- to provide an opportunity to develop family strengths;
- to practice some of the skills which improve the family's living together.

Problems Leadership Had to Meet

Problems arose when families did not attend the preliminary, introductory session in preparation for the weekend or when the leaders were not able to visit the families in their homes before the weekend. It seems there are certain anxieties and conflicts that can be discussed or clarified best in the home setting. If they are not dealt with before the cluster weekend, they can affect the whole group. The leaders try to make a point of meeting every family before the cluster weekend.

There were some problems in the Family Cluster being recognized as a viable form of family religious education. The best promotion of the program was the enthusiasm of the families who participated. Gradually the need for a family-oriented program has been recognized. Barriers toward an intergenerational model of education are *slowly* dissolving.

The approach of the leadership teams to this challenge is that as long as the program continues to meet the needs of families it will continue. As more and more families are touched by the experience, the more the program will be recognized. In the 1980 Year of the Family emphasis of the Catholic Church, the cluster program had a higher profile.

The recruitment of new leaders is an ongoing problem. Most of the husband and wife leaders have been involved as a couple. This has many advantages, such as keeping the family together as a unit for the weekend and being able to give more time together in the evaluation of the program and leadership. On the other hand, it implies that both partners have the desire and the aptitude for cluster leadership which may not be necessarily the case. The designing of a program which is based on the needs of a specific group is perceived as a value; this requires a great deal of time as well as design skills. Such requirements demand much commitment. For potential leaders who are already heavily committed, this can be a definite deterrent, and the problem has not been completely resolved.

Team Building

Team building among the leaders has been very important. If the needs of the leaders do not receive attention, the time allotted to the cluster task suffers. On the other hand, when some group building exercises are used, the group is energized for the task by the cohesion of the leaders. This is an ongoing challenge which requires constant attention.

Family Participation

Families have been in all stages of development and have included small babies, teenagers and grandparents. In one particular cluster the age range was from two-year-olds to seventy-six-year-old grandparents. Adolescents have been present through seventeen-year-olds. Although two-parent families predominate in the clusters, one-parent families participate as well. Most families are middle class.

Two of the clusters have been inter-racial, low income, single parent and mostly female. A lesson learned from these clusters was that the single parents needed to be brought together for a time without the children. This would have enabled them to meet some of their needs for quality time alone.

Couples without children have been involved, as well as families with a mentally retarded child. A large number of families involved have been in other groups such as Marriage Encounter, Transactional Analysis, Genesis II, Cursillo, Rochais, P.E.T. Most of the families have been open to experiencing growth in an intergenerational setting. The families have come from different faiths including Baptist, Anglican, Catholic and United-Disciples. Some single persons have also attended.

The family systems affect the cluster dynamic. The initial anxiety and dependency of families who are new to the cluster experience must be resolved if an atmosphere of trust and acceptance is to be built. The greater the number of "free" persons, the more freedom is called forth from the participants. A great amount of conflict within one family can cause tension within the larger group. If the struggle between "open" and "closed" family systems is not attended to with their different attitudes toward disciplining of children, tension will be created within the cluster group.

Contracting

Leaders and all members of the families attending meet together for an hour on a Sunday afternoon at least one to two months prior to the cluster weekend date. At that time information is given and the "stepping stones" (an agenda-gathering process) dealt with.

The sheet of stepping stones was originally given to persons to take home and fill out. With the last few clusters we have given the participants the forms to complete at the family gathering before the cluster. There are pros and cons for both ways. If given beforehand it seems there are persons who will wait until the last moment to fill them out; whereas, if they're filled out at the gathering the leaders have their use right way. However, persons find there is not enough time to think about their responses when filling them out for the first time at an introductory session.

Following the family gathering, a call is made to the families by the leaders and a date established for a follow-up visit. This meeting allows the leaders to become familiar with the families in their home-settings; establishes a personal contact; answers any questions the families may not have been comfortable asking in a group setting; as well as allows the opportunity to pinpoint problem areas within the family.

The cluster starts on a Friday evening and ends after lunch on Sunday for the weekend. This format is held three times a year. Each weekend has five sessions of 1-1/2 hours duration. The time format looks like this:

Friday

9:30-8:30	Cluster Session

Saturday

9:00-10:00	Cluster Session
10:00-10:30	Break
10:30-11:30	Cluster Session
	Lunch and Free Time
4:30-5:30	Cluster Session
	Supper
7:00-8:00	Cluster Session

Sunday

9:00-11:30	Cluster Session
	Lunch and Farewell

Along with the previous Sunday afternoon gathering, the group contracts during the *first session* of the Cluster weekend on Friday evening. One of the leaders is responsible for this. The group is asked to list those things they would like to see happen on the weekend. Following this they are asked to brainstorm guidelines they feel could be used to achieve goals for the weekend. The leaders model the process first. The group is encouraged to discuss the replies and to change any of the "rules" with which they may have had problems. They are asked to sign them; if unable to do so, they are to think about them, discuss them and sign them the next morning.

Problems always arise when we don't do contracting on Friday night. No matter how late the process goes, contracting must be done! One of the problems seemed to be that most people were not familiar with the process of setting up objectives for themselves and coming to an agreement on them as a group. They seemed not to be accustomed to taking responsibility for their own learnings and at times were actually unwilling to take such a responsibility.

The Group Process During One Weekend

The forces which helped build the group process of the particular weekend cluster from the leaders' points of view were:

Freedom of leaders
Location
Atmosphere/climate
People's attitudes
Giant hug—touching
Responsible participation
Acceptance of each person
Communication of ideas and feelings

Ice breakers (first evening)
Group building
Seclusion (At a camp where everyone is together at all times and not able to break away from the group)
Shared leadership
Authenticity

The following were taken from participants' evaluation sheets regarding forces which assisted the group process:

- Having to live for three days really clustered in one area, one has to live in the presence of others of not only your own but an extended family. The scheduled cluster time and a quiet time for sharing.
- Community sharing of sleeping and eating together.
- Recognition of participants who shared common interests and previous experiences, e.g. P.E.T., Marriage Encounter, Cursillo, etc.
- Large family concept of sharing for responsibilities and activities. "No frills" atmosphere.
- Getting to know people better and making new friends by talking and listening to others.

- I really think that the Holy Ghost was there working among us.
- Forces of love, understanding, communication, awareness of others.
- Working together on projects and sharing with one another. Singing together.
- Games, hymns, sharing, free time.
- Good leadership, spirit of love, openness, and patience.

The forces which deterred the group process, from the participants' points of view were:

- The time, lack of it. You're given good food for thought, not enough time to think and reflect, then share.
- Lack of promptness in beginning activities, but we liked the generous use of time in other ways.
- Failure to reach agreement on ground rules and approach to discipline.
- Shyness on arrival and nervousness over what was going to happen.
- There weren't any forces hindering our group that I know about. I truly feel there was no force hindering the group.
- There wasn't anything that hindered the group. Everybody got along just fine.
- Inattention, bad jokes.
- Teen peer pressure.

The forces which deterred the group process, from leaders' points of view were:

- Families not mixing.
- People coming in late the first evening.
- Negative attitudes.
- Unwillingness to participate.
- Poor communication of ideas and feelings.
- Lack of group-building activities when freedom of persons was stifled.
- Fear and anxiety.

The stages of group life through which the groups generally lived included moving from an initial apprehension and dependency on the leaders to a point where there was some sharing of leadership among the participants. As persons became more responsible for their own learnings, they were more able to confront some of the underlying hassles of the group.

The Educational Process

Each weekend usually had one theme for the five sessions with approximately eight hours being spent in sessions. Various themes which we have explored are: Christmas, Easter, Pentecost; Positive self image; Changing Seasons; "Cocoons to Butterflies," and Communication Skills.

From the leaders' perspectives, those things which were helpful were as follows: the use of scroll to portray the Easter story (this was used in a family worship setting by persons participating in that particular cluster); games where people and families reflect; communication skills; positive strokes; collages on the subject "I like you for _____"; image building; discussions; crafts; songs; name tags.

From participants' perspectives, the following were found helpful from evaluation sheets:

- Activities dealing with listening, reverse roles played out with the kids. The activities that make us look at our good qualities and own them. *Good News Bible* readings.
- Use of the "Bingo Game"; the plant; singing.
- The unplanned things for children to do.
- Looking at the "gift-ness" of each one and as a family.
- Incorporating prayer as part of the whole process, easy, comfortable.
- Planning ahead as family, i.e., planting seed allowed us to bring the experience home.
- Group discussions being open and frank; candor of children and teenagers.

- Making the scrapbook; enjoyment of sharing good meals and singing. Being with people of different ages. The church service, especially the Bread Ritual.
- Getting to know each other since our everyday life seems to divide the family. I felt we were working together as a family.
- Getting involved with others, sharing happiness, a feeling of well-being. A real closeness at meals. Campfire— everyone lost their shyness completely, and prayer time.
- All activities that took place. The poster was helpful for my family and me.
- Games, plays, spiritual services, sharing.

From the leaders' perspectives, those things which were difficult were as follows: certain kinds of collages; times participants were asked to find "things I like about me" (self-disclosure); questions, i.e., "What do I think about this?" "What do they want from me?" or, "What is it they want me to say?"; reflection times; allowing children time to talk first, prior to adult input; the difficulty for adults to let children reflect; allowing children to be responsible for their own learnings; contracting.

From participants' perspectives, the following were taken from evaluation sheets:

- The activities that touch our spirituality, our relationship to God; I feel inadequate to give this message of God's love (each one's uniqueness as a gift of God) to my *children* and others. I know it can't be done in three days, but must be lived each day; but it takes a time like cluster to stir up a guilty conscience. . . *That's good!*
- The candy search, although a fun exercise, revealed an inability to work together with one leader.
- Speaking to others when their back was turned to me (an exercise). Hard to get to the cluster on time.
- I saw my family working together and enjoying each other and singing.
- My five-year-old enjoyed it *all*. She didn't want to go home, and she loves home. I get excited even yet as I think of that wonderful weekend.

- Posters; lateness of bedtime hours.
- We felt there should have been a Mass.
- Leisure-time activities; I had the feeling that our family was really split, as the teenagers wanted to be by themselves.

Evaluation sheets were given to each person on the last day of the cluster to fill out before they left for home. The leaders evaluated after each session and at the end of the weekend. The participants made very positive remarks most of the time with comments having to do with the retreat setting and organization; very few of the comments had to do with cluster sessions. Comments made were very constructive, and improvements were made in other clusters based on suggestions from evaluation sheets.

How the Cluster Was Concluded

Each cluster event concluded with a Celebration; the following is a format for one:

Call to Worship
An Opening Hymn: "Amazing Grace," for example
Ritual of the   A. Making of unleavened bread (Activity)
Bread:

                B. Reflection on the meaning of bread and honey in our lives. (*Note*: Bread was left to cook as the group moved on to next ritual.)

Ritual of   A. Each person in the group planted a hyacinth
Planting the   bulb which they took home and watched grow.
Bulb: (Activity)

                B. The theme of the weekend was growth through change. (Reflection)

Reading from the Scriptures—reflection on the Word.
Prayer of Petition. (Spontaneous)
Lord's Prayer. Activity—Breaking and sharing of bread.
             Silent Reflection.
Prayer of Thanksgiving.
The Closing Hymn.

There were several meetings held after the first clusters; however, there was no definite follow-up with all cluster groups. It was difficult for leaders to undertake this, and participants were not interested in undertaking the responsibility. There was a Family Cluster Picnic, with attempts at having others; but, again, participants were not interested in doing this on their own. A number of families have returned to several other cluster weekends; others have gone on to other growth experiences.

Adaptations

The Family Cluster Model has been adapted in various ways. Some adaptations included: a day retreat for Catholic Deacons' families; two hour preparation sessions for Feast Days (e.g., Christmas, Easter); Family Worship; Single parents' Cluster. (In Family Worship a Scripture reading or theme is chosen. An intergeneration activity is experienced and reflected upon. This reflection is then shared with the group. The service includes songs and group building exercises as well.)

Resources

Purple Puzzle Tree. St. Louis, MO: Concordia Publishing House, 1971. (Series of 6 records plus books of 36 stories)

Larson, Roland S., and Larson, Doris E. *Values and Faith: Value-Clarifying Exercises for Family and Church Groups.* Minneapolis: Winston Press, Inc. 1976.

Simon, Sidney, et al. *Values Clarification.* New York: Hart Publishing Co., Inc. 1972.

"Purple Turtle" Rochester, N.Y. Family Clustering, Inc. A quarterly news-letter for leaders of Family Clusters.

Biographical Data

Doyle F. Prier, B.A., Panhandle State University, Goodwell, Oklahoma; Bachelor of Divinity in Religious Education, Central Baptist Theological Seminary, Kansas City, Kansas; minister in the United Church of Canada; minister of education; instructor of PET, YET; marriage enrichment leader; father of three; youth leader; Ad hoc committee of Children with Learning Disabilities, Bathurst.

Address:

Westminster United Church
247 Broadway
Orangeville, Ont. Canada.
(519) 941-0381

Loraine Penner Prier, B. A. in education, Panhandle State University, Goodwell, Oklahoma; Master's studies in Counseling, University of Kansas, Lawrence, Kansas; taught jr. high and sr. high English and Music; counselor in Juvenile Court Johnson County in Kansas; parish work — involved in various aspects of music, particularly with youth and children; instructor of PET, YET, TET; marriage enrichment leader; youth leader, mother of three children.

Address (see above).

Sister Agnes Burroughs, Sister of Charity, B. A.; teaching certificate from Mt. St. Vincent University; teaching for 15 years; pastoral ministry for 11 years; missionary for 3 years in Peru; instructor of PET, YET; spiritual director for Cursillo and Marriage Encounter in Sackville, N.S.; on various committees at parish and diocesan levels; involved in community organizations; designed, implemented and evaluated various workshops in communications, social awareness, consciousness-raising, and family values programs.

Address:

St. Joseph's College
90 Wellsley St. W.
Toronto, Ont. M5S C5, Canada
(416) 924-2121

Ruth Baxter, completed grade XI, secretarial training; mother of two boys, ages 14 and 10 and a girl, age 6; taught Sunday school; chaired various community committees; member church worship committee; co-leader of family worship service; PET instructor; attended Marriage Encounter, Genesis II programs; interested in ecumenical endeavors and family life education.

Address:

341 Highway No. 1
Lr. Sackville, Nova Scotia, B4C 2R7, Canada.
Tel: (902) 865-9403.

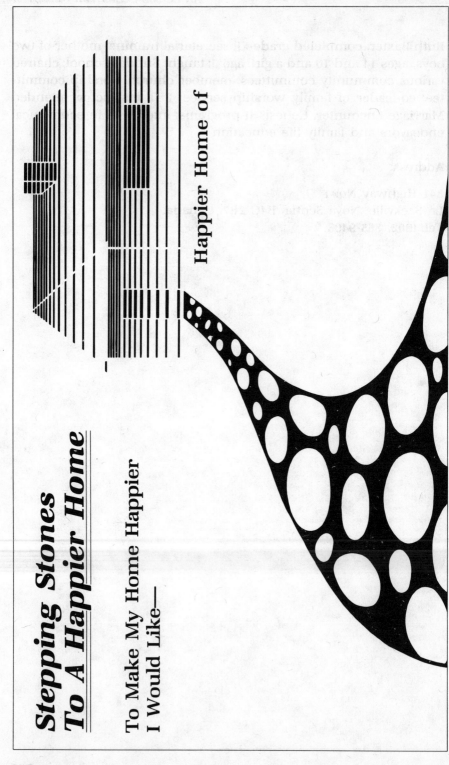

Stepping Stones To A Happier Home

To Make My Home Happier
I Would Like—

Happier Home of

Shalom
Family Cluster
Sam Matthews

Winston-Salem, N.C.

Family Cluster

The Family Cluster is nice and fun.
Also, it is nice to go to the family's house.

The food, fun, and fellowship
Have filled so many hours together.

Whobodies, love balls, sculptures, and giggles.
Big families, small families, small boys with wiggles.

What do you do there?
You have a great time!

Family Cluster is a place I know I can go,
To live and learn and love and grow.

To share with others,
With likeness and love we live.

Looking for special ways to give.
And knowing we will always receive ...

Love, hugs, care and tenderness.
What more could we ask from each other.

I always needed another brother.
Every other Sunday we did meet—

And we talked,
And a lot of food we did eat.

[The group poem on the previous page was written during a cluster exercise in March 1980. Each person wrote two lines, folded the paper so that the next person only saw the second line, and the next person wrote their two lines, and so on. The groups were simulated families of 4 to 6 people, children and adults. After the poems were written and shared in the family, they were read aloud for the entire cluster as a celebration.]

Beginnings

In May of 1979, approximately 20 families were contacted by Janice and Mahan Siler about their interest in creating an intentional Christian community using the Family Cluster Model. The conviction of the families who initiated the cluster was that the model presented an alternative context for Christian community in which the marks of the church—worship, fellowship, education, and ministry—could be realized. The Silers had been involved in pastoral care and various forms of enrichment and were interested in motivating clusters to get started.

The families contacted were somewhat unique in that all had had previous cluster involvement (including leadership for many) or had shared the deep concern for an alternative church experience with a focus on personal and family growth in a Christian context. Two exploratory meetings were held with the adults to explore fully the nature of the proposal and the commitment of time and other resources. Eventually eight families agreed to begin with the cluster, and an initial contracting session was held one evening in September with the entire family units together. This meeting was held to bring the children into the decision, clarify the purpose, outline the process and leadership roles, and answer questions. The families also decided on a date for an all-day retreat as a "kick-off" for the cluster.

The purposes agreed to were:
- To meet the primary needs for community or extended family.
- To provide experiences for Christian education and personal, marriage and family enrichment.

- To provide opportunities for worship in family settings.
- To share in the common mission for enhancing marriage and family life in our community.

The Commitment

Specific commitments were discussed in four areas: time, Christian growth and ministry, mission, and leadership.

Time. The cluster time frame was set as October 1979 to July 1980—ten months. Adult meetings and full family sessions were scheduled. The adults met every other Monday night from 7:30-9:30 in the homes. This provided for some 20 meetings on a wide variety of agenda items (discussed later). The full cluster met every other Sunday afternoon from 1-4:30, beginning with a covered dish lunch. This provided for 20 cluster sessions of 3¹/₂ hours in the homes of the families. Two retreat sessions were also planned for the total cluster, the kickoff in October and a weekend (Friday evening to Sunday lunch) in May.

Christian Growth and Ministry. The focus was the sharing of a common devotion to Christian discipleship. There would be flexibility in the response to each person's own needs at this point in his or her spiritual journey. Support for religious education and faith development would be a component of both the adult and full cluster meetings.

Mission. The primary focus would be the exploration of establishing a family enrichment center. This had been actively discussed among some in the group, and it was thought that the cluster—as a focus group—could determine the feasibility and timing of such a concept.

Leadership. The leadership would be shared by those having training and leadership experience initially. All other participants would be invited to share in the leadership as time passed. This would include youth and adults.

Leadership

The leadership for the cluster came from within the cluster membership. Eight adults from five of the families had previous training and experience in family enrichment which included Family Cluster education at Laurel Ridge Family Enrichment Training Workshop. Seven of the adults were also part of the Training Workshop conducted by Margaret Sawin in Winston-Salem during the fall of 1979. Four of the families had been in a cluster experience for nine months which added to the experience of the group.

The kickoff session and the first two months of the cluster sessions were led by the experienced adults. This was coordinated through planning and design sessions on a continuing basis. At the end of this period, leadership teams were formed voluntarily for the adult and family sessions to cover a three month period. Each team (for the family sessions) consisted of trained persons, other interested adults, and youth. As of this writing during the seventh month of the cluster, 23 of the 27 persons in the cluster have assumed some leadership role however small or large. This has added to the meaning of the cluster process for many.

After the three-month period, the leadership format changed. This followed an evaluation period where format and content were assessed. A new voluntary team was formed for the adult meetings, and the family hosting the Sunday cluster session agreed to provide leadership for that session, along with some of the other persons, periodically. This change grew out of the concern for additional meetings and the general pressure of time commitments felt by all.

The skills and experience which the cluster leadership found important are those which are well outlined in *Family Enrichment With Family Clusters*. Additionally, it was discovered that untrained, and yet highly motivated adults and youth, could be assimilated into the leadership teams with relative ease so that they could become even more involved in the full process. Guidance and support from trained leadership is essential. The leadership, arising from the group, actively participated also as a part of the experience at each level, i.e. as parent, partner, individual, etc. This added to the experience of all involved and further supported the modeling found to be so valuable.

The Families

The families came from varied Protestant denominations: Baptist, Methodist, Moravian, Episcopal. The level of participation in the church of each family varied from highly active to inactive at the time of the cluster formation. A graphic picture of the cluster system and the families involved is shown in Figure 1. The number of regular participants in the cluster was 27; however, as many as 35 have been in attendance with extended family members being present. Fifteen adults and twelve children have been the active and regular participants.

Two of the participating families had other family members in the household who chose not to be involved. In one case, this was the teenage son of a family and in another, it was the spouse of a dual-parent family who had no children in the home. In the case of the remaining adult of the couple without children in the cluster, it has produced some stress, due to meeting time, place, the Sunday meals, as well as the sharing of the experience itself. Two adults in the cluster had been in counseling for personal reasons, and this has added both positive and negative dimensions to the process. Both affirm that the cluster has been a significant support system for them during this period in their lives.

Two adult women from dual-parent families were also full-time graduate students. One found that she had to disengage for a period of time (approximately 2 months) due to time demands. This obviously affected the family involved, the simulated family designs, and the individual. It was done with disclosure to the full group so that they were aware of the situation.

All the families initially contracted to be in the cluster and agreed that it would be a significant commitment for them. Except for the situations outlined above, and the occasional absences of some for sickness or work, the families have held to the contract; this has been identified as a strength by the entire cluster.

FIGURE 1

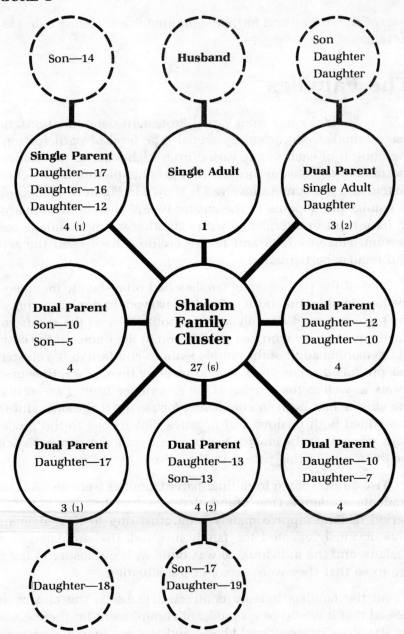

NOTE:

- Dotted lines indicate extended family members of immediate family
- Numbers in parenthesis indicate persons who participated occasionally

Contracting

Originally, each family was contacted by letter which outlined the purpose and general commitment for the cluster. The adults met then on two occasions to clarify involvement, leadership, and content. A third pre-cluster session was held with all family members present to involve the children and youth in the overall process.

During the all-day "kickoff" retreat, initial group contracting was begun. This was done using the "fishbowl"* method with youth and then adults in the center circle as they brainstormed agenda/process type concerns. The first two regular cluster meetings included also a continuation of the group contract. By the third session we reached concensus that all major items had been addressed and further concerns would be dealt with as they occurred. Additionally, the adults spent time contracting separately for their own Monday sessions. (See Figure 2 for areas covered during contract periods.)

The only significant problems to arise from the contracting were in two areas: the Sunday schedule and the bringing of guests. The initial contract called for a 1-5 P.M. time period. At the first two sessions it became obvious that a 1-4:30 time was more appropriate due to other family schedules, i.e., church youth groups, choirs, etc. The guest issue arose when one family brought another family with them to a full cluster session. The cluster family had announced this at a previous meeting, but it was not heard by most people because of the time period in which it was made. The "unannounced" family created some concern for several adults, and this was fully discussed in the next adult session. The scope of concern was group dynamics, the "closed environment," and some feelings of infringement on openness and freedom in the cluster. The open sharing led to two major changes in our contract: 1) a definite business or announcement time was needed at both sessions to avoid misunderstanding around issues of interest, and 2) that guests were welcome at the Sunday sessions with advance notice at the previous meeting.

---

*"fishbowl" is a technique where persons who are to talk sit in the circle of other persons who listen.

Contract Items of Family and Adult Cluster Sessions—Figure 2

FAMILY

—Dates and Time
—Discipline
—Decision making
—Topics + meeting types, i.e. trips, retreats, etc.
—Financial commitment
—Leadership
—Birthdays and holidays
—Duration
—Fun + games `

—Meeting place(s)
—Religious emphasis
—Meal responsibilities
—Level of participation

—Concerns/check in
—Attendance
—Expectations
—Process
—Friends + guests

ADULTS

—Process
—Leadership
—Expectations
—Dates and time
—Topics

—Place
—Children at meeting
—Concerns
—Attendance
—Level of participation

One area of the overall purpose and the contract which has received minimum attention has been mission. It was generally thought that the timing for our involvement has not "arrived"; that is, even though much time has been spent in meeting, this time has been needed for "inward" attention to each person, family, and the group. The only significant mission involvement to date has been the decoration and planting of a live Christmas tree at the Battered Women's Shelter of Winston-Salem. The shelter was in a new location with little landscaping and was filled to capacity with women and children during the Christmas season. Two cluster adults were on the Board of the shelter; during a session they raised this as an outreach project. It served as a good program focus and allowed for focusing on decision making and contracting within the cluster.

The Cluster Process

Through the use of an interim evaluation, the full cluster spent some time looking at the process. Those reflections are provided below under the categories evaluated:

- **What has helped bring the cluster together as a group?**
  —People sharing similar interests
  —Openness and caring
  —Shared leadership, particularly the children
  —Eating Sunday meals together
  —Simulated family groupings
  —Meeting in family homes
  —Fun and creative activities
  —Good planning

- **What has kept the cluster from being what it could be?**
  —Sharing of leadership caused a lot of organization time at first, and left some confusion
  —Hectic schedule, lack of more lengthy sessions
  —Irregular attendance at times
  —Focus, at times, on problem areas versus growth/ enrichment
  —Lack of focus on mission
  —Level of intimacy—still at surface level at times

- **Contracting: original or changed commitments**
  —At times, it still was not clear
  —Periodic reinforcement needed
  —Frequency of meetings, mission—a concern for some
  —Re-contracting around leadership was positive
  —Flexibility

- **Activities found to be helpful.**
  —Children acting in leadership role
  —Simulated family groupings
  —Activities focused on spiritual growth and reflection
  —Verbal and non-verbal communications
  —Adult meetings
  —Play and games
  —Meals together, all-day session
  —Sharing and trust activities

- **Activities found *not* to be helpful**
  —None other than those listed under what has kept cluster from being where it could be.

- **What has meant most to you personally?**
  —Positive "warm fuzzy" approach
  —Creative activities with art, other media
  —Being with my family and other families
  —Leadership of children
  —The caring shown
  —Worship and religious reflection
  —Different ages and types of families (dual and single parent)
  —Communication skills
  —Fellowship
  —Regular meetings with continuity
  —Seeing my children with other adults
  —Sharing of values

- **What ways has the cluster affected you and your family?**
  —We do more together
  —Having adult friends as well as friends my age
  —Worship in homes has been very helpful
  —Has helped us nurture each other more
  —More openness with spouse
  —Skills have helped us communicate better
  —We have felt loved and cared for by others.

The Educational Process

Using the agenda obtained from the "kickoff" session and the early meetings, sessions were planned to focus on the issues which seemed of major interest to the group. The adult meetings were also focused on issues raised during that meeting time.

Types of sessions we have had during the year have been:

Formation—Three meetings of two hours each in the evening with meal.

Kickoff—One day retreat from 9 A.M.-4 P.M. held at a nearby camp-site.

Adult meetings—Every other Monday evening from 7:30-9:30, in homes.

Cluster meetings—Every other Sunday, alternating with adult meetings, from 1-4:30 P.M. with pot luck meals.

Retreat—Friday evening through Sunday lunch with a program; to focus on "where we go from here"—the next year for cluster members. Held at local campsite for convenience.

The process of each meeting focused initially on individual concerns and then on the topic theme for the session. All topics were handled experientially, often using some writing or drawing followed by sharing with others in the family or simulated family. Often the adult sessions used dyads or triads for sharing of learnings. Singing and playing were very much a part also of the full cluster sessions. The sessions and list of topics for the cluster are shown in Figure 3.

Cluster Topics for Adult and Full Family Sessions—Figure 3

ADULT SESSIONS

—Reflection on first two family sessions

—Fantasy on where we are now and where we hope to be in 6 months

—Adult session topic brainstorming session

—Personal history sharing, using graph of significant events

—Topic brainstorming and leadership for Dec. to Feb.
—Christmas reflection—feelings, preparation for, and intentions
—Relaxation through head and foot massage
—Cross-roads of decision making in 1979 and plans for 1980
—Faith Development—journal writing
—Parenting—needs, communications
—Nurturing Parent—self nurture
—Aging—Images and relationships to parents

FAMILY SESSIONS

—Group building
—Personal and family strengths
—Contracting
—Family rituals
—Jesus' ministry of touching
—Self-esteem—"I Am Lovable and Capable" (The IALAC Story, Niles, Il.: Argus Communications, 1973.)
—Trust walk
—Family history sharing
—Our feet as instruments of carrying God's message
—Family sharing around birth experience of each child
—Jesse Tree—symbols of Christmas
—Advent wreath service
—Family Christmas traditions
—Homemade decoration of live tree for Battered Women's Shelter
—Share fun things of Christmas just past
—Collage group get well card—for girl who broke ankle
—Form simulated families with skits and name game
—"Paper Castle" exercise of non-verbal communications
—Barriers and gateways to communications
—Relection on communications with God.
—Communication styles—Satir
—Communication styles of Jesus
—Story telling and games
—"Whobody" story (Charles and Ann Morse, Whobody There. Winonoa, MN.: St Mary's College Press, 1971.)

—The whobodies in our life

—Film, *Jesus of Nazareth* (Genesis Project, Inc., P.O. Box 37282, Washington, DC 20013.)

—Relationship of Jesus to God as Father to Son

—Nurturing and critical parenting

—Loving and caring using *Being a Lover* from (David Marquis, *Making Love a Way of Life*. Niles, IL: Argus Communications.)

—Parenting—changing roles with children and relection on the roles played by each. How did it feel?

—Hugging—(David H. Ross, *A Book of Hugs*. NY: Thomas Y. Crowell, 1980.)

Evaluations

· Interim evaluations have been held within the cluster—both for the adult sessions and the full cluster. These were done at mid-point in the year and were handled differently. The adults used a force-field approach where each person listed expectations and the forces which worked for and against them. These were shared with an emphasis on where we go from here. The total cluster was done by family groups and then shared in the total group and listed. Again, the focus was on the future and was of assistance in planning for those sessions. Some of the evaluation input which was found to be most helpful was:

ADULT SESSIONS	TOTAL FAMILY SESSIONS
Leadership for three months at a time was too long	More "unstructured" time desired
Frequency and length of meetings beginning to cause conflicts in spring	More play and games
Lack of focus on mission	All day or weekend time needed
More emphasis on faith issues	More simulated family activities
Parenting emphasis desired	

The Future

At this point of writing, the cluster is in its seventh month. We plan to re-contract for the future in a weekend retreat where ample time can be spent on reflection and plans. The two options tentatively explored to date have been a continuation of the cluster as is and a possible splitting, with three or four families becoming the nucleus of new "extended clusters" which might meet jointly from time to time. Almost everyone seems committed to the cluster process as a meaningful one and wants to be a part of some continued effort next year.

Resources

Agard, Bonnie. *Family Cluster Resources*. Chicago: Evangelical Covenant Press, 1977.

Briggs, Dorothy. *Your Child's Self Esteem.* Garden City, N.Y: Doubleday & Co. Inc., 1970.

Gordon, Thomas. *Parent Effectiveness Training*, New York: Wydan Books, 1973

Satir, Virginia. *Peoplemaking*, Palo Alto, CA: Science and Behavior Books, 1972.

Biographical Data

Samuel C. Matthews is an active layperson in the Moravian Church. His enrichment training includes Marriage and Family Enrichment, Family Cluster Education, and Couple Communications. Sam has been active with his wife, Peggy, and two teenage daughters in the participation and leadership of two 9-month clusters. He is a local businessman who is also active in many civic organizations.

Address:

1220 Forsyth Street
Winston-Salem, N.C. 27101
Tele. (919)-748-1066

Family Clusters Outside the Continental United States

Clusters are adaptable in countries with industrialized patterns, for the need to have support communities is strong among families in such settings.

1 *Family Clustering: United Church of Canada* by Valerie M. Griffin
A cluster in a smaller community, representing a local congregation of the largest denomination in Canada.

2 *Clustering Comes to Australia* by Moira Eastman and Helen Praetz .
The story of a cluster composed of Catholic families in the large city of Melbourne.

3 *Family Clustering in England* by Martin Goodlad
A cluster composed of Anglican families in the city of London.

Family Clustering: United Church of Canada

Valerie Griffin

Hornby, Ontario

With the backing of the Christian Education Committee, Hillcrest United Church in Hornby, Ontario, Canada, sponsored a ten-session Family Cluster held weekly in the Fall of 1979. It was a follow-up to two concurrent clusters which had been held to give a taste of clustering to families who were curious, but might be unwilling to make a long-term commitment. All who attended were enthusiastic and readily agreed to be a part of an ongoing group. About half of the families wanted some further sessions. With the addition of one new family, we started another cluster. With leaders, the group totalled twenty-four people, ten of whom were children, ranging in age from three to sixteen years.

Leadership

My husband, John, who is the minister of the church, and I were leaders. Our roles included planning and executing the weekly programs according to the needs and interests of the families. Much of our combined education and experience proved helpful at this time. We both had participated with our family in a Family Cluster Laboratory Training at Five Oaks Centre in Paris, Ontario, taking turns receiving the training in two Labs. In 1979 I returned to Five Oaks to take Track II Training under the leadership of Margaret Sawin. It was an exciting and challenging time.

John's sixteen years in various aspects of the parish ministry were certainly an effective preparation for clustering. Here he could relate small group skills and Christian nurture principles. My own background is in elementary school teaching, church work with all ages, parenting, and counseling teenagers.

As John is the musician of the family, the task of teaching songs and accompanying the group on the guitar naturally fell to him. I usually taught the games, as I was more familiar with them. Most of the other leadership responsibilities were shared equally.

In planning often we did some work alone, then pooled our resources. Together we added ideas, made changes and came up with a fairly polished outline. We then marked down our timing, responsibilities, and materials needed.

On the whole we worked well together. However, being married, we tended to procrastinate our planning sessions. (When we had shared leadership with others, in the first cluster experience, we had to have set times to meet.) Sometimes our different needs and temperaments caused tension. I tend to initiate thinking about planning and want more detailed preparation, whereas John can be more spontaneous and less anxious. Co-leading made us more aware of our differences as a couple in style, timing, needs and values. Working out those differences was often painful and time-consuming but always rewarding in the long run. Love, patience, common objectives and much humor helped us through the rough spots. All these factors aided our growth as individuals and as a couple. At the cluster conclusion, one thirteen-year-old thanked us for being "kind, thoughtful, neat people." If this is what came across in our combined leadership style, then we fulfilled our purpose.

The Families

The Kozaks were our newest family, having moved recently to the area from western Canada. The father is Ukranian in background and travels a lot in his business. The mother is an artist and runs a boarding kennel for dogs. They have three daughters, fifteen, thirteen and nine years, all with different personalities and skills.

The Summers are a family with a daughter, age twelve, and two young boys, three and five; they had had a lot of illness at the time of the cluster. The father travels widely in his Government work as an environmental scientist in atmospheric research. The mother is interested in early-childhood education and country living. She sometimes experiences frustration at being housebound.

The Harrises consist of the father who owns his own company, the mother who enjoys her many animals and amateur dramatics. They have two children, a boy of eleven and a girl of eight.

The Kellys are an Irish family. The father is a rising executive who sings in a barber-shop quartet. The mother is starting to work part-time for a travel agent. They have a girl of eleven and a boy of eight.

The Schmidts are German immigrants who run a large dairy farm. Attending the cluster with them were their two daughters, eight and sixteen, the older of whom is president of the church's youth group. Their other three older children were busy with their studies and jobs.

On the whole, these families had open systems with good communication. By attending the cluster they expressed their desire to grow and change. Naturally, they all were at different stages of development; but this only added to what they could share with each other.

Having a new family prevented us from being "cliquey." They brought "new blood" and interest to us all. Shared parenting was sometimes needed and happened quite naturally. It was unfortunate that there had to be occasional absences, but we made adjustments as any family unit must do.

Contracting

All the families, except one, had participated previously in a cluster so they were familiar with the process of contracting. The other family was visited at home, data was collected, and all aspects of clustering were discussed, including the contract. The total group dealt with the cluster contract early in the sessions without any problems. Contracting was accomplished in a light-hearted way through a game. As a wrapped package was passed around the group, a record was playing. When the music stopped, whoever was holding the parcel ripped off a layer of paper to find a note concerning an aspect of clustering. These included such topics as: time, place, meals, clean-up, shared parenting, etc. As each subject was discussed and a decision made, it was recorded on the flip-chart, and the parcel moved on. This process kept the interest of the children, and they all participated readily. The last person to receive the diminished package was our youngest member who delightedly discovered a bag of jellybeans inside, which he was persuaded to share with all of us. The final contract was then checked over and signed with unique hand and finger prints of each person. The time commitment was for ten sessions.

Although everyone agreed with all the items in the contract, we leaders felt that sometimes it was not taken as seriously as we would have liked. Most of the difficulties had to do with attendance, which was out of our control, because two men had to travel for their businesses and the farmer had to take his turn on a milking schedule. These matters were discussed, and allowances were made for absences. There was hardly a week with everyone present which made for frustrations and disappointments.

The following week there was opportunity for further planning, which was done in peer groups. The adults met by themselves, John organized the younger ones, and I helped the older children. All contributed good ideas regarding programs, games, food, etc. These were worked into our further planning as leaders. It seemed to be an effective way to meet individual needs and to make sure each person was heard.

The Cluster as a Group

The group process went along naturally in some ways, because friendships were already present. And yet, sometimes this could have been a hindrance with an "in" group and an "out" group. We did our best to incorporate the new family into the cluster, and I feel it went smoothly. They seemed to enjoy attending and participating, and yet I sensed some reserve. They did not seem too comfortable showing affection; one of the teens said when asked what she liked the least—"the hugging game." We tried not to push the affection issue, but trusted the family felt care from the others.

Sometimes the Schmidts seemed to be on the edge of the group also. They had been in a former cluster, and the parents had been involved with us in some study groups. However, the other three couples and ourselves had continued together in a closer situation which included a lot of personal sharing. At the time of the cluster, John and I were the leaders officially of the other group; but the roles were often rotated with the other members which resulted in feelings of equality, nurturing and trust. It developed into a support group for all of us, so an unofficial group already existed within the cluster. Naturally, our expectations for continued intimacy and openness were colored, as this relationship continued within the new cluster.

John and I felt very responsible for leadership of the cluster and were less personally involved than in some other groups. There were always many details needing to be checked to ensure the program running smoothly. Sometimes this prevented me from just "being" with people about whom I cared. However, I benefitted from the experience in many other ways. Being appreciated as a person and also as a leader was an advantage, as well as seeing family closeness being developed. I could see some of the cluster concepts being lived, i.e., participants recognizing the worth and opinions of each individual. Moreover, I experienced a loving community which made me humble and thankful. Cluster provided a valuable experience through sharpening my skills which will assist me in leading other groups. The more I learn of the ideals of clustering and the potential of individuals and of families, the more I realize how far there is to go!

The stages of group life progressed fairly predictably. I sensed that some of the early stages of inclusion were omitted for many of us, due to the past history of families being together. There was a distinct movement from separate families to a "cluster family" with its own identity. As experiences were shared, trust and openness developed. Control did not seem to be an issue for the total group. The members seemed to be genuinely appreciative of our leadership. However, patterns of control within families became obvious.

We attempted to deal with them by having families ask themselves questions about their control issues in relation to decision-making.

The group stage of affection is a complex one. Individuals brought to the cluster the injunctions about touching, differing ethnic and cultural backgrounds, their self-esteem, different personalities, their feelings about their bodies and sexuality, as well as fears of being rejected or hugged! Along with all of these, they brought their existing norms for affection in their families. Even these are sometimes in a state of flux, depending on the degree of marital harmony and the developmental levels of children. As leaders, we felt that we should be able to facilitate a group of people in a few weeks who showed affection spontaneously and constantly. No wonder we were disappointed! This may happen in some clusters, but I think there is a danger of affection becoming an expected ritual, rather than a genuine expression of caring. Our hope may be to feel close and warm equally to everyone, but it is not humanly possible. This does not mean that any cluster member is less deserving of affection than any other; rather, it means that some people are more comfortable giving and receiving physical affection. It is an area which must be dealt with tactfully, realistically, and sensitively. It might have been a good idea to discuss the matter within the group. We thought it unnecessary at the time, but possibly we did not want to take the risk of tackling such an emotionally-charged subject!

During the time of the cluster there was a good deal of affection shown, but it had been in effect prior to the cluster sessions. To hug a small child is easy, natural, and socially acceptable; with a self-conscious adolescent or unresponsive older person, it may be a threatening and uncomfortable experience. We felt, as many others do, that to force hugs on people is not kind nor loving; rather, we reached out in friendship and hoped affection would be reciprocated. If it wasn't, we preferred to let the individuals remain at the level with which they were comfortable. After the cluster experience, one mother reported to me that family members were asking for hugs from each other. Virginia Satir had made front page news in Toronto when she stressed our constant need of hugs for survival, maintenance, and growth. Her article was posted on their refrigerator. All the family members had enjoyed the challenge of getting and giving plenty of hugs.

The stages of group development are varied and yet predictable. Different persons were at different stages during various times, yet the group momentum continued through the stages of inclusion, control, and affection and, then, deeper stages of inclusion, control, and affection. Each person gradually felt a part of the larger identity.

The cluster sessions were two hours long, starting with a meal and leaving one and one half hours for recreation and program. We met over ten weeks of time.

The Educational Process

Our study sessions were separate units each week, using the general topic of communication in the family. We had two seasonal programs. The craft projects, songs and games were always related to our theme for the evening. After supper, we were updated with "News Time."

One ritual which brought us together was a birthday cake for those celebrating during the coming week. Once we had an "un-birthday cake" for all those born at different times of the year.

One activity which many found meaningful was an outdoor trust walk. For this exercise, a child chose an adult to lead blindfolded; then they reversed the process. This was done early in the life of the cluster. Many feelings were shared about readiness to trust each other and to co-operate as equals in the larger family.

Many families enjoyed working on craft projects such as a collage box. On the outside were pasted pictures of how others see their family, including shared interests and individual activities. On the inside, they could symbolize concerns that were more hidden. One family put all their garbage in their box—how fitting! In general, people felt more free to share achievements and adventures than to expose needs and weaknesses.

When Hallowe'en came, it seemed like an ideal time to talk about roles. We played the "Owl Game" by pairs. One person is the owl and keeps asking, "Who?" The other partner responds with all the roles that he or she plays. Then they reverse parts. This provided a fun way to discover how many roles we play and how much is required of us in different situations. In families we shared our feelings about these roles and made plans to trade some, share others, and drop those which were unnecessary. We concluded our evening with a progressive, scary ghost story which brought out the role of "ham" in many of us!

The collage boxes were used again near the end of the cluster when the topic was "Blocks to Communication." During a suitably quiet moment at the beginning of the program we had a visit from the devil! John had left during a game. He returned all dressed in red and brandishing a foil-covered pitch fork. As he burst through the door, he knocked over the boxes, which had been piled against the door, representing family togetherness. The effect was electrifying, hilarious and highly memorable. A lively discussion followed on how our closeness was sometimes ruined.

In simulated families we wrote on new cardboard cartons all the factors that we see blocking effective communication. The acquired list of comments was long and thorough and included the following: "T.V., silence, acting busy, being 'mouthy', misinterpreting, worry, stubborness, lack of explanation, not 'being there' enough, and one person thinking he's always right."

These boxes were piled to make a wall which, literally and symbolically, kept family members from each other. Then each person was reunited with his or her own family to discuss changes that could be made in communication styles. Each family chose a box with negative statements on it, reversed it and wrote positive suggestions. Some examples were: "make family time, be more considerate, remember to listen, don't interrupt, ask necessary questions, express worries and fears to each other."

The total group shared ways of transforming the wall into something more optimistic. The most popular suggestion seemed to be "build a bridge." This we did, using our original collage boxes which showed our good times, as foundations for our new structure. To conclude, we joined hands and paraded around and under our bridge. We felt we had really reached out and found new ways of connecting with each other.

Since the Canadian Thanksgiving comes in early October, we thought we should hold a cluster family celebration. Everybody became involved in the planning and preparation. When the day arrived, we sat down to a traditional turkey dinner, complete with candlelight and background music. The children decorated placemats, while the others served the feast. It was a joyous time as our voices blended in a singing grace, "Thank You Lord . . ." to the tune of "Edelweiss."

Afterwards, we relaxed and reminisced about Thanksgiving customs from our childhood days. The memories were rich and varied. Some favorite old hymns from the various countries of our birth were taught and sung. Then we each picked an apple from a basket, studied it and returned it to the basket. Later we could easily identify our own fruit. This led to a discussion of how each of us are all similar yet unique, as are families. Our mood was one of warmth and reflection as we shared appreciations for our own family members. These were written on red paper "apples" to be taken home and treasured. Some had extra time to share similar feelings with others in the total cluster.

Wanting to close the evening in a prayerful way, we wrote our "thank you" notes to God and tucked them into colorful balloons. We planned to let the wind take our messages "heavenward" but the elements were not with us. The balloons fell to the ground where they all popped on the frosty grass. However, our sentiments were expressed and heard as we sang, "We are one in the Spirit." It was not a solemn time, but certainly a happy one.

The children suggested that each week a family should teach us a new song or game. It seemed like a natural introduction to the topic of "rules." First John and I tried to get a game going with very inadequate instructions. The resulting chaos dramatized the need for clearly understood rules. Each family then received a bag containing "odds and ends" such as egg cartons, newspapers, buttons, a grapefruit, etc. Using these materials and their own ingenuity, families were to create and to teach a new game. We enjoyed sharing our creativity and providing fun for each other. Families discovered their own styles of cooperation or disagreement. Each person then drew a floor plan of the family home, listing rules related to each room. A lively discussion followed as individuals shared their perceptions of the family rules. Many feelings were aired, and misconceptions cleared up. Unnecessary rules could now be abandoned in favor of democratic decision making.

The least structured session turned out to be the favorite one for many of us. On a beautiful fall Sunday, we decided to reverse our schedule by *closing* with supper. We spent a relaxing time hiking through a local conservation area. We returned to the church with armfuls of wild flowers and colored leaves to decorate our supper table, consisting of a simple meal of soup, sandwiches and fruit.

Near the end of the cluster we decided to tie-dye T-shirts. It was a messy but enjoyable evening. The church kitchen even looked better after we cleaned up! While waiting for the colorful dyes to work, we paired up to draw outlines of each other on large pieces of newsprint on the floor. These projects were continued the following week until each person had a life-sized replica. We dressed the replicas with old scraps of material.

The families seemed to respond positively to all our cluster activities. There did not seem to be any program that caused difficulty.

Evaluation

Each session had included a short evaluation, usually in the total group. We tried to incorporate the feedback into our further planning. At the end of the cluster series, we had each member fill in a written questionnaire. Here are some of the questions and samples of answers:

Q. What were your expectations of Family Cluster? Which ones were met?
A. I hoped for warmth, acceptance, togetherness—all were met. (Adult female)
A. I wanted to get to know everybody better and to share experiences. These were both met. (Sixteen-year-old girl)

Q. What did you enjoy the most?
A. Having a new family. (Eleven-year-old girl)
A. Warm, fuzzy feelings. (Eight-year old boy)
A. Working and sharing with my family. (Ten-year-old boy)

Q. What did you enjoy the least?
A. Nothing. (Five-year-old boy)
A. Going home. (Eight-year-old girl)
A. Doing the dishes. (Adult male)
A. The "before hand" rush. (Adult female)

Q. What discoveries did you make about yourself, your family and others?
A. I love myself, my family loves me, others like me. (Eight-year-old boy)
A. I felt much closer and more warm towards my family. (Adult male)

Q. Would you like to be part of a cluster again? If so, what suggestions do you have?
A. Yes, with a new group to meet more great people. (Adult female)
A. Yes, but I'm sure we'd commit ourselves to a contract of several weeks immediately. (Adult female)
A. Yes, Sunday night was a good choice—it wiped out blues, blahs, and family obligations!

Q. Any further comments?
A. The more we communicate the more we realize we aren't alone. (Adult male)
A. I love you. (Thirteen-year-old girl)

We felt we kept fairly close to the original Family Cluster Model. However, concessions were made in the number of the cluster sessions and in the area of compulsory attendance. This was necessary to fit the realistic needs of the participants' busy life styles.

Conclusion of the Cluster

For the closing session we all wore our tie-dyed T-shirts which was symbolic of our unity and diversity. We shared a party meal of take-out pizza and fried chicken, which simplified the day for the family chefs. To give each other some parting "warm fuzzies," (Richard Lessor. *Fuzzies.* Niles, IL.: Argus Communication, 1971) we wrote notes on each other's paper people. In this way we took ourselves home, along with some part of everyone else. We had humorous reminders of what we had made ourselves along with concrete, positive feedback on how we were seen. We ended with favorite songs and many hugs.

Follow-up

No official follow-up activity has taken place. However, we are friends and neighbors who continue to socialize and worship together. We see each other as having very special connections within the church and community. Our "Circle of Love" is not broken, but expanding.

We will probably hold another cluster within the next year; possibly in the spring, so we can enjoy the out-of-doors. There seems to be some interest in a more concentrated experience such as a weekend cluster. For others, a monthly enrichment program would meet their needs. I see both as worthwhile alternatives.

Resources

The following have been most useful:

James, Muriel M. *Born to Love.* Reading, MA: Addison-Wesley Publishing, 1973.

Johnson, David W., and Johnson, Frank P. *Joining Together.* Englewood Cliffs, NJ: Prentice-Hall, 1975.

Satir, Virginia. *Peoplemaking.* Palo Alto, CA: Science and Behavior, Inc., 1972.

Biographical Data

Valerie Griffin is a wife and mother of three children who works part-time as a high school counsellor. She enjoys reading, writing and listening to music. She finds experiential education is an exciting process to share with small groups of all ages. Facilitating learning and growth in herself and others is one of the most difficult, but ultimately most satisfying challenges in her life.

Address:

308 Steeles Ave. East
R.R. #1 Hornby, Ontario, L0P 1E0
Canada
Tel. (416) 878-4749

Clustering Comes to Australia

Moira Eastman
Helen Praetz

Melbourne, Australia

The Beginnings

In 1976 Margaret Sawin visited Australia as a guest of the Australian Council of Churches' Education Commission to introduce churches to the Family Cluster Model and to train leaders in Family Clustering. Garry Eastman coordinated her visit.

Garry and his wife, Moira, had been part of a Family Cluster for several years prior to this visit. They had developed their own model of clustering which differed from Margaret Sawin's model in that they had shared leadership; were not as nearly as strong and as clear about contracting; and the group was an on-going, not a time-limited one.

Helen Praetz came in contact first with clustering during Margaret Sawin's 1976 visit to Australia. As President Couple of the Teams of Our Lady (an organization of couples who meet for support, sharing, prayer in their life as married Christians), the Praetz's were invited to attend a five-day Family Cluster led by Dr. Sawin at Easter 1976. Helen said of the cluster, her first experience of experiental learning, "I would never have believed how much you can learn in this way." In 1978 Peter and Helen went to the University of Rochester in the United States to do further work and study. While living in Rochester, Helen attended leadership training in Family Clusters with Margaret Sawin.

In September of 1979 we (Moira Eastman and Helen Praetz) began co-leading a Family Cluster in St. Dominic's Parish, East Camberwell, a suburb of Melbourne, Australia. The families were Catholic, all with school age children.

Our decision to run a pilot cluster program stemmed from a number of motives. We were both convinced that there was a great need for family enrichment and support and that the Family Cluster Model was an excellent response to that need. At the time we started this project there had been no follow-up to Dr. Sawin's visit in Catholic parishes in Melbourne (although there were clusters in other states). Despite the fact that family is such a high value for Australian Catholics, they also see the family as under attack and needing support. There was a growing desire being expressed that large parishes introduce a small group component. Parishioners talked of basic communities, of street churches, of wanting "something" that will support and challenge them in their faith, that would be "more meaningful" and more personal than they found the present parish to be. Family Clusters seemed a flexible, adaptable and workable model that would enable parishes to respond to this need.

It would also be true to say that having been trained in the method we were personally motivated to try it out! Moira was also anxious to see how Sawin's model compared with the cluster she had already experienced. Thus, there was no sponsoring organization or group who encouraged us to begin, but we decided to take the plunge.

Skills Brought to the Project

At the outset we were conscious that our skills were complementary. Although we had both taught in high schools, undertaken PET courses, trained as cluster leaders and wrestled with family dynamics in our own domestic settings, we both had some separate areas of competence. Moira is a skilled group leader, being a member of the Victorian Council of Churches Group Life Training Team, and a trained leader of group life laboratories. Her work as an editor and writer of religious education books and her long experience in her ecumenical group means that she knows where to locate resources and how to plan for group sessions.

Helen has taught in a variety of settings, including a county jail, and can play the guitar and sing loudly. Her training as a sociologist alerted her to the need for an assessment of Family Clusters as an educational model. She was aware that new educational models cannot be successfully assessed by instruments designed for traditional methods. She therefore proposed that careful records should be kept of all that took place, that outside observers be invited to help with assessment and observation, and that techniques be used of the participant observer, the focused interview, plus open ended questions to gather data on the effectiveness of the cluster experience for the participants.

Although we did not know each other well at the outset of this venture, we were confident that we could plan and organize together. We found that, throughout the cluster, we developed a rhythm of joint work and that leadership tasks flowed from one to the other. One of the great joys of co-leading the cluster was the depth of friendship and mutual affirmation which we came to offer each other.

Recruitment of Families

Having decided to lead a cluster, our next step was to find families and a venue (meeting place). We knew of a suitable space in a parish education centre; when we tentatively broached the idea with the parish priest, he applauded the idea, gave us the venue (site) rent-free and suggested seven families who might be interested in clustering. As we were hoping to show that clustering was a suitable model for adoption by parishes, we thought it best to start with highly involved parishioners rather than with families on the outer fringes of parish life. Several of the married couples we approached were already members of the Teams of Our Lady, a Roman Catholic movement for marriage enrichment, and hence had already showed some commitment to group experiences. To our relief, six of the seven families we contacted readily agreed to join the cluster.

Although time was short, we decided to follow Margaret Sawin's advice and to make a home visit to each family. At this visit we described as well as we were able what a Family Cluster is and what membership would involve. We found this quite difficult as most people have really no experience of intergenerational or experiential learning. A typical question in response to a description of cluster is,

"Who minds the children?" The idea of adults and children really learning together (not just filling in time), is something our system of age segregation has suggested just *cannot* happen. We stressed that joining a cluster would be one of the few opportunities for the family to do something together. It would involve games, songs, and a shared meal. There would be an opportunity to learn things related to everyday life as a family. Besides giving adults and children a chance to make closer friends among their respective age peers in the group, there would be an opportunity for adults and children not of the same family to make closer friends. We suggested they would learn things of value from seeing other families working together, and other families would learn things of value from this family. We tried hard to get to know the children and to find out something of their interests and what they would like to happen in cluster. At one home Helen sat on the floor, apparently the signal for the children to deluge her with talk and to keep running to their rooms and bringing out their favorite toys and things they had made to show her. We felt it was important that the children *want* to come to cluster, so that the parents weren't "forcing" them to come and would see cluster as yet another parental burden. In fact, once cluster started the children kept arriving earlier and earlier. Usually puffed out from walking because they couldn't wait for the family car, the children caused us leaders to hurry our last-minute preparations!

We felt the home visit was an essential part of the process. From our point of view, it enabled us to meet each family separately. If we had started with 11 adults and 17 children in one room, we doubted we would ever have sorted out who was whose. At home, the family is on their own ground, more relaxed, and surrounded by their own things. It is easier to learn what their interests and concerns are in such a setting. Meeting the families this way was reassuring to us that we would be able to do what we were offering to do.

From the family's point of view, they have a chance to hear first hand what cluster is about and to ask questions. Each person has met the leaders, so no one is turning up with the feeling 'I don't know anyone there.'

The questionnaire which we left with each member of the family to complete and to send to us was modelled closely on the one Margaret Sawin devised in her book *Family Enrichment With Family Clusters*, (p. 135).

We saw the home visit as an opportunity to start the contracting process. From our point of view this involved making as clear as possible what cluster would be like and what we intended to do, including our leadership role.

Example: "Will you be, er, sort of leading this?"

Helen: "We won't be sort of leading it. We'll be leading it."

We also made clear that if the family decided to join, we would expect a high commitment in terms of attendance and participation when there. The cluster was to run for twelve sessions on Wednesday evenings, from 6:15 to 8:30 P.M. The leaders met about three hours each week to plan.

The Cluster Families

All the families in our cluster had school age children, the youngest being two four-year-olds and the eldest being fifteen-years-old. There were 17 children. They all belonged to St. Dominic's parish and were highly involved there. Three of the adults were not themselves Catholics, but this in no way deterred them from a very active part in the parish life. All the children attended, or had attended, the parochial elementary school or one of the adjacent Catholic high schools. This made an added bond between families and meant that, while not all members knew each other well, they all knew the other members (both children and adults) at least by sight.

One of our assumptions was that this group would have expectations of some explicit religious content in the cluster sessions. (It seems that Catholics in Australia have been less affected by rationalism and secularism than some other urban groups. In particular, the Eucharist is a living symbol that still draws full participation from many Catholics). This was supported by the answers to the questionnaires where many responded that what was most important to them was the family and living their religion.

The make-up of the participating families was as follows:

Family A	Family B	Family C
Mother/Father	Mother/Father	Mother/Father
3 boys—11, 9, 7 years	2 girls—10, 4 years	1 boy—11 years
1 girl—6 years	1 boy—6 years	

Family D	Family E	Family F
Mother/Father	Mother/Father	Mother
3 girls—15, 11, 8 years	1 girl—6 years	3 boys—14, 11, 6 years
1 boy—6 years	1 boy—4 years	

In one family the husband had died suddenly only six weeks before cluster began. The bereaved wife was influential in gathering the cluster together and enthusing people with the idea.

A feature of this group of families that is different from a similar Protestant group is that it seemed the families had taken part in few "fellowship" activities before. In Australia, the Catholic Church has always pursued a policy of Catholic schooling for every Catholic child. This was done without any government help for buildings or administration until 1974, so enormous energy and commitment were devoted to Catholic schools. It also came to be expected that the schools would 'do' the major tasks of religious education, and they tended to become the focus of parish life. It seemed to us that our families were not as practiced in the skills of playing games, singing or group processing as a similarly involved Protestant group would be. A very pleasant corollary of this was that they were extremely open to learning cluster-type activities and very ready to enjoy and take full part.

The Setting

The setting for the cluster was the Parish Education Centre, behind the church. It had originally been the parish school and was now a carpeted, heated hall about 40 feet long and 18 feet wide.

There were some comfortable old chairs and moveable straight back chairs. A pool table was a great attraction to the children, and tractor tires and a few other toys gave the younger children opportunities for play. There was a small kitchen off the hall for food preparation and washing up. It was an ideal setting for cluster, and it became a centre where everyone felt at home. Surrounded by lawns and gardens, there was plenty of play space.

Expectations of the Group

The questionnaires indicated that the things that most bothered people about their families were fighting, bickering, and misunderstandings. Questions of organization, T.V. watching and discipline were also raised. The family which had been so recently bereaved expressed the need to eliminate some of the tensions and resentments that were causing friction in the home. They wanted to value themselves as unique, despite the loss of the father. The wide range of hoped for outcomes of the cluster can be summed up as wanting games and fun; to be together as a family; to meet and share with other families; to make new friends; to understand and appreciate each other more.

We decided that the more direct techniques of conflict resolution would wait till later sessions, but that even in the first few sessions we could be planning to fulfill many of these expectations. We knew we needed to do the contracting in the first few sessions (and in this we would be modelling a key conflict resolution and prevention technique).

The Cluster Session

The Straggle-in. Cluster began at 6:15 P.M. with a 'straggle-in' time. We arrived about an hour earlier to arrange the room and to put up sheets of paper for compiling the contract and recording other discussions, to prepare the materials for the learning activity and to check over our plans made earlier. As early arrival soon became the norm, we were usually interrupted and had to hurry with these last-minute preparations.

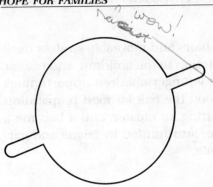

We prepared games of fun things for this period. It could be a series of large scale enigmatic drawings that people were asked to name. This example was variously, a Mexican riding a bicycle, the planet Saturn, and a well known bald politician seen from above.

Another night, people were given a sheet of paper marked in squares with a fact about a different cluster person in each square: 'someone who sails,' 'someone who has 2 sisters,' 'youngest person here,' and so on. Filling in the sheet required checking with many others in the group. We aimed to make this activity something fun to do and an 'ice-breaker' in that it provided an entrance back into the group and required numerous one to one conversations, including adult to child. Often we planned an activity that we could build on later in the learning sections.

Shared meal. The meal began at 6:30 with a sung grace. The food was spread on a tablecloth on the floor, and people sat in groups around the edge to eat. Our suggestion that it be a sandwich tea was met with some reluctance at first. Several mothers felt this would not satisfy their families, as the evening meal was the main meal of the day. After a few cluster sessions though, it was the mothers who were quite adamant that the meal would remain basically sandwiches and fruit (despite requests for 'carpet-bag' steak, garlic prawns and quiche from the men, and for fish and chips, hamburgers and pizza from the children). The time-saving involved had come to outweigh other factors.

There was a pool table in the room where we met; before and after the meal, the children played pool, or with lego blocks; inflated tractor tubes, or just each other. It was soon obvious that the simplest games were much more fun in the setting of a number of families together.

Games and songs. At 7:00 we began the evening's program. We always started with games and songs. We aimed here to teach some new songs and games that the families could add to their own collections. Many of the songs were fun songs or action songs, and the games drew heavily from the New Games repertoire (New Games Foundation, P. O. Box 7901, San Francisco, CA 94120). They allowed physical involvement, activity and competition in a form that all ages could enjoy together. Games encourage spontaneity and fun to emerge which in turn allows warmth, friendship and trust to grow more quickly than in our usual more formal and controlled interactions. As the weeks went by, everyone participated more and more enthusiastically in the games. Some fathers and sons occasionally battled mightily which aroused frenzied cheering by men and boys and much laughter among women and girls. When asked in the final session to name one thing that each member had liked about cluster, one father said, "Acting like a big kid," and another, "Seeing the other adults acting like big kids."

Contracting. In each cluster session there was a 'cluster-time.' In the early sessions this was when the contracting or covenanting was done. In later sessions it was a brief time to review the covenant, to hear about future absences, change of venue (site) or particular plans, such as outside games or a fish and chip tea.

Helen introduced the contracting with the Old Testament covenant story, showing how keeping the covenant was the way the Israelites showed they wanted to be part of this people. "What is *our* covenant to be? How do we want to *be* together?" The group fairly quickly decided what to do about absences and late-coming (if possible let the group know in advance), the kind of food for the meal, how the attention of the group could be gained (ringing a bell which meant 'freeze'), and so on. As the children realized that they had a say, some of the negotiations became more lengthy. The question of who is responsible for the safety of the children and for any discipline required raised the suggestion from one mother—"Let's all take care of all the children. I don't mind if someone else corrects my child." When the children's opinion was asked they emphatically said, "No." They did not want to be corrected by adults other than parents. However, when they realized that they could remind *adults* of the cluster rules the solution was reached that everyone was responsible for the covenant and could remind anyone else of it!

The most difficult issue in the contracting was the use of the pool table. In the first two sessions there were heated arguments among would-be players. Those who were victorious over possession of the cues were nevertheless defeated by their rivals, who stole the balls and hid them. There were constant scuffles and tears. In the second session parents expressed their irritation and also concern for the safety of little children running into billiard cues. All the adults agreed the table should be dismantled. However, the children were unhappy with this solution and various groups argued their case for sole access to the table. The final solution was to place a line of chairs to protect running children from the area of play, and that children under twelve could play during arrival time and those over twelve after eating. This decision involved some parents to relinquish their desire that the children remain seated during the meal.

The contract was finalized and signed at the third session. After that it needed only a brief review at each meeting. It was clear that everyone had had to compromise something. For example, we had assumed the group would sit on the floor—with the advantages of the spacing between people not being determined by the rigid spacing of furniture. (Adults and children are on one level on the floor and there is freedom to move as the group changes from sitting to games or other activities without the cumbersome moving of furniture.) However, some members declared they hated sitting on the floor, so the rule became that those who want to sit on chairs could. The leaders' desire to invite evaluators to attend sometimes was refused for the first few sessions until the group felt more at ease.

The contracting process modelled for families a method of power-sharing within the family, and a conflict-resolution method of setting clearly defined rules of access where sharing was a problem.

Learning time. The learning session usually took about one hour and involved some activity (clay modelling, painting, role-playing, model-building, fantasizing, talking and listening) on which participants later were helped to reflect. Observing what happened, identifying feelings, trying new behaviours in a secure group, having the opportunity to practice it, and being affirmed by others made this learning time involving, interesting and efficient.

Prayer time. The last ten minutes of each session was spent in closure. We often took the opportunity to find out how the session had been perceived by the members. "What was helpful?" "Was anything not helpful?" or, "What is something you learned tonight?" We developed a ritual of turning out the light and gathering around our cluster candle for a few moments of silent reflection on the evening and for shared prayer. One of the leaders sometimes said a few words to link the theme of the evening to a theme of the gospel or of church teaching. The fact that the families were all committed to the church, and at ease with ritual and (in most cases) accustomed to shared prayer made these moments particularly close.

The Learning Program

Sessions 1-3: Inclusion, Contracting, Affirmation
We knew that there were some good friendships and many acquaintanceships within this group. We assumed, however, that the early sessions would need to provide opportunities for people to meet and share with those they didn't know or at levels not yet reached. Margaret Sawin says that people come to a group with many questions, such as: "Will I be safe here?" "Will I be O.K. here?" "Will my family be acceptable here?" We wanted the answers to be a very clear "Yes."

The first three sessions then concentrated on completion of contracting, inclusion exercises that gave people the chance to get to know each other better, and opportunities to practice listening and affirmation—both within families and across family boundaries.

For an affirmation exercise we taught families to make a 'family chain.' Each member was given two pieces of paper for each other member of the family. On each piece of paper she or he was to write something she or he liked about the person whose name was on it. There were signs that members needed practice at affirming each other. Some members had to struggle for a long time to think of something they liked about some other family members. When it came to giving the gifts, none of the families were able to give the gifts verbally and strongly. They tended to shove a few cards at another family member, saying, "These are yours." At a later session cluster members gave 'pats on the back' to each other. This followed a reading of *The Fuzzies,* (Richard Lessor, *The Fuzzies*. Niles, IL.: Argus Communications, 1971). Each person had a large sheet of paper pinned to his back and other cluster members gave 'pats on the back' messages of appreciation for that person. Group members quickly improved in their ability to affirm each other and also seemed to visibly relax and enjoy each other's company more. On the first evening, families left as soon as the program finished, but after a few sessions there was a period after the closing where adults finished some conversations and children enjoyed unstructured play.

Sessions 4 - 6: **Family Systems and Roles**

Sessions four to six focused on family systems. Families took the opportunity to observe some of their own ways of operating, to learn about some common family roles, to appreciate the uniqueness of their family style, and to do some creative work as families.

For the fourth session the whole group arrived early to attend the First Communion of one of the cluster children. At the end of the Mass, which was held at twilight in the beautiful candle-lit medieval-style church, cluster members lit sparklers from the church candles and carried them back to the hall.

By this session, we felt that our aim of capturing the children's interest and cooperation was well achieved; however, the fathers seemed to be tolerating the cluster experience rather than being really engaged in it. The fathers tended to join in the singing half-heartedly and to often hang together at the back of the group.

Therefore, we decided to divide the persons over twelve from those under twelve for a period of reflection on the experience of each family making an insect cooperatively from an unlikely heap of scrap materials. This was the only time we worked with adults separate from children, but it certainly seemed to have the desired effect of allowing the adults to see that the reflection on the experience could raise very absorbing issues. We asked the adults in each family to reflect on what had happened, especially on how the decision of what to make had been made, who had led, who had followed, had anyone not been involved, how had the family coped with members who disagreed on the chosen solution, and so on. The adults then shared with each other what they had learned about their own family. Some were ill-at-ease with the role they had played. Some came to the conclusion that someone has to lead, but that leading is not the only valuable role in a family; also there can be no leading without following. One family was astonished by the ability of their ten-year-old daughter to muster support in the family and to be the one who led in this situation.

Family Roles

We decided that Kantor and Lehr's model of family roles (see Resources) would provide a helpful model to follow up the observation and reflection on family systems which the insect-making activity had started. Kantor and Lehr suggest that in any sustained interaction four roles must be played. The mover initiates an action, the follower supports the mover, and the opponent opposes him. The bystander observes what is going on and usually refuses (at least initially) to say what side he is on. Using role-play, we attempted in the fifth session to give everyone an experience of each role. (This was not very successful as the role-play relied on being able to read to get into each part, and too many of our children had difficulty reading sufficiently well.) Later, members grouped themselves according to which role they played most often and each group decided on a body posture which showed what they liked about this role. Trying to reach agreement in a group of opposers or a group of movers led to some discussion of what are the agreeable and disagreeable aspects of this role. There was also some reflection regarding what are the difficulties of *always* being in the same role and the need to change roles around and to give family members a chance to try out different roles. Kantor and Lehr suggest that all roles are equally powerful. Any role may be the one that decides the outcome of an interaction. All these roles can be played negatively or positively and all these roles are essential to both families and groups.

The sixth session was a much more relaxed and 'messy fun' time. Families made collages to show certain aspects of their family life.

Sessions 7-8: Communication

Sessions seven and eight took up the communication theme again, particularly non-verbal communication, and developed increased awareness of feelings and a language to express feelings. In using body language to convey certain feelings, it became clear that role-playing and acting were real strengths in this particular group. Fifteen of the members were under twelve years of age, and we had discovered in our first few sessions that exercises that involved a fair amount of talk (or worse, reading or writing) caused problems.

In the seventh session we recalled and told statements that made us feel really good and statements that made us feel "yukky." After some role playing of 'building-up' and 'putting-down' statements and their effects, everyone made clay images of themselves as they felt receiving the two different messages. Many of the adults had never modelled in clay before and discovered they could express themselves very adequately in this medium. One father's representation of a 'hollow man' spoke strongly to many in the group.

Sessions 9-11: Negotiating Conflict

Having done some ground work on listening, being aware of and expressing feelings, practicing affirmations, observing, and being aware of some family roles, we thought it was time to try some more direct work on conflict resolution. In the ninth session we took common conflict situations that were raised by the group in an earlier session. The group divided into simulated families to role play a family in such a conflict and then attempted to find a solution to the problem. For this exercise, the children played the adults and the adults played at being children. This was probably the session that produced the most laughter of all. Many of the adults showed they knew every trick concerned with not eating meals, staying up late to watch T.V., getting permission to take a part-time job or negotiating an extra outing for the week. One leader wrote up on newsprint the attempted solutions. After each role play the attempted solutions and the final solution were assessed. The value of being negotiable and of seeking alternative solutions was clear in some of the situations. In others, the best solution seemed to come from a parent firmly, calmly and consistently reminding children of the rule and of the necessity of keeping it.

Session ten focused on rules in families: What are they? Do we agree on what they are? Where do they come from? How can they be altered? Do any of our rules need to change? Do we need any new rules? The eleventh session looked at the values behind our rules, in particular, the sources of values in family history. This session seemed to give parents a great encouragement as they realized that some of their most treasured values had been handed on—not by someone 'telling' them so much as by what the person was. They seemed to feel reassured that these values were in them and would just as inevitably be handed on to their children.

Session 12: Closure

In the concluding session we celebrated fulfilling our covenant and that we were people who could say we would do something and do it. Everyone made 'memory bags' and decorated them. Then each person in turn went to the centre of the group while the rest of the group filled his or her memory bag with messages of the gifts seen in this person. We called this 'giving the good news' to each person.

Evaluation

To evaluate this pilot Family Cluster project we visited each family one month after the final cluster meeting. We were able to see every member of the cluster in these family groups. We had previously drawn up a list of questions to guide our interview (see page 164). Each family interview took about an hour and was recorded on tape.

The cluster was unanimously declared a success, and the expectation of having fun together was clearly achieved. The success was usually attributed to the leadership and to the process of contracting. Members seemed to think the leaders' ability to get people to take part in games, songs and various other unorthodox behaviour was a particular gift verging on magic. We are more inclined to the view that it resulted from careful planning, the confidence that comes from a clear contract and the effect of modelling what you want. In other words, we feel we could teach our adult members to have exactly the same success.

Another reason given for the success of the group was the caring and closeness that developed between the members—commented on by at least one person in most families. We felt that the closeness and caring grew from the modelling of the leaders and from the opportunities provided for it to develop, especially the structured communication exercises, the opportunity to share in depth about matters of both individual and family concerns, the effect of affirmation, and the spontaneous sharing of role-plays, games and fun.

There were almost no criticisms of the program or things that people would have liked changed. One mother said she wanted to drop out of one section of the program one night. We had said this was OK, but because it was not cearly written on the contract she didn't feel free to do so.

Other signs of the success of this project were the high level of commitment to attendance. Despite a bereavement, work interstate, sickness, moving house, and other high priority commitments, there were very few absences.

The cluster was due to finish the last week in November. During one of the later sessions an eleven-year-old said, "Christmas Day is on a Tuesday. Will we be having cluster on the Wednesday?" The families had noted some changes from their participation in cluster.

1. In some cases the definition of conflict had changed. Mothers in three families commented that an awareness of the positive role of opponent in a family system had eased tensions between themselves and their frequently opposing adolescent or pre-adolescent. In one other family, the husband's bystanding role had been accepted more philosophically by his wife. Respondents in several families mentioned that conflict was inevitable, if regrettable.

2. Every family had constructed and signed a written contract, which was usually hanging in the kitchen. In all but one case, the contracting process learnt in the group had been followed. In three families, joint timetables and schedules had been devised, and in all cases the former generalised parental expectations of children had been translated into specific behavioural norms. For example, one mother commented that, although she had always demanded but seldom obtained help with chores from her four children, the family's mutal allocation of tasks had eased the problem. In three cases, adults had accepted their own need to comply with family rules. One mother said, "I always thought rules were just for the kids before." Two families had instituted weekly family meeting times.

3. All families had discussed aspects of the group experience together, and several families had adopted strategies learnt from others. For example, one family's self-selection style of food serving had been widely emulated.

4. Self-esteem appeared to have increased. When asked what had surprised her about the group experience, one eight-year-old said, "People don't look as if they like you. I never knew that so many people liked me." In every family, children made similar comments. One father, whose company had been sought often by an unrelated six-year-old, recalled the pleasure he had felt on being singled out.

Further, group membership seemed to have boosted family self-esteem and identity. The group provided an arena in which the talents of the whole family were displayed, both to others and to themselves. Numerous parents throughout the sessions commented on new and attractive facets which they had perceived in their own children. After working in simulated families, adults often noted a child's appealing words or deeds to an attentive parent. However, sometimes parents also saw less attractive sides of their children.

It seemed to us that Family Clustering has much to offer Australian parish life, expecially where there is concern to do something for families. Some added impressions that we formed are:

> *No family can offer everything to its members. For example, in one family of four children there was only one girl. She was used to playing with boys but was not at all used to playing with girls.*

> *The opportunity to gather seems to be a value in itself. It was amazing to see how much fun people had doing simple things with a group of varied ages. No wonder they and we want to continue with clustering!*

Family Cluster Evaluation Sheet

1. How would you describe a family cluster to a family thinking of joining one?
2. How many people were in the cluster? Was it too many?
3. Did you feel that the families involved in our cluster were alike? Would another cluster benefit from having different styles of families?
4. Did you feel that the cluster was a success? If so, what would you attribute success to?
5. What did you like most about the cluster?
6. What would you change?
7. What would you like more of?
8. Can you think of anything else, apart from clusters, where you would have gotten the same kind of experience?
9. What did you get from clusters for yourself?
   What did the family get?
   What did the whole group get?
   Did the parish get anything?
10. Did you get what you expected to get?
    Did you get something unexpected?
    Would you have preferred not to have gained something?
11. Did you ever talk together in the family about what happened at cluster?
12. What do you think you will have remembered from clustering in six months?
13. What possibilities do you see for clustering in a parish setting?

Resources

Agard, B. *Family-Cluster Resources*. Evangelical Covenant Church of America, 1977.

Benson, J., and Hilyard, J. *Becoming Family*. Winona; St. Mary's College Press, 1978.

Kantor, D., and Lehr, W. *Inside the Family*. San Francisco; Jossey Bass, 1975.

Sawin, M. *Family Enrichment With Family Clusters*. Valley Forge: Judson Press, 1979.

Biographical Data

Moira Eastman is a graduate student in the Faculty of Education at Monash University, specializing in the sociology of the family. Until 1979 she worked as an editor and writer of religious education books. She is a member of the Victorian Council of Churches Group Life Training Team and travels widely conducting seminars in religious education. She is married with three children, ages 10, 14 and 15.

Address:

5 Nigretta Court
Mt. Waverly
Victoria,
Australia, 3149
Tel. 233-1284

Helen Praetz lectures in the sociology of education at Monash University and has specialized in the study of organizations and ideologies with particular reference to Catholic schools. She is married and has two children, ages 12 and 10.

Address:

23 Belgrade Rd.
E. Malvern, Vic.
Australia 3145

Family Clustering in England
Martin Goodlad

London, England

How It Began

Family Clusters started in England in a very roundabout way. With my family I attended a family enrichment weekend, organized by the Church of England's Board of Education. One of the staff at the weekend had been to Canada where she was introduced to Family Clusters. She presented the concept in the design of the weekend, and this was my first acquaintance with the model.

When we returned home we shared the experience of the weekend with a discussion group which my wife and I attended. A number of the group members showed an interest in the concept, so I called a meeting in the fall of 1975 for interested persons to discuss the idea further. I managed to obtain a monograph written by Margaret Sawin in 1973 entitled, "Educating by Family Groups— A New Model for Religious Education," which I used as a basic document for our first meeting. Six families attended and discussed the ideas in detail, and agreed to contract for one year's time, meeting for a full day (9:30 A.M.-5:00 P.M.) every two months.

Background

At this point it is helpful to give some background information on the original discussion group mentioned previously. All of us lived in the Church of England parish of All Saints, West Dulwich, which is in South London in the borough of Lambeth. Lambeth itself is one of the poorer London boroughs with a large immigrant population, mainly West Indian, living within it. There are large pockets of middle class families living in the borough, and our group came from this type of situation.

All of the adults had undertaken some type of further education since leaving school. All but one of the parents did some kind of work outside the home. Four members of the group were qualified teachers, and two others trained marriage guidance counsellors.

There was quite an age range, with the children's ages spanning from four years to 18 years and the parents' from 34 to 50 years. Four of the families had three children, and these happened to be the youngest in the group. The two older families had four children, but only two youngest from one family and the youngest from the other attended the cluster.

History of the First Year

The first meeting was held in January 1976. My wife, Mary, and I agreed to design the programme and to lead the day's session. Both of us had conducted weekend experiences for young people and adults, but we had never designed a programme for such a wide age range. During the next year we were to learn about the advantages and disadvantages of intergenerational education. In our first year the program evolved. To incorporate all age groups, we used different exercises: constructing, drawing, role playing, making music, and playing games both indoors and outdoors.

Each day had a similar pattern—an introductory game began activities, followed by a family exercise (i.e. building a vehicle, drawing a family coat-of-arms) which included discussion and sharing. Each family brought a contribution for lunch. In the afternoon we experienced some outside activity, usually in a local park, much to the surprise of neighborhood residents. Thirty people running around a park doing all kinds of strange activities is bound to raise a few eyebrows! Finally, we returned home to do one more activity together (such as making music with newspapers), and then the day was evaluated with all persons expressing their likes and dislikes and proposing various ideas for the next session.

All of the meetings were held in the home of each family by turn, as we all had fairly large houses. After the first meeting, the programme was planned and led by my wife and me in cooperation with the host parents. The host children were encouraged to offer their ideas, and they would organize a particular activity. One of the major problems we faced was that the children became very bored when the adults talked too much. The adults wanted to discuss their experiences, but the children wanted to get on to the next activity. Another problem, which was to develop more in the second year, was that every month the adults met in the discussion group mentioned previously. This had the effect of creating a group within a group; also, unresolved business from the cluster often spilled over into the discussion group.

Dynamics in the Cluster

By the end of the first year some interesting dynamics had occurred. Three of the men, who were used to operating from a cerebral standpoint than from an emotional one, felt that they were not getting much from the sessions. Two of the wives were beginning to discover their own power, as were the older children; and this began to have an effect on their families. All of the children enjoyed themselves; they liked the attentiveness of so many adults, and even the most unruly and energetic child could find someone to give attention. Next to the children, the women were the group which clearly derived the most benefit from being in the cluster.

All of the men held demanding jobs, with most working long and unsociable hours. They also involved themselves in the community through politics, church, and neighborhood activities. All of the men were hard-working, highly competitive, achieving, middle-class males. The fact that they would relaxedly spend a whole day every other month made the cluster beneficial to them.

The first year concluded with an agreement that the families would evaluate the year together, and the parents would attend a meeting to decide whether or not to contract for another year.

Evaluation

In the evaluation it was agreed that we needed to find a way for the parents to discuss issues in more depth. On one occasion we had tried to have separate activities for the children from the adults; although this had worked to a limited extent, it still didn't meet the needs of the adults.

For the new contract, it was agreed that we would continue to meet for a full day (11:00 A.M.-4:00 P.M.) on a Sunday, the later start allowing people to attend church services. The parents also agreed to meet during the evening of the cluster day (8:00-11:00 P.M.), which would allow the adults to have in-depth discussion related to the theme for each session.

It was agreed that each cluster day should have a topic, so we brainstormed ideas to be dealt with over the year. Also, the choosing of themes tied in with an additional task the group had agreed to undertake. In 1977 the World Council of Churches (headquarters: Geneva, Switzerland) began a social action/research project, and our cluster agreed to take part. This agreement brought some significant changes. First, the group had to undertake filling in the necessary papers for the project, as well as having the meetings recorded in writing. Secondly, since I was national co-ordinator for the project, one of the members of the cluster agreed to act as leader and recorder since she was a trained marriage guidance counsellor.

The Second Year

During the second year, the programmes for the cluster followed a similar pattern to that of the first year. The introduction of family sculpting in one session was much appreciated. Towards the end of the year we decided to have a walk, eat a picnic meal and visit a zoo which was different from our usual pattern. The children enjoyed the outdoor activity best, and this led to the whole day being spent outside.

Reflection

Some of the issues and dynamics created in the cluster over the two years were as follows.

Leadership. The cluster had experienced a change in designated leadership within the two years. Although Helen was leader in the second year, Mary and I were still members of the group and made major contributions to the designing of the programmes. Helen had a more confrontative style of leadership which led to some interesting developments within the group.

Throughout the two years, Helen, Mary and myself were regarded clearly as the experts. All three of us were trained in group work; Helen and Mary were trained as marriage guidance counsellors, and I was educated as an Anglican priest. Although labeled as the experts, we were not allowed to use or we failed to use our skills to the fullest. Meanwhile, skills in planning and leading were being developed by many members of the group.

Clearly, there are advantages in using outside leadership; but, despite our problems, I believe there was enough skill within the group to overcome the difficulties. In retrospect, we might have improved our performance if we had established feedback on leadership as well as on the value of a particular exercise. By doing this, it would have been possible to develop the skills of other members in a more effective way, apart from the trained leadership.

Contract. The main features of our contract were: time commitment (how long and how often), topics to be covered, regular attendance, and methods to be used. Also, there was an expectation that everyone would take part in every activity. From the start it was clear that this expectation would cause problems. Quite often children chose to opt out of an activity they didn't like, and the parents or other children tried to persuade them to participate; but what if adults wanted to opt out?

In the first year one of the teenagers declared that this wasn't her "scene" and didn't attend again. With this particular family, only the parents remained. Halfway through the second year another teenager decided she had had enough and left.

The real "crunch" came one afternoon while boating on a lake. The day had gone very well, and the afternoon activity consisted of rowing in small boats on the lake. Mary and Helen, the two "leaders," didn't fancy rowing so went for a cup of coffee instead. The rest of the group enjoyed the activity and had alot of fun. On the way home there was moaning from the adults that not everyone had joined in the boating activity. In the evening matters came to a head in a variety of ways. There was alot of annoyance expressed about opting out, and Helen challenged John about opting out of the evening session by looking as if he'd gone to sleep. The meeting continued late with the issue still unresolved. I share this issue in more detail, because it indicates what can happen with an issue when it is not effectively dealt with in the contract. This issue arose from misperception of the contract, but I would identify it as one of the most crucial issues concerning commitment to relationships in the group, as well as in the wider society.

The following cluster session saw another example of opting out. Some of the parents didn't want to go to a commercial zoo for the planned activity. All kinds of reasons were given from "too commercial" to "not my scene." Again, the adult evening session explored the situation; Helen's report states:

> "There was alot of strong feeling about the contract being broken by some members; we had not stayed together as a cluster, so what was the point? How had we decided to spend a day out and not have the usual structured day? It seemed as if some were very disappointed and angry with the day being different, though some had a good day and 'got what they wanted.' "

It's worth noting that the Pepper family was about to leave for South Africa where Ben Pepper was being sent by his employers. This was their last meeting. It seemed that the break-up of the group had begun! It's not surprising that the topic for the last cluster meeting of the year was death. My reflection on these sessions is that it is not sufficient to make a contract at the beginning for the whole year's time; a clear understanding of procedures for negotiation of the contract is also needed.

One process noted in our contracting was that discussion of it was held in each family and then negotiated by the parents on the family's behalf. This procedure seemed to work well, although I can see the point for involving the whole cluster in the process. A final importance I would make about contracting is that each family must take responsibility for helping to meet its expectations of the cluster experience. In a society like Britain's, many social benefits are offered as part of the welfare state; and it is too easy to expect that everything will be provided, including self satisfaction. In short, it is easy to look for a scapegoat when our expectations are not met. Participants may blame the leaders, the programmes, or even the weather; but unless we all understand our responsibilities in making the contract work, the group can find itself in difficulty.

Commitment. Following the discussion noted previously, the question was raised about the nature of commitment. Is each individual adult and child from the families committed to the basic philosophy of Family Clusters? It is clear the children enjoyed the days, but might they not also have enjoyed any day where adults, particularly their parents, gave them attention? The adults had varying motives for being present, so their commitment depended on that motive. If they were present for "the sake of the children" or "because my spouse wanted to attend," the commitment was low, and the possibility of meaningful learning remote.

Methods of Learning. All of the adults in the cluster had been educated in a cerebral manner. Their schooling was mainly didactic, with the "teacher-tell" method predominating. Further, we are encouraged in English society to hide our feelings and to exercise our thought processes. The children are more fortunate today in their education which encourages the experiential and are used to playing games and working on projects. Some adults had experiences with new educational methods, and three persons had also participated in the area of personal growth. There was a constant conflict between thinking vs. feelings and didactic vs. experiential.

Jim continually declared, "I've learnt nothing." Ted claimed, "I've learnt nothing, but my wife has; she's much better at this sort of thing." Don asked, "Is there a book I can read which will tell me what it's all about?" Many of the group repeatedly said to Helen, Mary and myself, "It's all right for you being open; you've done all this sharing of feelings before."

It's interesting to reflect three years later and know that Ted can say for himself, "I've changed!" Jim has a grudging respect for experiential education, thanks to a discussion on the methods of Saul Alinsky (an American social activist). Don still wants his books but also would own up to having changed. It is clear to me that using experiential methods does allow for learning and change to take place, although it doesn't produce instant results. This is difficult to understand for those who have been taught by more traditional methods. In a society where feelings are hidden behind the "stiff upper lip," it is difficult to share thoughts from an emotional level as well as a cerebral one. It is all too easy to put ourselves down, to say such things as, "I can't change," "I'm not really a very good person." The need for confrontation and affirmation is clear; when this happens growth does and can take place.

Teenagers. It has already been written that two of the teenagers left the cluster; by the next contracting time the remaining one was to leave. Since the time of the beginning cluster, we have had some changes with new and younger families joining, and the two older families leaving. In the new cluster group where there were six teenagers (four girls and two boys), three of the girls stopped attending the sessions, and the fourth girl is contemplating it. In the first cluster the girls were 16 years old when they left, and the boy was 18 years old. In the present cluster, the departing girls are 14 years old.

The Present Day Cluster

At the completion of our second contracted time, we rethought the whole structure and invited others to join us. The Pepper family was in South Africa; the Golders and the Etons were giving consideration to leaving. We held a typical cluster day when all the original cluster families and four new families met and shared. In the evening session three of the new families agreed to commit themselves to a contract. The two older families, whose children no longer wanted to attend, decided to leave as well as the Eton family because the father was not prepared to attend regularly.

Five families contracted to meet and follow the same pattern of the former cluster with an additional evening for parents. The planning for the cluster was done mainly by the parents when one representative from each family attended the planning meeting. In addition to the cluster day, we also arranged other activities such as weekend camping, visiting the theatre, swimming, and bowling. The outside activities, except for camping, were not part of the contract, so all members did not feel obliged to attend.

Some results now showing are:
- the Pepper family returned from South Africa and couldn't wait to rejoin the cluster.
- a group has been formed to look at marriage and family in the parish, and all the original families are represented in the assemblage.

The effects of Family Cluster still continue after five years of growing in the parish.

Resources

Freed, Alvyn, M. *TA for Teens*. Sacramento, CA: Jalmar Press, 1978.

Pfeiffer, J. William and Jones, John E. *A Handbook of Structured Experiences for Human Relations Training*, Vols. 1,2,3,4,5. San Diego, CA: University Associates, Inc., 1973-75.

Sawin, Margaret M. "Educating by Family Groups: A New Model for Religious Education," 1973 (rev.1977). Available from Family Clustering, Inc., P.O. Box 18074, Rochester, N.Y. 14618.

Biographical Data

Martin Goodlad was born in 1939 of working class parents in Yorkshire, England. Marrying Mary in 1962, they now have three children. Trained as a teacher, he is an ordained clergyman of the Church of England and is currently Youth Officer of the Church of England Board of Education, Church House, Dean's Yard, London SW 1P 3NZ. Telephone: 01-222-9011, ext. 244.

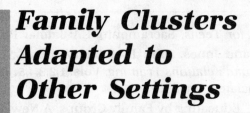

Family Clusters Adapted to Other Settings

Because the cluster model is a process one, it is easily adaptable to other settings and can be used with many different types of family groups. The following stories tell of some of those adaptations:

1 *A Mental Health Experience* by Bruce Brillinger
This is a story of how an agency uses Family Cluster with potentially dysfunctioning families in an enrichment manner.

2 *Pre-School Children's Experience* by Joanne Hanrahan and Joyelle Proot
This account shares how a church-sponsored pre-school helped its families, as well as its children.

3 *Public School Experience* by Barbara and Bill Reeder
Clusters have been used in numerous public school settings to enhance both children and family members with learnings concerned with interpersonal relations.

4 *Divorced and Separated Families' Experience* by Gregory Dunwoody
A narrative showing the use of the cluster model to help divorced and separated families experience enrichment for their family units.

5 *Air Force Families' Experience* by Charles Prewitt
An account of the use of Family Clusters with Air Force personnel in a retreat setting.

A Mental Health Experience

Bruce Brillinger

Toronto, Ontario

"I enjoyed talking with other parents ... you know, we don't talk about what goes on in our family usually ... and I don't feel so strange about our family now."

"It was encouraging to see my children playing with others ... and to see other people's children acting up too!"

"I liked playing *Upset the Fruit Basket* with everybody in the big room upstairs."

"I liked helping to get the breakfast ready."

"I want to come next weekend, can I?"

"I haven't played in the snow like that since before the children were born!"

Comments like these are often heard from adults and children in the Family Cluster groups at the Dellcrest Children's Centre.

Sponsorship

Dellcrest, a Children's Mental Health Centre, established in 1961, is situated in the city of North York, formerly a borough of Metropolitan Toronto in Canada. The Centre has evolved a wide range of innovative treatment services. A family systems approach is the underlying theoretical framework.

In 1977 I introduced the Family Cluster Model as an innovation within the Dellcrest Child and Family Clinic's range of services to families. I wanted to see families as they functioned in a broader social context, to see how the children related to each other and to adults, and to see how the parents handled real behavioral problems as they emerged. This information is not readily available in a traditional one family interview. In addition I feel there is a hunger for "community" on the part of parents, a desire for feedback and recognition from their peers as to how they are doing, and a deep need for caring and support around the challenging job of parenting. I believe parenting is a lonely task in our day. This need is heightened by a society which promotes individualism to the point of isolationism and alienation. Our society also promotes segregation of the ages by defining 'peers' as people of the same age. The Family Cluster Model counteracts these tendencies by establishing a "community" based on intergenerational exchanges and by enabling groups of people to benefit from the "wisdom of all ages." It actually creates a forum for the exchange of perspectives across age boundaries and across family lines that is enriching, stimulating and all inclusive of the people involved. Community is created when individuals and families meet this way. So, cluster has become not just a matter of collecting information about a given family's functioning in a social context, but a way of creating a supportive network of care-givers, a way of including all ages of persons, and a way of building the self-esteem of parents, children and families. If these needs are not met, reactionary behavior can develop which can lead to serious dysfunctions which require intensive treatment.

Two practical considerations also played a part in the introduction of the cluster concept. One is the desire to reach out to other helping agencies in the community with a service that is supportive and supplementary and that will yield important assessment information for them. Secondly, the Child and Family Clinic is facing increasingly long waiting lists, and the cluster approach is a way of responding to a number of families who would otherwise wait up to six months for regular service to begin. In the three years Family Clusters have been functioning at Dellcrest, families have been drawn from the Clinic's waiting list, other agencies, other Dellcrest services, or from the community at large.

I have adapted the cluster model to Dellcrest's situation in a variety of ways:

1 Live-in Residential Weekends (from Friday 7:00 P.M. to Sunday at 4:00 P.M. for four to six families in total.

2 Ongoing Groups (four to six families in total) that meet for two-hour sessions every two weeks for a maximum of six sessions.

3 Assessment Groups (four to six families in total) for *either* two sessions (three hours each) or for one full day, usually a Saturday (approximately 7 hours).

These various forms serve to meet different needs. For example, the weekends are the most intensive because of the length of time the group spends together without outside interruptions. These blocks of time are especially helpful to a family in getting a change process started. The ongoing groups span a longer time frame and, although less intense in nature, can more effectively monitor change over time. There are also practical reasons for the various formats. For instance, some families find it difficult to set aside a whole weekend. Weekends are also more difficult to organize because of the complexities of overnight accommodation and food preparation. Seasons of the year seem to affect the weekend format, with the winter season being the most acceptable time. There are emotional issues, too. For example, the issue of trust and risking exposure is very high during a weekend event. Families are not accustomed to having professional people and agencies respond to them in these ways. Fear of leaving home overnight, for long periods, is a particular problem for those from the poorer, subsidized housing area. Therefore, I have tried to devise a variety of formats to accommodate as many of the circumstantial and emotional concerns as possible.

Cluster Leadership

Leadership for all of the cluster adaptations has been provided by myself and a core of selected volunteers.

The role of the professional. I have worked with Margaret Sawin in a variety of ways over the past seven years. Initially, I attended a summer Family Cluster Training Lab with my own family, followed by being a Staff leader-in-training member at another Training Lab and then as a trainer of cluster leaders at a Lab. All of these were held at The Five Oaks Centre in Paris, Ontario. I led clusters in my home community as well as at Dellcrest. My skills as a therapist and as a parent educator enabled me to bring additional resources to the cluster model which helped to create the adaptations being reported here. My theological training and experience within the religious community gave me an important perspective on the depth-dimension of the model, especially in relation to the concepts of caring, community and the enhancement of self-esteem.

My role has been to conceptualize and create the adaptations and, to a great extent, design the programs. I have assumed the responsibility for evaluation and research as well as organizational accountability. However, in terms of actual content used with a given group of families, I have drawn heavily on the insights, abilities and sensitivities of the volunteers. Over the past three years a number of these volunteers have remained consistent. They have acquired a wide range of skills now and are able to have a perspective on the whole process that facilitates planning and designing.

The use and training of volunteers. One of the major innovations that has come with the introduction of clusters at Dellcrest is the heavy involvement of volunteers in direct, fact-to-face service with families. These people have actually functioned as "caseworkers." The volunteers have received three types of training:

1 the regular eight-week general training provided by the Centre for all volunteers;
2 an eight-week course in interpersonal communication skills;
3 specialized training and orientation to the Family Cluster Model.

In the first year the volunteers who were selected were invited to bring their own families or their family of origin to a Family

Cluster Training Weekend in which they experienced and practice-led some of the cluster program components.

Selection. The volunteers are selected by me in consultation with the Volunteer Coordinator of the Centre. Skills in group leadership, music and recreation as well as interpersonal skills in relating and communicating are considered desirable. Life experience and how the volunteer relates to that experience is important. Personality characteristics, such as sensitivity to self and others, and a sense of responsibility, as well as maturity, are rated as highly desirable. Work experience and level of formal education are not significant factors in the selection. The core group of cluster leaders are men and women who range in age from 20-55 years, with a variety of educational backgrounds. In some cases they are parents, married people without children, or single people. Their paid occupations range from factory foreman to teachers, from social workers to full-time students or housewives.

The volunteers have assisted in the leadership of specific elements of the program, have helped with planning and designing sessions and have served as liaison or contact persons for specific families. In this latter role the volunteers play a significant part in the recruiting and contracting with families as well as conducting follow-up visits in the home. The volunteers work in teams consisting of two of three persons with myself in each cluster event. These teams change their composition as the volunteers change from event to event. Specific roles are worked out on the spot or just before the family group sessions occur.

The natural abilities and personalities of the volunteers are fully utilized. For example, a young mother who sings well and plays the guitar is heavily used in that way. She has also made a tape of songs to be taught and sung in groups where there is no such talent present. A young father, a foreman in a warehouse, has the natural ability to relate to a wide range of people and is particularly effective with working class fathers with whom he can converse readily and play poker after the formal program ends. An older man who has experienced divorce demonstrates extreme sensitivity towards single parents and can be supportive to them. He is also a grandfather figure for the younger children and provides them with much nurturance. A young female student, also a product of a broken home, can relate extremely well to the quiet, withdrawn or depressed children within a family. Programs are designed so as to give as much opportunity as possible to these people to use themselves in the process of helping to create a climate of comfort, acceptance and nurturance that is conducive to learning and is growth producing.

Problems of leadership. One of the problems faced by the leadership is that of time and time management. Because the volunteers are giving their time, it is difficult to demand much beyond the actual experience with the families. This means that time for planning and reflecting are at a premium. This is a particular problem during weekend events when the leaders tend to be "on" all the time. The emerging design is most evident then because planning meetings have to be held "on the run." The problem is being resolved by setting some times for meetings for de-briefing and planning, apart from the events. We hold open staff meetings to which parents can come late in the evenings. These serve to involve parents in the planning and to conserve time. For the most part, the volunteers have been trained on the job, and that experience has been invaluable. However, they have not had the benefit of a Family Cluster Leadership Training Lab or a Design Skills Lab that would provide them with the broader view needed for designing and conceptualizing. This problem has not yet been totally resolved.

Benefits for the volunteers. As a result of their involvement in the various cluster adaptations, the volunteers have reported significant positive changes in their attitudes toward themselves, their own children and family life; positive changes in behavior within their relationships, and a greater sense of self-worth. Several of these people have given three to four years of significant service to the Centre as a result of their training and experience in cluster groups.

The Families

All of the families that have been a part of the cluster experience at Dellcrest have been identified as "troubled"; that is, they are families who have come to the attention of the school system, the medical profession, the courts, or the welfare system. They are families who are considered to contain one or more 'troubled' children. They are families who in many cases are attached to some form of helping service before being in a cluster.

They are families who represent all social classes and who represent the major current family life styles such as single-parent families, reconstituted families, traditional two-parent families and two-parent families in which the parents are not married. Children in the cluster groups range in age from 1-19 years. Clusters at the Centre contain highly dysfunctional families in which both adults and children lack basic social and nurturance skills. They have families with severely and mildly retarded children. They have families in which child abuse is a documented fact. And they have well functioning families.

By virtue of the fact that the participants for clusters are recruited primarily from the client lists of helping agencies, our selection is somewhat random; and the resulting group is often a mix of the above features. This mix has proven to have an interesting effect on cluster dynamics resulting in exciting learning for all members of the group. For example, I observed a number of middle-class children sitting around the dinner table making quiet complaints about the food but not saying or doing anything about their problem. However, an eleven-year-old girl from a poor family, with brutal honesty, announced in a loud voice, "I'm not eating that garbage!" This episode not only represented the true feelings of most of the children but it also resulted in some important learning for those preparing the food, namely, that children from poorer homes did not recognize food that was prepared in a fancy, casserole style. The more controlled families also tend to model positively for the chaotic families. They demonstrated the need for greater organization in order to accomplish tasks and solve problems. This cross pollination is one of the positive effects of mixing families of different lifestyles and socialization skills.

Special Problems for Dellcrest Clusters

Families in which there are major behavioral problems create more control problems in clusters. This demands that the cluster program be ingenious and fast-moving in design so as to hold the interest and attention of people who are not used to, but need, structure in their family life.

Families who are identified by some community agency as "families in need of help" tend to feel low self-esteem and low corporate esteem as they come to the Centre. The Family Cluster Model is an excellent way to create a normalizing effect or climate. At no time is any family or individual identified as "the problem." All of the activities of the cluster, in content and in method, are designed to build the self-esteem of individuals and the family.

Families, in which the common tendency of the parents is to suppress their children, present a major challenge to cluster leaders. This tendency works against the nurturant philosophy of clusters. However, by attending as much to the self-esteem needs of the adults as to those of the children, the tide soon turns. Our research has focused on self-esteem and use of power within the family with encouraging results that support the Family Cluster Model as not only an educational but a therapeutic resource.

Contracting with Families

Because the majority of participant families in clusters are clients of the Dellcrest Child and Family Clinic or some other therapy resource and have been referred to Dellcrest, in a sense, the contracting process is accomplished. They have completed an Application for Service form and are waiting for family therapy to begin, or they are already engaged in some form of service from the Centre. Therefore, individual families are invited by me or by a volunteer to come to the cluster event which is described to them in advance. A minimal fee is charged for each event.

During the cluster group, the contracting process is much abbreviated from what is recommended in the model. For example, during a weekend event contracting takes approximately thirty to forty minutes on the Saturday morning. The content is focused largely on ground rules for living together during the weekend. On some occasions, the contracting might also contain such issues as shared parenting, rules for discussion, opting in and out depending on the nature of the group, the ages of the children, the level of activity, etc. Some form of group signing of the contract always occurs no matter what the nature of its contents. No special problems have been encountered with this modified version, and in every case the exercise of doing it helps to bring about group cohesion.

Factors of the Weekend Cluster

Although several different adaptations of cluster have been used at Dellcrest, the major one being reported here is the live-in, residential weekend format. This format has been used each year for the past three years with three to four weekend clusters per year. Each weekend has involved four to five families. Some families have been in attendance all three years; some for two, with the majority attending one such event.

This weekend format has many strong features. First of all, the shared living (we use a large residence in downtown Toronto, owned by Dellcrest), plus the continuous forty-five hours (Friday evening until Sunday afternoon) quickly builds community. All members of the group tend to relax, open up and trust, including the leaders. This atmosphere facilitates sharing, makes conflicts seem natural, and enables problem-solving to occur constructively within family systems, across family lines or in the total group. A definite feeling of "we're all in this thing together" draws people close together.

The credibility of the leadership is enhanced through this format, because the leaders expose themselves as human beings by living with the families. This comes as a surprise to the participant families because they have formed expectations of professionals and helping agencies tending to be aloof, controlling and willing to work only between the hours of 9 and 5. The use of volunteers has proven to be a major step in breaking down the barriers between the "givers" and the "receivers" of service. The volunteers function without any professional airs about them.

Another strength of this format is the deemphasis on the "problem-child" or the "problem family." Cluster is an educational, enrichment, learning model, holistic in its approach to human behavior and interpersonal relationships. When operationalized, cluster becomes a caring community of people who have much in common, although they may be different in appearance, and lifestyles. Within the context of community they discover, affirm and celebrate their similarities. Such an experience combats the feelings that most clients have that they are somehow different from the rest of humanity, are less adequate, more troubled and somewhat weird. Families who experience the cluster phenomenon realize their common humanity as expressed in their sharing of difficult family life issues. Within the cluster they are able to share their strengths and weaknesses without reproach, labelling or judgment.

The weekend format best highlights the above strengths. Its major shortcoming is that it occurs at a point in time and that's it! The more utilized form of clusters in church settings with contracted periods of ten sessions occurring weekly, has the major advantage of continuity over time. Due to this major difference, the weekend experience does not allow for the group to pass through as many developmental stages as would occur in an ongoing group. However, a very clear pattern of movement has evolved in the weekend format.

What Happens in the Cluster?

Friday evening and Saturday morning sessions are spent in group building and inclusion activities designed to help participants feel comfortable and begin to trust and open up. The children are always the first to achieve these at this point. The adults take longer to overcome their anxiety, fear, and suspicion.

Saturday afternoon usually includes a lot of free time for everyone, structured and unstructured play for the children (indoors and outdoors) and a parents' discussion group.

Generally, the latter part of Saturday afternoon is for parents only, and Saturday morning and Sunday morning are the "work times" for everyone. By Saturday noon the leaders have observed enough to sense what some of the issues are within individuals, families, and the group. On the basis of this information, programs are designed for Saturday evening and Sunday morning that enable families to begin to address some of their issues.

Sunday afternoon activities centre around affirmation, contracting for change back home, closure and reentry. Usually this is a heavy time emotionally with most participants struggling with separation issues in a positive way. At this stage the adults tend to have a difficult time as they realize the strength of the community support they have had in contrast to the loneliness of parenting and the challenges of family life back home.

What Is Learned

In the course of a weekend a number of group formations are used to facilitate sharing, learning and problem solving. These are family groups, simulated family groups, subsystems of a family (for instance, mother/child, father/child, parental team, sibling group), peer groups and total group. Most of the tasks given to these groups are preconceived and structured; for instance, each family makes a collage that they can use to introduce themselves to the group. Activities used also might be talking to a partner or small group about what it was like to be you in your family of origin; to identify as a family what you would like to do as a group for the next hour, plan it, carry it out and evaluate it afterwards. These various activities bring out different features of a person, reveal different dynamics at work within a family, and begin to break down some of the inhibitions or barriers to communication. For example, a child in a simulated family may be able to express himself, without reproach, about an important issue that was suppressed at home. An adult may gain a whole new perspective on the behavior of his or her adolescent son by listening to someone else's teenager. In the total group, all persons realize their importance as each is recognized for his or her contribution. In the family groups various members discover, through a shared task, an important feeling or desire that someone has had but never expressed before because the family seldom does anything together that focuses on its members as persons. In the parent group the adults discover they are *not* alone, weird, or sick and that other people *do* care for them. They also discover the importance of caring for themselves and the connection between feeling good about oneself with the quality of their parenting.

Because of the live-in feature, there is always a lot of free, unstructured time before and after meals, at bedtime and in the latter part of the two evenings. These times often yield some of the most significant learnings as a group of parents, over coffee or a cigarette, discover a commonality, share an experience or a solution that works for them. It is also during the free times often that the children form alliances and make new friends. The moments of shared house-keeping, such as preparing breakfast, setting and cleaning off the table, are important times of meeting and recognizing individual worth. For instance, a father who was a reluctant and peripheral member of the group came into a position of importance and prominence when he was able to fix the kettle and the toaster that weren't working. A little mongoloid boy of five won his way into the group by dancing with his own shadow in the sunlight as the group sat and sang. And a single parent mother who hadn't danced since she was a teenager let herself go as we did the "Hokey-Pokey." A middle-class, middle-aged mother "let her hair down" and really had fun at the park sliding down a snow covered hill in a plastic garbage bag. A hyperactive seven-year-old boy learned to accept a back rub and lie quietly for several minutes as the group sang.

The children benefit from the accepting and nurturing environment which was created. They enjoy the content that has to do with meals, games, songs and crafts. They find talk times and discussions uninteresting.

The adults benefit from times together to share feelings and ideas. They gain encouragement from seeing other children misbehave and other parents becoming bewildered as to what to do. Parents obtain helpful reference points and benefit from learning communication skills. They like to have some input and feedback from the experts or the leaders.

Evaluation and Research

Various methods for evaluating have been used. In all cases we have tended to look at the relationship between the cluster experience and such factors as family cohesiveness, self-esteem, and the structure of the family's life. Does it alter at all? What are the negotiation skills which a family has before and after the weekend? We have used pre- and post-measures. We have done follow-up home visits. We have used various forms of satisfaction questionnaires. We have used tape recordings and drawings to collect information from children who tend to have difficulty with written questionnaires. We are continually refining our methods. To date, the evidence suggests that the cluster weekends definitely enhance the self-esteem of family members, increase communication skills, lead to positions of greater equality in the family and facilitate collective ability to solve family problems in constructive ways.

Each weekend cluster is concluded on Sunday by suggesting to the families that they engage in a planning session about their learnings as individuals or as a family during the weekend and how those relate to their life back home. If they choose to do that, they are asked to write out their contract for change, sign it and have it witnessed by someone of their own choosing who is outside their family.

Follow-Up

Very little specific follow-up has been done with families. In part, many of them are on the Centre's waiting list and go on for family therapy as originally planned. In other cases the continuity of service is maintained by the agency or professional who referred them. In a few cases, informal contact is maintained by me and/or the volunteers. Several families have returned, of their own volition, for a second and third experience. With some, no other formal service has been required. One single-parent mother explained, "We get so much out of the Weekend that we can manage on our own for about six months. By then the children are asking, 'When can we go for another weekend at Dovercourt?' [the downtown house]. If I can promise them a definite date when we can go again, then we are able to manage until we get there. I just wish we could go twice a year, that would be just right."

Summary

After three years with ten weekend events, I am convinced of the value of this service for our client families. I am also convinced that there are more "variations on the theme" to be developed. I am convinced that the multi-family or cluster or intergenerational group is a helpful way to build a network of support for families, and I want to develop it further. I am developing services designed as preventive, skill-oriented, awareness enhancing, self-esteem-building so that individuals, couples and families can move in healthy, functional directions instead of dysfunctional ones. I see the caring community nature of the Family Cluster Model as one which provides the experiential basis for ongoing family and individual help. Often the need which motivates a family to seek professional help is simply the loneliness of the task of parenting, a lack of recognition and feedback from outside the family system, the lack of knowledge about what to expect, and reference points for checking it out. The need for help is great, because the stresses of modern urban life are often too much for any set of parents, no matter how strong they are as individuals or as a team. The nuclear family is under heavy pressure as it is cut off from its extended family network, isolated in high density housing without neighbourhoods, and alienated from historical and traditional institutions such as the church and the "little red schoolhouse." Left to its own resources, it may manage but not really develop to its full potential as a place for promoting the health of its members. Highly specialized, high cost, professional treatment services should be reserved for those families needing "intensive care"; but the Family Cluster Model has proven to be an excellent vehicle for transmitting basic care through a community network.

Resources

Briggs, Dorothy Corkille. *Your Child's Self-Esteem: The Key to Life.* New York: Doubleday & Company, Inc. 1970.

Gordon, Thomas. *Parent Effectiveness Training.* New York: Peter H. Wyden, Inc. 1970.

Satir, Virginia. *Peoplemaking.* Palo Alto, California: Science and Behavior Books, 1972.

Biographical Data

Bruce A. Brillinger, B.A., B.D., M.S.W., is a supervisor in the Child and Family Clinic at The Dellcrest Children's Centre, Toronto, Canada. He is a professional family therapist and parent educator who brings together clinical, educational and theological perspectives. Bruce is married and is the father of four children, ages 8 to 15.

Address:

The Dellcrest Children's Centre
1645 Sheppard Ave. W.
Downsview, Ont. M3M 2X4
Canada
Tel. (416) 633-0515

Pre-School Children's Experience

Joanne Hanrahan
Joyelle Proot

St. Louis, Missouri

Maria Center for learning and life-enrichment is a commitment to the mission and ministry of education by the St. Louis Province of the School Sisters of Notre Dame. The Center fosters an integration of the personal, spiritual, and professional dimensions of life for persons of all ages and provides learning opportunities within a Christian community environment. The philosophy of Maria Center reflects the belief that

- —learning is an integrative process that is lifelong
- —learning is experiential and reflective
- —learning is participative and mutually enriching
- —learning is planned collaboratively by staff and participants
- —learning is flexible in place and time
- —learning respects diversity and fosters interdependence
- —learning builds on the gifts of faith and nature
- —learning takes place in a community of shared gospel values
- —learning is a freeing, creative act.

Maria Center offers programs and services in four major areas, one of which is family enrichment.

Beginning in August of 1978, we began a search for models of family education that involved the total family. During this time we met Dr. Margaret Sawin and became acquainted with the Family Cluster Model of family enrichment. After meeting her and participating in a Family Cluster Training Lab sponsored by the Mennonites in Winnipeg, Canada, we came to understand that Family Cluster activities are intergenerational, experiential, participative, and integrative. Through building upon family strengths, cluster experiences enhance both personal and relationship growth between family members. A Family Cluster is an enriching experience that takes place within a supportive community environment. Because this model is consistent with the philosophy of Maria Center, it is now an integral part of the family enrichment program.

How We Began

In early June 1979, we began piloting the Family Cluster Model in various school and parish settings. We chose Notre Dame Pre-School in St. Louis as our first pilot group. Because of its proximity to Maria Center and the interest of pre-school families in family growth, we believed that a cluster composed of these families would be an excellent beginning. With the support of the principal and her recommendation of families, we initiated contacts with thirty families during the month of July. We sent letters of invitation that introduced us and briefly explained the Family Cluster Model. Each family was invited to participate in an introductory session. A week later this letter was followed by a personal phone call to answer any questions about family enrichment and to see if the family was interested in coming to the session. The calls gave us the opportunity to answer questions and clarify expectations. The conversations often involved discussions of values, religious beliefs, concerns and hopes about family life. Of the thirty families contacted, seventeen expressed an interest in the project. Twelve families actually committed themselves to the introductory sessions which included cluster-type activities.

From the attendance in two introductory sessions, five families expressed an interest in forming a cluster that would meet once a week for five additional sessions. During September we began the process of obtaining final commitments from the five families and setting dates for the cluster meetings. We used the introductory sessions as a substitute for the home visitation and sent each family member a data collector which all filled out and returned. However, before the initial evening two families withdrew for reasons of conflicting schedules. This experience with the two families caused us to re-evaluate our process for recruiting families to contract for the cluster.

We made the decision to go ahead as planned with three families. Their enthusiasm, interest, and commitment, as well as our own need for experience, convinced us we had everything to gain and nothing to lose in trying. By early October we started the cluster with these pre-school families whose eleven children ranged in age from two months to five years.

Leadership

We undertook the leadership of this Family Cluster because of the focus of Maria Center and its commitment to family ministry. Our roles as leaders throughout the cluster involved the planning, facilitating, and leading of the sessions. As leaders of a cluster of young families, we found our teaching backgrounds to be an invaluable asset in terms of understanding the developmental stages of both children and adults. Skills of organizing, synthesizing, and creating custom designed learning activities were particular talents we had developed in our teaching experiences within innovative school settings. Our professional experience with individualized learning helped us to be flexible and adaptable with pre-school families. It was easy to transfer our educational skills to the design and leading of cluster activities with an intergenerational focus. In addition to our educational experience, we found that our training in the Family Cluster Lab gave us a better understanding of cluster theory, practice in design skills, and the opportunity to observe behavioral changes in families.

In discussing our leadership roles in the cluster, we decided to work as a team in planning and leading the sessions. We set objectives and designed activities together. As one of us led an activity with the families, the other acted in a supportive role by facilitating family interaction and caring for children. With eleven young children involved, the leaders' roles demanded a lot of flexibility and teamwork in facilitating activities and games. It took energy and persistence. As the cluster sessions developed, we appreciated the supportive role the parents began to assume.

As we continued our team building and planning for further sessions, a difference in approach began to surface. One leader looked at the possible obstacles connected with the activities, while the other leader was willing to experiment with anything once. One leader's apprehension coupled with the other leader's enthusiasm lent a creative tension into the planning sessions. However, our mutual commitment to the cluster, our ability to work together, and our desire to work with the pre-school families were the conerstones of our success. We agreed to the goals, format, and activities of each cluster session. We steadily gained experience in designing and adapting activities that were appropriate and meaningful for the families.

Families

The families that composed this delightful cluster were three sets of younger parents with pre-school children. The McCarthys have four children, the Deckers have two, and the Antons have five children, including twins. Steve, Mike, and Karen were five years old. Susie was the four-year-old. Randy and Robby were three-year-old twins. Tommy was two and the infants were Jenifer (9 months), Kevin (five months), and Brian (two months). Tom and Pat McCarthy, Joe and Carol Decker, and Jim and Joan Anton were the parents in their late twenties and early thirties. All lived in a suburban setting.

Two of the fathers worked at an Air Force base. When the cluster dates were established, neither the families nor the leaders anticipated the effect this factor would have on the cluster. Due to job demands and the unpredictable travel schedules of these two fathers, we had to adjust and change the dates for the sessions. The length of time between the re-scheduled sessions was a disadvantage. However, the willingness of families to adjust and accommodate each other was edifying. Although the families had not met prior to the cluster, they cared for each other, waited for each other, and wanted to do the sessions together.

Other unique features of the cluster were the presence of three-year-old twin boys, three infants, and the fact that all children were five years old or younger. This necessitated the designing of cluster activities that would provide opportunities for the twins to relate as individuals and enable the infants to move freely in and out of structured activities. The experiences and dynamics of this Family Cluster were especially shaped by the presence of so many young children. At the beginning of each session one leader would spend some time with the parents, while the other leader took the children apart. This helped set the theme for the evening and it also gave the parents an opportunity to share insights and ask questions about the goals of the session as their children were engaged in activities appropriate for them.

The Group Process

During the five sessions together over a period of eight weeks, the families grew steadily in a common bonding. The data from their initial collectors was used as a springboard for the themes and activities of the sessions. Special care was taken to create a rhythm within the two-hour period to include intense activity, quiet listening, and mutual sharing.

Common family make-up of young children and parents, trust in cluster leadership, and the inclusion of all family members created a bond of togetherness during the eight weeks. That all the families had toddlers and infants opened an increased understanding of active child behavior as normal and healthy. Parents began to see the change of mood and interest level of their own children as acceptable and appropriate. Although the children did not verbalize their own increased understanding about parent roles, their behavior seemed to indicate that they, too, were growing in appreciation of the vocation of parenthood. They began to accept both encouragement and correction from any parent within the cluster and relate to these adults in friendship.

Parents voiced a trust in the cluster leadership. They observed our working together and genuine out-going concern. The sincere love and spirit of playfulness we shared with the families also stimulated further bonding. Finally, both the parents and children appreciated the opportunity for all members to be engaged in a common event. In a setting where children and adults were welcomed and loved, the evening became a non-threatening and nurturing event in their lives together.

Along with the factors that fostered group cohesion, there were also forces that slowed the group-building process. The learning facility, the two-hour length of the sessions, and child illness became sources for creative problem-solving during the eight weeks.

By consolidating books and removing empty shelving, a large open and free space was designed within a former college library to accommodate the family evenings. The elements of temperature-control, open space, carpeted area, play area, and moveable furniture all contributed to the making of an environment that was welcoming and flexible to meet the learning needs of the families. However, the volumes of remaining college books on metal stacks that surrounded the perimeter of the open area seemed to demand awe and respect. The "message" of library was a cause of concern for parents who wanted to insure that their children did not playfully harm any of the texts. No amount of leader reassurance, indicating that there was no cause for anxiety, allayed parental fears.

The evening two-hour sessions began at 7:00 P.M. and overlapped the usual bedtime for many of the children. However, differences in father/mother work schedules within the families made the seven o'clock evening time the most convenient for coming together. An earlier starting time or sessions that were an hour and a half could have eased the problem of child tiredness.

Pre-schoolers and infants easily indicate the strains of not feeling completely well. The stress begins to show itself in impatient behavior and tears. In one instance an infant continuously crying as a response to not feeling well, almost caused a domino effect on all the other children. However, the concern of other children and parents for an ill child more often was a cause of strength within the cluster experience.

The creative tension present in the life of a Family Cluster is real to family life and a source that can stimulate positive growth. As both leaders and families evaluated the solutions used to ease tensions and encourage growth, they recognized that every lived experience mixes both pain and delight. The unique problems characterizing these sessions may not be present for other families participating in a different cluster, but the reality of creative tension always exists.

As a group sharing in family education together, the three-family cluster and leaders experienced phases of growth which moved easily from one to the other. Initially, the beginning with a sense of uncertainty and apprehension was coupled with a sincere eagerness to put forth only the best to enhance group life. The dedicated energy present in this first phase enabled leaders to maximize the willing efforts of the family members for forming a cluster. There was positive openness and a zest for trying to make each of the sessions a success. By the third week a familiarity with each other and the process of family cluster continued. This familiarity encouraged ease in conducting sessions and building relationships. A security evolved that allowed each person to reveal personal attitudes and feelings. In the presence of the new-found security, the tensions, the highs and lows in each parent and preschooler were free to surface. These moments of tension became significant building blocks of creative growth for the families. These were remembered months later when making informal visits to the families; it was the role-playing, puppet-making, and block-building activities dealing with anger, family conflict, lying, and cheating that were first recalled. By session five both adults and children expressed a sadness about not returning to share life in the Family Cluster context. A sense of community waited to be nurtured in new ways. Now, a year later, these same families express a hope for coming together again to share growth, learning, and religious values.

The Learning Process

The five sessions with the pre-school families focused on topics indicated in the data collectors which were completed by both children and adults. One session was appropriately designed for each of the following themes:

> I am special, my family is special;
> Ways to strengthen family togetherness;
> Family cooperation and outreach;
> Lying and cheating hurt me and my family;
> I count me, I count you.

A range of 10-to-15 experiential activities reinforced each evening's message. To us, facilitating our first Family Cluster group, each session was both exciting and challenging. It is tempting to describe each activity because of the personal investment of love and creativity we put into each design. However, there are three activity-events that offer significant insights:

> Session 2: Light of the world,
> Session 4: Getting rid of the garbage,
> Session 5: You be me, I'll be you.

"Light of the world" illustrated the familiar Gospel parable that encourages each person to share his or her unique gifts with others. The world is a darker place for each talent that remains hidden. The library facility used for the cluster sessions has a master switch that turns off each light, one by one. As family groups the cluster participants sat in a circle. A small candle vigil light flickered brightly on the floor before each family. The library lights were extinguished one by one. The children became mesmerized by the pattern of light fading into total darkness. As the final light went off, there was a hush of awe that hung in the air. Only three vigil lights burned, revealing meditative expressions on the faces of both adults and children. Now the message from Scripture was read and related to the lived experience of sharing personal talents within the family as a way to strengthen family life. Then each vigil light was blown out by a child until there was a blackness which symbolized the same darkness that exists when no one shares. The candles were then re-lit one by one, as each family member verbally shared a gift he or she brings to their family life. The warm hues of candle flame returned. This activity revealed the Gospel message: "Let your light shine so that all may see."

After session three we chose to include both a verbal check as well as the weekly evaluation to discover if there were any topics the families wanted included other than those on their data collectors. In this now secure environment, they readily suggested we explore some of the experiences that can hurt family life; anger, lying, cheating. In session four an activity titled "The Angries and Getting Rid of Them" was used to enable family members to participate in non-destructive ways of releasing anger. Each child and parent was given a large, empty cardboard box. They were asked to crunch newspaper into a pile of "wads" as ammunition for this activity. Each family member now sat securely behind their box fort with a ready source of harmless artillery. While they sat in waiting, we further explored what if feels like to be angry with brothers, sisters, parents, or friends. The instruction was given to fire the paper wads in order to get rid of any angry feelings. The wads jetted through the air until the ammunition piles were exhausted, and delightful laughter filled the battlefield. On all fours the war players gathered the scattered wads in a hasty clean-up strategy. Sitting in a circle we shared ideas for other non-destructive alternatives of getting rid of the angries: throwing marshmallows, balloons, nerf balls. The parents especially found these to be refreshing solutions for better coping with the common tensions that exist in the daily sharing of life.

Throughout the five weeks the children showed themselves to be very adept at role-playing. Our favorite, and most revealing, role-play event came in session five during an activity called "You Be Me and I'll Be You". Children were each paired with an adult who was not their parent. Because the three infants amused themselves by just watching or scooting on the floor, it was possible to couple one child to one adult. The two within each pair exchanged shoes as a symbol of their new role. Adults became children and children adults. In the new roles the players carried on mini-discussions of the following topics:

> We will watch my favorite TV show tonight
> I do not want to go to bed now
> Will you do something for me?

The insights were profound for both children and adults. Children enjoyed their new authoritative roles, and parents rejoiced that they did not have to continue to be subjects of their children. Two children were empathetic, tried to be understanding, and not dominate these role play child-parent discussions. Although no child was over five, the level of discussion and attitudes assumed for the role play indicated amazingly clear perceptions of parenting tasks.

Evaluations and Results

A willingness to try anything once characterized this cluster of pre-school families. Perhaps this open attitude was the cause for seeming success with all activities. In the weekly evaluations both children and adults gave valid suggestions for improvement of the sessions. They identified ways of better handling materials and giving directions as areas of growth for us, the leaders. We responded by lessening the scissor-cutting, gluing, and magic marker coloring. We continually tried to present clearer and more direct instructions. Through the five sessions we eagerly worked towards building a cooperative community spirit.

The simple weekly evaluations were designed for quick response. "Cold pricklies" or "warm fuzzies," made of paper, were used for positive and negative comments. Other times a grid was used to indicate a response ranging from "boo" to "yeah" for each activity of that evening. While these simple evaluations for feedback were key to the ongoing improvement of the cluster sessions, the visits to each of the families two months later provided a better image of the impact of the cluster on these families. During the home visitation the parents shared observations of the changes and growth that continued to happen after the completion of the cluster sessions. Joe and Carol, parents of five-year-old Mike and two-month-old Brian, enthusiastically commented on the change they observed in Mike's attitude toward his infant brother. Before the cluster Mike always wanted little Brian left home or with a sitter. He tried to exclude his brother from being a part of away-from-home family activities. However, since the cluster experience included all family members, his attitude changed. He no longer wanted Brian excluded from any family event. Both Tom and Pat thought the presence of other infants in the cluster and the positive attitude of letting these little ones be themselves made an impression which enabled Mike to change.

Jim and Joan, parents of Karen, Randy, Robby, Tommy, and Jenifer, related similar attitude change in themselves and their children. As parents of five small children so close in age, they were uncertain about the benefits of including all family members in the cluster. They were apprehensive about the high activity level of their children as a possible source of anxiety for the entire cluster. At one point they even considered leaving their two youngest at home with a sitter. However, two months later, they expressed gladness in the fact that they had all shared in the family evenings together. For their family, too, the five sessions were a source of bonding and common sharing, a time to learn and grow together without excluding even the youngest.

Some of the techniques used in clustering have been integrated into the day-to-day living of these families. Even the throwing of paper wads as a constructive release for anger is still helpful. Cooperative games that provided learning and laughter in the cluster evenings also continue to bring variety into the everyday-ness of living together.

The couples shared the growing sense of community they watched happen. As three couples of small children they were able to observe the common experience of the peaks and valleys in the moods of their children as normal and healthy. They were also able to perceive their own uncertainties and insecurities as a normal part of living. One evening when Joe was out of town, Carol received supportive help from the other four parents in caring for her children and insuring easy participation in the cluster activities. This spontaneous concern enabled her to be a gracious recipient of the growing community spirit. Finally, all parents appreciated the activities suggested for at-home follow-up to each cluster session.

In looking to the future, Pat suggested a way to further emphasize family togetherness in worship. She and Tom explored the possibility of having the clusters on Saturday afternoon followed by Mass, their weekend worship service. For each of the three families it is difficult to take all members to church. They would appreciate opportunities to worship together without being concerned about child behavior as a disturbance to congregation prayer.

All three couples generously offered to talk at any future introductory sessions in order to allay any fears of new family participants. They also expressed the hope to come together again in another cluster event.

Adaptations

In working with the pre-school families as our first cluster attempt, we tried to be pristine in our use of the cluster format. Each session was two hours, based upon data collector information and other family feedback, designed with activity variety and smooth flow, and was both educational and religious. However, we did make adjustments in the approach to contracting and in the number of sessions. Because we held introductory evenings to identify the families who were genuinely interested in committing themselves to an ongoing cluster, we did not use the formal contracting method accomplished in home visitation. We accepted family commitments by mail and phone. If we had visited homes, perhaps two families would not have withdrawn their commitment before the first cluster session. Yet the actual cluster event revealed that six parents and two leaders were needed to easily involve the eleven children under five years of age. The families also appreciated the bonds of friendship that developed within the group size of eleven children and eight adults. They thought that having more than three families may have not allowed for adequate personal attention to one another.

We made a second adaptation by conducting five instead of ten sessions. By doing this, we tried to insure our own success in getting families to participate in family enrichment. It seemed more feasible to get a commitment from families for five sessions rather than for ten. This proved true, but after session five, both we and the families realized that there is wisdom in going beyond five cluster evenings. Having now shared growth, change, and bonds of friendship, we were in a stance of eagerness to pursue family education as a community of friends.

Each family evening included a closure activity for the purposes of summarizing and stimulating at-home follow-up for each theme. The fifth evening accomplished this same purpose for the entire cluster experience. Each family went home with a prayer jar containing the names of all participants. The families were encouraged to pull names from the jars and include these persons in their prayers as a way of continuing care for one another. Also the family members each carried home a puzzle piece from a 4' × 5' puzzle that summarized the themes and activities of the two months together. Particularly these two activities provided closure and opportunity for ongoing bonding.

Friendship is fostered through the cluster event. Today we still keep in contact with these families by mail, phone, and occasional visits. We all share in a new mutual richness that cannot be measured.

Resources

Benson, Jeanette and Hilyard, Jack L. *Becoming Family*. Winona, Minnesota: St. Mary's College Press, 1978.

Braga, Joseph and Laurie. *Children and Adults*. Englewood Cliffs, New Jersey: Prentice-Hall, 1976.

Jenkins, Jeanne Kohl and MacDonald, Pam. *Growing Up Equal*. Englewood Cliffs, New Jersey: Prentice-Hall, 1979.

Biographical Data

Joanne Hanrahan, S.S.N.D., is a program designer for Maria Center, a project of the School Sisters of Notre Dame to further their mission and ministry of education. She is the Staff Director for Family Enrichment. She received her Ph.D. from Saint Louis University and focused her doctoral research on the social history of the American family.

Joyelle Proot, S.S.N.D., is a program designer for Maria Center, a project of the School Sisters of Notre Dame to foster learning and life enrichment for persons of all ages. She coordinates the area of Older Adults and works as a supportive staff member in the area of Family Enrichment. She is the recipient of the 1980 *Creativity Award* given annually by the Adult Education Council of Greater St. Louis.

Address:

The Maria Center
320 E. Ripa Ave.
St. Louis, MO. 63125
Tel. (314) 544-0600

Public School Experience

Barbara Reeder
Bill Reeder

Rochester, New York

The case study presented here will focus on the Family Cluster Program used in the City School District (CSD) of Rochester, New York in March 1979. This program was sponsored by Education Resource Network (ERN), a non-profit organization under the auspices of Genesee Ecumenical Ministries, and federally funded under the Emergency School Aid Act (ESAA). ERN's main goals are to identify and break down racial and cultural isolation in the city schools, and to encourage and promote community/parent involvement in the educational process. The Family Cluster was sponsored as part of these goals.

Background

Two years before, during the school year 1976-77, a Family Cluster pilot project was held in a school classroom using the classroom teacher and school social worker as leaders. Financial support had come, in part, from Education Resource Network. The decision was made then to include Family Cluster as one of the components in ERN's 1977-78 funding proposal. This called for the allocation of federal funds for a second Family Cluster to be held within the Rochester City School District. In April, 1978, a Family Cluster was held with seven families from School #42. Funding covered the families' residence at a local college for two weekends, a paid consultant, and leadership team of four.

Based on this successful and very positive experience, Education Resource Network again chose to include the program in its proposal and sponsored a Family Cluster for the school year 1978-79. When the money was allocated, federal cuts in the proposed budget severely limited the financial resources. This prevented ERN from using a residential setting and hiring outside leadership. Sufficient funds were available, however, to train one salaried ERN staff member and one consultant. Therefore, the decision was made to do this and to proceed with the Family Cluster program. This case study describes the cluster experience for that school year, 1978-79.

Leadership and Beginnings

Barbara Reeder, a Human Relations Coordinator for Education Resource Network, was the staff person chosen to attend leadership training in the Family Cluster process. She had previously attended a weekend workshop on the Family Cluster Model and was somewhat familiar with the process. Her husband, Bill, a minister and professional marriage/family counselor, was hired as consultant. The Reeders attended a week-long Training Laboratory for Family Cluster leaders during the summer of 1978 at Five Oaks Centre in Ontario, Canada.

A husband/wife leadership team is not the usual combination for leading a Family Cluster, and there is always danger that they might bring years of unresolved conflict and difficulty to the process. If the cluster is to work well and to be free of leader-produced tension, the husband/wife team must have done some thorough work on their own relationship. In order to be effective, they would have to have resolved may of their problems around competitiveness, "one-up-man-ship," and their acceptance of one another as persons and competent leaders. Anything less could produce a disastrous cluster experience for all concerned.

Both Barbara and Bill had extensive experience in small group leadership, couples and family retreats, and were trained leaders of Marriage Communications Labs (a marriage enrichment model). They each had good listening skills and were skilled group facilitators. They came to the Family Cluster process with a reputation of being able to lead in a flexible, cooperative and non-competitive style. All of this proved to be a very valuable background as they assumed the leadership role for a Family Cluster in the city schools.

This leadership role included the following responsibilities and preliminary procedures:

After an initial meeting to review plans with the Education Resource Network director, it was decided to contact the staff person from the City School District's Parent Center who had been involved in the previous year's cluster experience to ask if he would be part of the leadership team. He agreed to co-lead with the Reeders, making this a cooperative venture of ERN and City School District.

The CSD ESAA Office was contacted to request their aid in identifying a target school and to obtain their approval for the project. The leaders suggested that they work again with School #42 because of the "groundwork" which was laid through the previous year's cluster, and this choice was approved by the CSD ESAA Office. A meeting was then set up at the school to talk with the local administrators. The group agreed to have the cluster consist of School #42 families, with publicity to go through the PTA organization and school newsletter.

The design model for the cluster experience was prepared and presented for the approval of the ERN Director, William Benet. The cluster was designed to be held on two consectuive weekends, consisting of nine sessions. Five sessions would be held the first weekend, using Friday evening, all day Saturday (9 A.M.-9 P.M.) and Sunday afternoon. Four sessions would be held the second weekend, using all day Saturday and Sunday afternoon. Limited financial resources eliminated the possiblity of overnight accommodations, so the cluster was scheduled to be held in a local church building with families returning home at the close of each day's session. Arrangements were made to have dinner meals prepared by the women of the church.

The leadership team met, and the two weekend cluster dates were chosen. Arrangements were also made with School #42 PTA for the leadership team to make a presentation at the January PTA meeting. The Reeders attended, made the presentation and talked to a number of families in an effort to recruit them for the cluster experience. Two publicity flyers, with a tear-off slip to be returned, were prepared for distribution to School #42 families through the school newsletter.

All families who indicated an interest in attending were contacted by telephone, and an appointment was made for a home visit by the Reeders with the entire family. The leadership team visited each family, discussed plans and schedules for the two weekends, and answered questions. Each family member completed an 'Information Collector' and contracted to participate in the entire Family Cluster process. A few days before the first weekend, information sheets were mailed to each family reminding them of the schedule and the items they were to bring.

Supplies for the weekends were gathered together and/or purchased, and arrangements were made for the use of a neighborhood YMCA pool. The Reeders' 18-year-old son was recruited as photographer and guitarist, and all plans were re-checked and finalized.

Special Problems

In preparing the design model for the Family Cluster process, the leaders chose the following objectives:

1 To provide an opportunity for families to participate in activities designed to enrich and strengthen the family unit;

2 To provide families of different cultural and racial backgrounds with an opportunity to share experiences and build a greater understanding and acceptance of each other;

3 To provide some experiences designed to enhance the development of appreciation for the dignity and worth of oneself and others.

Major problems evolved in the effort to fulfill the second objective. (This objective was chosen purposely to fit into the overall goals of Education Resource Network.) The plan was to recruit a racially-mixed group of families and to use a racially-mixed leadership team, as had been done the previous year.

In arranging the additional leadership, the Reeders had contacted a CSD Parent Center administrator who had been involved the previous year, to help co-lead the experience. This proved to be more problem than help. The CSD staff person agreed to be a part of the team but failed to attend most planning meetings. He subsequently helped with approximately one-half of the home visits, but family obligations prevented his working as a leader on the two weekends. As a substitute activity he agreed to be an observer/evaluator the second weekend, but never appeared.

Families

Originally, two black families, one hispanic family and four white families had indicated their intent to be a part of the cluster weekends. Before the home visits were completed, one black family had to withdraw because of revised work schedules, and one white family decided not to participate after learning that the cluster included a commitment to attend each session and not just "drop in and out." The second black family failed to attend the first Friday night session and after repeated phone calls, it was determined that there was a transportation problem. The leaders arranged to provide transportation when needed. The father in this family did not attend the first weekend because of a changed work schedule and then decided not to participate in the second weekend either. One family did not appear at all and calls to their home received no answer. Subsequent calls to their home and to the school during the interim week still did not reveal their whereabouts. No one seemed to know what had happened to this family. It was several days after the Family Cluster ended when the leaders discovered that the family had left Rochester to answer a subpeona to testify in a legal action in New York City and, thus, were not in the area to participate. Needless to say, the second objective was met with minimal success.

Four families finally participated in the two Family Cluster weekend sessions. They are described as follows:

A A white family, consisting of father, mother and three children: Two boys, ages 9 and 7, and a girl, 18 months. The father is a white-collar worker, and the mother a homemaker. They live in a one-family home in an older area. All members of the family were present throughout both weekends.

B A black family, consisting of two older parents (around age 50) and their two adopted children: one girl, age 12, and a boy, 10. Both parents are employed. The father is a maintenance worker for the city, and the mother a hospital aide. They live in a two-family inner-city home on a street where the houses are in generally good repair. The parents have an older married daughter of their own. The two children took part in all but the introductory session. The mother missed the first two sessions and a small part of another due to a changed work schedule. The father did not attend at all.

C A white, reconstituted family with six children. The first three: a girl, age 13 and two boys, 12 and 11, were the progeny of the mother's first marriage. The last three: a boy, age 5 and two girls, 3 and 6 weeks, were the children from this marriage. The father is a blue-collar, steadily employed production worker, and the mother a homemaker. They live in a one-family home in an older middle-class neighborhood. All family members were present at all sessions of the cluster.

D The fourth family involved the second marriage of a widow with three children: one boy, age 15 and two girls, 9 and 5. The step-father, who is considerably younger than his wife, is a blue-collar skilled worker. The mother owns her own small craft studio. They are a white family living in a one-family home in an older suburb. These parents were married less than a year, and this was the first family event of this type they had shared. Both parents hoped it would be an experience to bond all of them closer together.

E In the absence of the third leader (from CSD), the Reeders' youngest son, age 18, served as part of the leadership team as song leader, guitarist, and photographer. He also joined in family activities as part of the "leader family," but most importantly became a comrade to the 15-year-old boy from Family D.

Sharing leadership responsibilities with each other was a new experience for the Reeders and their son. This combination provided the participating families with a model of cooperative and non-competitive family interaction and behavior. Because their son had been with them during previous family retreats and family camp experiences, he was familiar with his parents' style of leadership, was able to blend his own skills into theirs, and contributed to a cohesive "whole."

Contracting

As stated previously, the leadership team scheduled interviews with each family to discuss plans and schedules for the two weekends, to answer questions and to have them fill out the 'Information Collectors.' This was also the beginning of the individual families' contracting process. During the home visits, each individual was asked to contract to be present for the entire Family Cluster process. All family members agreed to do so.

On Saturday morning of the first weekend the contracting process was continued. The leaders presented an overview and schedule, and then led the families on a tour of the church facilities. They felt it was important to satisfy the children's curiosity about the building and at the same time share with everyone the limitations placed upon the group by the church trustees.

The group returned to the meeting room and listed, on newsprint, some "do's and don't's" pertaining to the use of the church. The families were asked to contribute additional ideas relative to sharing responsibilities around meals, clean-up, caring for one another and arrangements for walking to the YMCA pool, two blocks away. They also listed things like "be on time for sessions; tell someone (preferably an adult) if you leave the room; it's O.K. to 'opt-out'; stay off the stage, etc." When there were differing points of view, alternative suggestions were asked for and the contract was achieved by common consent.

During the two weekends, both adults and children called attention to violations of our agreements and suggested revisions when some part of the contract was unworkable, unnecessary or needed improvement.

The major problems around contracting were related to the B family. No one from this family came to the first Friday evening session, even though the Reeders thought there had been a clear agreement with the family that they would attend all sessions. A phone call to their home that evening indicated there was real doubt that anyone from the family would appear for the next session on Saturday. The parents' work schedules had both been changed and they would be working in the morning, although Mrs. B was free the rest of the day. The Reeders provided Saturday morning transportation for the children, and Mrs. B promised to come right from work at noon time. Several conversations underlining the importance of the contract, finally convinced Mrs. B to be present for most of the remaining sessions. Mr. B was another story! He was the one who had originally signed up his family to come to the Family Cluster (at the PTA presentation), but a changed work schedule prevented him from attending the first weekend. The following weekend produced several different excuses, e.g. fixing his car, working around the house, brother-in-law coming over ... etc. Several phone contacts with him just were not effective and he didn't attend at all. The reason was never very clear. In any event, Mr. B seemed to have breached the contract more overtly than any other person in the cluster. During the follow-up visit to this family, the leaders talked to Mr. B about this. His response was such that they both received the impression he thought Family Cluster was a good idea for his kids, but really had no intention of being a part of it himself.

Family D also breached the contract by being consistently late for beginning sessions when they had to come from home. The other cluster families reminded them of the contract kiddingly each time they were late, until the last day when they made a special effort to be the first ones there.

The contract was reviewed several times during the cluster weekends. It was revised, added to and subtracted from. It proved to be one of the more valuable components of the cluster process.

The Cluster as a Group

The total cluster came together as a cooperative, caring and concerned group rather quickly and with seeming ease. The initial group-building process used by the leaders was casual and non-threatening, but also very informative. This provided the participants with some knowledge about each other as persons and as families to begin their time together.

Several other factors contributed to the group-building process also. At least two children in each family attended or had attended School #42 and, therefore, had some acquaintance with each other. At least one parent from each family had participated in School #42's PTA events and some had been active as leaders in this organization. Most families had had contact with some of last year's participants in the Family Cluster and were already aware of the positive impact it had or could have on family life. Therefore, many were "sold" on the cluster process before they began. They came, willing and eager, to join in the shared exercises that helped to build the group. The small size of the cluster—seven adults, twelve children, two adolescents, plus the leadership—was another factor which aided the ease of group building.

There were two primary deterrents to the group process. First, was the absence of the father of Family B during the entire program, and the absence of the mother for the first two sessions and part of another. The behavior of the B children was greatly affected by these absences. The son became loud, hyperactive and undisciplined, while his sister (two years older) tried to "boss" and correct him with little success. The leaders and other parents stepped in to fill the void as the cluster became more of a "family" itself. The B children were the only ones to experience parental absence, so therefore were the only ones who could take advantage of such an "opportunity." Their behavior altered drastically when their mother was present.

The second deterrent was the almost-chronic lateness of Family D. The first session each day was always delayed from 20-30 minutes because the D family was never on time. The leaders used extra recreation or songs during this waiting period but, because of the cluster's small size, chose not to start the main activities until the D's arrived. Reviewing the contract and requests from the leaders didn't seem to help. They were always apologetic, but stated that this was the way they operated in all areas of their family life. It was as if they felt they had no control over their tardiness. Their statement that they "just never seemed to be on time" was reflective of the chronic nature of their problem. The other cluster families began to chide them, gently and kiddingly at first, and then more strongly as the cluster went on. At the start of the last session, Family D was the first one there!

The Educational Process

The First Weekend
Goal: To get to know one another as families and to discover and appreciate likenesses in the ways we operate as individuals and function as a family unit.

During the first weekend, we began with a variety of shared activities designed to help the members of the cluster learn each other's names as well as get acquainted with other families. The program was designed around the information gathered and expectations expressed at the home interviews, and was aimed at encouraging the participation of family members of every age.

Among the activities included during the first weekend were:

—A unit on their own names, first, middle and last. This included the history of their family name; who they were named for; who chose their name; what their name means, etc. This was planned to help each person recognize and affirm their own uniqueness and gave them the opportunity to look at this quality in other members of their family.

—Another unit involved the construction of a family treasure chest. Each family decorated a cardboard carton with pictures, drawings, words and descriptions of what their family "treasured" in terms of their living and playing together. Inside the treasure chest went feelings and thoughts (written down) of appreciation about each individual member of the family which had first been shared verbally.

—A review of the cluster contract led into another unit on family rules and their rule-making process. A shared discussion took place around the need for all families to have rules and guidelines within which to operate, and a realization and appreciation of family similarities and differences grew out of this process. Each family discussed ways they would like to improve their at-home interactions with regard to their own family rules and proposed revisions to be tested out during the week between cluster sessions. The group contracted to report back the following weekend.

The Second Weekend

Goal: To continue to become better acquainted and to begin to appreciate and affirm differences between individuals, between families, and between individuals from the same family.

During the second weekend, we continued the process of trying to enrich the interaction within families, but also focused on broadening each person's contacts with adults and children from other families and other backgrounds.

Some of the activities included during the second weekend were:

—Reporting back on the revised behavior, pertaining to family rules, which had been tested at home during the preceeding week.

—A unit on family "listening" interaction was opened by the reading of the children's book *Nobody Listens to Andrew* by E. Guilfoile (Chicago: Follett Publishing Co., 1976). An exercise in which each family drew a diagram of their family table to illustrate the patterns of communication and the nature of their interactions was a very valuable "eye-opener" to some families. Family C discovered that their oldest daughter did not participate in family discussions around the table. She felt unable to compete with so many people talking, and therefore remained silent. The family realized their loss and resolved to take steps to include her.

—One of the meals was shared with a new "set of parents (or children)" as an introduction to the next activity. The cluster was formed into "simulated families" (father, mother, and children from different families) to share in a decision-making and idea-sharing process. After these "new" families shared their decisions and ideas in the total cluster, participants re-assembled into their real families. They then shared their "likes and dislikes" of being a part of a different family, and what they appreciated or what adjustments they might make on their own.

—A focus was also made on appreciating the larger "cluster family" members; time was taken for affirmation and exchange of "fuzzies" made from cotton balls within the whole group (Richard Lessor, *Fuzzies*. Niles, IL: Argus Communications, 1979). As these tokens were exchanged, persons expressed, verbally or non-verbally, some of their feelings about each other and the sharing that took place over the two weekends.

The second weekend ended with family planning for continual reassessment of their interactions, a discussion of plans for a picnic-reunion of the cluster, and written evaluation of the two weekends.

Evaluation and Follow-up

At the close of the second weekend, families were asked to complete a written evaluation (using one person as recorder) with each family member having input. The evaluation questions were put up on newsprint. During the first two weeks of May, each family was re-visited in their homes and asked to complete a copy of the same evaluation. Then, each individual responded to an additional evaluation of what affect the cluster had had on their families and themselves.

The families had suggested a picnic-reunion, and plans for this were finalized at the follow-up visits. The picnic was held near the end of May in one of the area parks. Each family came with a game to share and brought its own food. It was a time of relaxation, recreation and the renewal of friendships.

Evaluation Results and Feedback

The results of the evaluations at the close of the cluster and at the follow-up visits were almost universally positive. They indicated a preference for expanding the cluster to cover a longer period of time, and some persons said they would prefer a cluster experience with over-night accommodations further away from home.

Individual evaluations from the follow-up visits clearly indicated that families were continuing to use better communication methods. They also expressed improved cooperation among family members and new knowledge of one another as persons. Families were aware of an increased cohesiveness in their family life and were more conscious of the expressions of caring.

The cluster families had mixed responses to questions about improved understanding and acceptance of families of different racial/cultural backgrounds. Some indicated growth in their understanding and acceptance, while others felt there had been too small a representation of other cultures for significant changes to occur.

Parents shared that they also found themselves gravitating toward one another at School #42 functions and sharing latest family news.

Some of the verbal feedback from participants revealed the following:

—One father stated that their whole family was paying more attention to "family rules" and he, in particular, was becoming more aware of family interaction as a result of some of these rules.

—A mother said, "It was heartening to see other families, no matter what their racial background, having the same kinds of problems and operating very much like ours."

—A teen-ager commented that he agreed to come to Family Cluster because he knew that others in the family wanted to go ... but he really didn't want to participate. "Even when I first got there ... I was saying to myself, 'this is going to be a drag,' but when the group started to do some of the activities and exercises together, it started to be fun and I was really anxious to come back the second weekend."

—A couple of parents from white families said that they wished there had been more black families involved, and most of the children asked if their families could "come again next year."

In addition, a few observations by the leaders included the following:

—One family's tiny baby falling fast asleep in another mother's arms.

—One family's arriving the second weekend with the depressing news that the 11-year-old child of friends had just been diagnosed as having leukemia. The response to them by other families was most supportive ... full of hopeful words and offers to pray, etc.

—An 11-year-old boy (the 'live-wire' of the group) sitting quietly holding another family's 18-month-old little girl.

—The cluster as a whole, taking on the characteristics of a real "family" ... kidding, joking and cooperating on projects ... and becoming more and more verbal as the time went along.

Even though the Family Cluster process reaches a small number of families at a time, the Reeders feel very strongly that it is a significant step toward real understanding between families and family members and is most helpful in promoting acceptance between families of different racial/cultural backgrounds. Their hope is that this process will be used in many city schools ... in many other areas ... in the future.

Resources

Jeannette Benson and Jack L. Hilyard. *Becoming Family.* Winona, Minn., St. Mary's College Press, 1972.

Virginia Satir. *Peoplemaking.* Palo Alto, CA, Science and Behavior Books, Inc., 1972.

Sidney B. Simon. *Meeting Yourself Halfway.* Niles, Ill., Argus Communications, 1974.

Biographical Data

Bill and Barbara Reeder have been married since 1950, have raised four sons and have lived in United Methodist parsonages since 1962. They are trained leaders in the Family Cluster process and Marriage Communication Labs (a marriage enrichment process). Bill has earned a M.Th. in pastoral counseling. As well as being pastor of an urban Methodist church, he is on the staff of the Pastoral Counseling Center in Rochester, N. Y. Barbara is a Human Relations Coordinator with the Education Resource Network in Rochester where she leads "Better Parenting" workshops and provides other services to parent groups in the City School District.

Address:

1122 Culver Rd.
Rochester, N.Y. 14609
Tel. (716)288-5331-Home

Divorced and Separated Families' Experience

Gregory Dunwoody

Winnipeg, Manitoba

In the late spring of 1979 I was approached by three people from a group of separated and divorced Catholics in Winnipeg, Canada. They were hoping that the Catholic Pastoral Center of the Archdiocese would be willing to initiate a live-in weekend for their families as well as for some single adult members. The group had already reserved a live-in facility outside of Winnipeg, and they estimated about seven single-parent families along with four or five single adults would be attending (see Appendix A for families and age groups).

A team of three from the Catholic Pastoral Centre had just finished two years of parish renewal work with local church groups. A conclusion was that we were trying to renew entire local congregations and help them build a sense of community, when there was not yet a sense of the family being a community. We considered the forming of smaller Christian communities which would include a small group of families along with single adults. The Family Cluster Model seemed to us to be one way to begin the formation of these basic Christian communities. Thus, our priority for the coming year was to work with families and to facilitate family growth within the context of four or five other families. We received the request from the separated and divorced group with ambivalent feelings.

We were pleased to have been asked to conduct a family oriented workshop and excited that a group, usually viewed as being on the fringe of the Catholic church, might in fact be responded to by the Catholic Pastoral Centre (or the institutional church). On the other hand, we were anxious as this was to be our first Family Cluster experience. Only one team member was married with a family, and he was the only one who had received Family Cluster training at St. Thomas College in St. Paul, Minnesota. The divorced and separated group had a wide range of expectations for the weekend from having a good time with the family to healing all the hurts that family members had experienced through the separation and divorce processes.

Contracting with the Individual Families

Before the actual live-in weekend no contracting with individual families had been done. In retrospect, and according to the Family Cluster Model, this should have been done because of the number of anxieties and expectations people revealed during the first hours of the actual cluster event. Only hours before the weekend, two teenagers were told that they would be going on the weekend. The leaders were called upon to be supportive and understanding of these teenagers during the initial contracting stage of the cluster event.

Many persons in this group of separated and divorced people were hurting very much and wanted to handle their hurt in different ways. While all had agreed on a family weekend in the initial planning stage of the weekend, some wanted an "intellectual" weekend (interpreted as lectures by experts, followed by group discussion), others wanted only children to attend who could read and write, and still others wanted to divide the group according to age groups to discuss hurts and angers. However, other parents wanted a fun weekend for their families with some structured activities to encourage family growth. All participants felt that the Christian faith meant a great deal and the weekend should include the faith dimension. Eventually, the theme of the weekend became, "Separated and Divorced Families Seeking Wholeness Through Their Christian Faith."

Before the actual weekend, one of the frustrations during the initial planning phase was that the group of separated and divorced Catholics did not have any formal structure (e.g. a coordinator nor president) and did not have any committee that was clearly responsible for planning the weekend for families. As a result, three different people from the city of Winnipeg had been asked by three different group members to facilitate the weekend.

Contracting with the Cluster Group as a Whole

In the initial planning of the weekend, someone from the divorced and separated group asked a university professor to address the group at the beginning on Friday night. For this reason we cluster leaders felt it would be best not to jeopardize the spirit and contracting trust of our workshop by starting Friday night and then having it interrupted for an hour while someone gave a lecture! Although the professor knew it was a family weekend, he did not know that young children would be attending as well. His talk, which was a philosophical interpretation of Freudian concepts in terms of the divorce experience, did not relate to the children at all!

The cluster leadership agreed to design an initial get acquainted/welcome activity for Friday night, but the cluster event for all ages with contracting would begin Saturday morning. This proved to be a wise decision, as people forgot about their reactions to Friday night's lecture (especially the children), and they viewed Saturday as a totally different event.

As families came Saturday morning, they made name tags and went around to a variety of learning centres suited according to the ages of the participants. One of the learning centres had instructions to draw a face to show how each felt at that moment. Then these faces were used in the entire group to surface hopes and feelings people had about the weekend. An agreement or covenant was proposed to the group (see Appendix B), and participants were invited to meet as families (single adults formed a group) to discuss the agreement and whether or not they wanted to adopt or make any changes. No changes were proposed, and each person was invited to show their agreement by signing their name or drawing a personal symbol or picture on the contract.

orces Which Helped Build the roup Process

Among the forces which gave a sense of security for the group, rust and reassurance was helped by the rural, religious setting vhere the weekend was held. For most of the adults the Christian aith was of value to them, and the fact that they were gathered ogether in a setting administered by a religious community of isters made them feel at home. Some participants had experienced the church as an institution and sought answers for their nurts and life dilemmas from the official church. However, the 'amily Cluster experience gave them an opportunity to discover hat caring and support can also come through friends and families as well as the "church." Since all participants were from Winnieg, the adults, and especially the children, reacted well to the ural setting.

Another force which helped build the group as a unit was the act that the mothers were very eager to put some effort into helping their children have a good and happy experience. During the re-planning stage the expression "We're hurting families" arose, ut the mothers wanted a successful weekend and quickly suported the weekend with the activities suggested.

In the initial phase of the weekend, the facilitators expressed cceptance of whatever feelings persons had upon coming to the veekend, especially "low" feelings. This imparted the message that ll feelings were OK in our group and could be expressed. Once nese feelings had been faced and accepted, especially fear, they ould be allowed to dissipate.

Early in the weekend, the facilitators made a special effort that ne contract would be seriously kept (e.g. one could opt out and use ne activity corner); the group responded to the openness and ncerity of the facilitators. The facilitators also respected the freeom and emotional life of each participant, and this affected the roup as a whole. In the activity of making a personal/family crest, ne of the single adults thought about it and came up with a ɔlank." The group experienced acceptance when she presented her ersonal crest "empty for the moment; sometimes in life one has to be empty in order to receive and be filled again." The facilitators accepted it with the same enthusiasm and response given to others

Forces Which Deterred the Group Process

One force which broke the process of building trust and commitment for the entire group was the presence of a family which dropped in Saturday afternoon of the weekend. The parents came to see what everybody else was doing and had no commitment to become involved in any exercise, even when invited to do so. The parents had both experienced other marriages; so the discipline of the children, which was harsh and physical, was left entirely to the husband since both the children were from his first marriage. When the parents mentioned they might drop in again on Sunday one of the cluster leaders met with them and explained the process of the weekend and received agreement for their return only at the end of the weekend of the activities. This particular incident pointed out our failure to anticipate what families might think and gave another reason for individual contracting with each family.

Another force which deterred progress was a few adults who were trying to approach the activities on a very intellectual basis. One individual, a separated father who attended without his children, was hurting and yet avoided expressing his feelings by sermonizing. Early Sunday morning, he remarked to one of the facilitators that we should have talked more about God's love for us. The facilitator replied by asking, "All day yesterday what did you feel. . . what did you experience?" The father said, "Well, yes. . . but we could still TALK more about God's love for us."

Most families in doing a "family flower" activity did not include the absent husband/father. This was not dealt with since we were trying to get the family members who were present to affirm each other, but it does indicate some kind of blockage, according to the belief that anyone (living or dead) who has ever been part of a family has an impact on it. In another family, an older delinquent child (who was not present for the weekend) had been omitted also from inclusion in the family flower.

Units of Study and Activities Used

As mentioned at the beginning, the Catholic Pastoral Centre team had been doing Christian community renewal workshops. These were designed around the belief that each person was special and gifted in the eyes of God, and that a living Christian community would have three characteristics: praying together, witnessing to others, and caring for one another. Since the theme for the family weekend included the words "seeking wholeness through our Christian faith," it was decided to have a learning session on each of the above three characteristics. For our model of the Christian community we made use of *Ministry to Word and Sacrament* by Bernard Cooke (Philadelphia: Fortress Press, 1976). For the educational design and activities of the sessions we used *Family Enrichment With Family Clusters* by Margaret Sawin (Valley Forge; Pa.: Judson Press, 1979), with some activities picked up from previous readings and experiences. Since this group had all experienced a separation or divorce, we felt that the initial unit had to be affirming the specialness of each person in the family and in the group.

The five learning sessions went as follows (see Appendix C for timetable):

1 Session One on "Affirmation" had families sharing the "family flower exercise" where each family member cuts out a petal for himself/herself, puts their name on it, draws or writes something special about themselves, and then passes it around to other members of the family who, each in turn, write or draw what they appreciate about that person.

   The single adults had to blow up a balloon and decorate it with what was special about them. Then they had to present their balloons to each other. The exercise was concluded with each family sharing their family flower with the entire group, single adults presenting their balloons, and everyone singing, "He's Got the Whole World in His Hands," substituting family names in the verses.

On the whole, this exercise was well received. There was a little awkwardness on the part of some single adults in their initial activity with balloons. While some really got into it, others felt it was kind of silly and wanted a more intellectual approach. One mother later told us she liked the activity because it led her son to say and write something nice about his older sister. For many families, having experienced the pain of a separation, the use of family names in the song and the cheering that was received for presenting family flowers was the first time, during a long period, that someone called them a "family."

2 Session Two on "Christian Witness" had families reading the story of Jesus and Zaccheus, discussing how Jesus welcomed Zaccheus and how Zaccheus, in turn, welcomed Jesus. Then each family filled out a sheet that was entitled "The Welcoming Customs of the _____ Family." They were to list on the "welcoming sheet" the people who came to their house, what they did with them to welcome them, and then each family member was asked to sign the sheet in some way or another. Again, the exercise was concluded by families sharing their "welcoming sheets" with the entire group. We also sang a song called, "Will You Come and Follow Me?" that allowed us to put in people's names; the chorus is built around the phrase, "Yes, Lord, Yes, I will come and follow you now." The single adults met together to read and reflect on the story of Jesus and Zaccheus (Luke 19:1-10).

3 Session Three was about "Caring for Each Other" and had each member of the family draw the floor plan of their home. Then each person was asked to draw a happy face in the room where they go to have fun, to draw an "A" in the room where they go to be alone, and a heart in the room where they go to receive love and care. Then the family shared together their floor plans and eventually were asked to talk about the ways they give love and care to each other.

By the end of session two, the single adults were asking to be incorporated into the activities of the families. In order to do this, we asked them to create a short advertisement about themselves in a word or song of what they would give to a family and what they would like to receive. A few ads were very creative, but some of the single adults were uncomfortable with thinking of an advertisement. However, once they were all actively working with a family we felt a sense of ease and inclusion.

4 Session Four on "Family Prayer" had the families go through the process of listing what each individual and their family had lived that day which could form the reason for evening prayer. Then they designed the prayer together as a family and, prayed together in the way the family designed. The 'single adults met together as a group and went through the same process. All participants then reassembled half-hour later for five minutes of group prayer around the symbol of incense.

5 Session Five was on "The Family Community." Each family made a family banner which included a drawing or cut-out from each member of what he or she liked to do as a family, plus the creation of a family motto. The single adults made an individual crest which included symbols to express an activity that they liked to do with close friends, a religious symbol of special importance, an important event or moment from their past life experiences, and a hope they had for the future. Then we gathered together for the sharing of family banners and individual crests.

Afterwards we spent twenty minutes planning our Sunday celebration in prayer as a "Faith Community." The archbishop of our church joined us for the Sunday Eucharist.

How Did the Family Systems Affect the Cluster Dynamics?

In some cases rule enforcement or family discipline was entirely the role of the mother, and instructions from facilitators were rigidly interpreted by some of the mothers initially. It seemed as if children's behaviors were most questioned during the initial phase of the weekend. As the mothers were affirmed and accepted, and as the facilitators intervened into families to model other ways of doing some activities, the mothers became freer in allowing children to seek alternative patterns for following instructions. As the mothers realized that we were serious about keeping the group contract, they relaxed more about their children's behavior.

Initially, most communication within families was one-way direction, i.e., parent to child. As the weekend progressed, there was a noticeable shift to two-way patterns of communication.

The absence of father figures affected some family exercises in two ways. The family had to decide whether or not it would include the father in some of their exercises (e.g. the family flower); and the men facilitators found themselves modeling as adult males to some of the children during the weekend. Two male participants also became father models on a couple of occasions.

There was a chance for families to look at some of the overt and covert rules by which they were operating: welcoming customs of the family; ways caring was expressed or withheld; ways of expressing family prayer; and who was about to say what, to whom, and how. Families were given space and time to try out some new behaviors as well as to observe a variety of behavior patterns in a supportive milieu.

The single adults present were "adopted" by families for some sessions. This gave the children other adult models and was particularly helpful in that all the families were headed by women while most of the singles were men. It was a chance for some families to feel "good" about males.

The weekend was a time to savor the uniqueness and value of being a family and a member within one. Prior to the weekend, the emphasis of the planners from the divorced and separated group was consistently on the problems and special needs of divorce and separation. While there is truth in the reality of this, the weekend gave families an opportunity to discover ways of meeting those needs and to find resources they might have for meeting problems in inter-family and intra-family relationships. The hurt they were experiencing could be dealt with in a different way, as families discovered more of their strengths and fulfillment of their dreams. Families also learned ways of enhancing one another's self-worth through experiences together.

The fun component (breaks for songs, games, the Bar-B-Que) was important as was the late night exchanges among adult members. There seemed to be a growing excitement about, "I'm not the only person, and we're not the only family who feels this way."

One twelve-year-old stated that he had detested coming because he thought that it would be like church or school with everyone sitting in rows. His only wish at the conclusion was that the weekend would last longer because he was having such a good time getting to know so many friends.

How Was the Cluster Concluded?

Before planning together for our Sunday prayer, we held a closing farewell outdoors. The ritual we chose to use comes from a custom among our Canadian native Indians where everyone forms a large circle, then one person begins by going around "giving thanks" individually to each person. Once he passes the first person, that person follows him and goes around giving thanks to each individual. Those who are standing in the circle cannot say anything—only "receive thanks" from those who are giving it; their turn for "giving" will come when they enter the circle and go around. When the original leader has finished giving thanks to each person, he will find himself back at his original place. He then stands there "receiving the thanks" of those who are now going around.

Evaluations and Follow-ups with the Families

Although an evaluation had been planned by the facilitators to be introduced after the parting ritual, it seemed inappropriate to introduce it from the emotional excitement and enthusiasm of the group. In the one-to-one contact of the parting ritual, people overwhelmingly asked for another weekend . . . especially the children. The weekend experience was subsequently heard about in the city, and another weekend has now been established. Over the last ten months some of the families have re-incorporated themselves back into the regular community and congregational life, and seem to no longer need extensive ties with the divorced and separated group.

No follow-up was planned for the families, and none has been carried out. However, many of the adults have established ties with the facilitators of the weekend and have visited to get resources for their church life and their family life during the year. A survey on the church's support for family life was recently done in our archdiocese. Among the responses from the separated and divorced group was the comment that the church generally failed to respond to separated families, but last summer's family weekend provided one exciting time in which the church did respond.

Adaptations of the Family Cluster Model

The initial response from the Catholic churches in our archdiocese was that of reluctance to enter into the Family Cluster format of once-weekly evening sessions. However, good response has been received from churches for weekend day sessions that run from 10 A.M. to 4 P.M. with lunch or from 12 noon to 4 P.M. or 5 P.M., again with lunch. After ten months of this format, we are now receiving requests from families who wish to repeat the experience.

I feel that some pastors see themselves and their time so heavily taxed that they respond to families according to the medical model ... a crisis or pain must arise before a response will be given ... rather than choose to spend some time in nurturing and supporting family life.

Biographical Data

Mr. Gregory Dunwoody is Director of Adult Christian education for the Roman Catholic Archdiocese of Winnipeg, Canada. He received an M.A. in religious education of adults from Fordham University in 1973. He has been working in the field of adult Christian education since that time and has published *Adult Christian Learning: A Facilitator's Guidebook*, available from the Winnipeg Catholic Pastoral Centre.

Greg and Rhonda, his wife, have three boys and a girl, ranging in age from one to six years. He received Family Cluster training in the summer of 1979 and has been offering family workshops in the Roman Catholic Archdiocese of Winnipeg since that time. Greg has also led conferences and workshops dealing with adult Christian education and the Christian family in various parts of Canada.

Address:

Catholic Pastoral Centre
788 Wolseley Ave.
Winnipeg, Manitoba, R3G 1C6
Canada
Tel: (204) 774-2556

Appendix A

Participants on the Family Cluster Weekend for Separated and Divorced Families

Facilitating team

Mr. Gregory Dunwoody, from the Catholic Pastoral Centre, adult Christian education.

Rev. Albert Lafreniere,o.m.i., from the Catholic Pastoral Centre, liturgy department.

Sr. Veronica Dunne, R.N.d.M.., a family life counsellor

Sr. Denise Kyup, R.N.d.M., a pastoral worker

Participating Families

Family A: mother, daughter 10 and son 12

Family B: mother, daughters 13 and 10, son 12

Family C: mother, daughter 12 (plus an 18 year old who was absent)

Family D: mother, daughters 8, 6, and 5

Family E: mother, daughters 13, 12, 7, and son 9

Family F: mother, daughter 11 and son 9

Family G: mother, daughter 8

Participating Single Adults

—two separated women

—a separated father whose family was not present

—a priest who is a family counsellor

—a married woman (Her family did not attend, but she works with divorced and separated adults in her church.)

—two Catholic sisters from the religious community where the cluster weekend was being held

—one separated man

Appendix B

Our Agreement with the Cluster Group as a Whole

Our Purpose: Separated families seeking wholeness through their Christian faith.

1 First try an exercise and after that a person can choose to "opt out" in the activity corner but cannot leave the room.
2 Rules for the "Activity Corner"—play quietly; toys and books to remain in corner.
3 Everyone is treated with equal respect.
4 Group discipline is the responsibility of each other.
5 Leadership of the weekend is in: Greg, Denise, Albert, and Veronica.
6 This agreement can be changed by a meeting and agreement within the whole group.

Appendix C

Timetable of Family Cluster Weekend

Friday August 24, 1979

7:00 P.M.	Registration, settling in
7:30 P.M.	Getting acquainted activities
8:00 P.M.	Lecture presentation
9:15 P.M.	Refreshments and snacks

Saturday, August 25, 1979

8:00 A.M.	Breakfast
9:00	Beginning of Family Cluster event: —name tags and learning centres —contracting —Session #1: Affirmation
10:15	Coffee and snack; free time with games outside
11:00	Session #2: Christian Witness
12 noon	Lunch
1:30	Session #3: Caring
2:30	Coffee and snack: free time
4:00	Practice of hymns for Sunday's church service

5:00	Dinner
6:30	Session #4: Prayer
8:00	Bar-B-Que and Sing-a-long

Sunday, August 26, 1979

8:00 A.M.	Breakfast
9:00	Session #5: Family Community
10:00	Coffee and snack
10:15	Closing ritual outside
11:30	Sunday Eucharist in Chapel with the Bishop presiding
12:30	Lunch

Air Force Families' Experience
Charles Prewitt

North Carolina

My Evolvement into Family Enrichment

The encounter movement of the sixties was encountered and found severely wanting. I heard radical psychiatrist, Claude Steiner, conduct the funeral service for the human potential movement in Atlanta in the mid-seventies. I was sad/mad/glad that the "fads" had been had! My sadness was related to the people I had come to know in the "groupie" experiences but who had disappeared. I was mad that I had invested so much in a way of growing, and now "they" seemed to be saying it was all a waste. I was glad when I realized that out of those experiments would come some lasting contributions to human community in America.

The human potential movement frequently neglected consideration of the "shadow side" of the human, our sinfulness, and the need for grace. To be sure, the emphasis on the positive side of humanity was long overdue in our culture, but it was time for a more balanced picture of ourselves.

I was challenged to look for models of relating that survived and still retained the openness and caring of the small group movement. I should not have been surprised to find among the surviving models one which included families. Families are tough and have a way of outliving cultural onslaughts. Families tend to invite people out of their private corners of existence and into relating. This could combat the individualism (if not narcissism) of the human potential movement.

To me, the Family Cluster seemed to be one answer for the need to combine our time-tested religious values and faith with skills learned from the behavioral sciences. Suddenly, we had new tools for achieving the old job of nurturing and growing without fragmenting our families. We would learn about God, others and self as a family joined with other families in an experiential educational event, designed to fit our needs.

Discovering the Family Cluster Model

Shortly after joining the United States Air Force Chaplains' Resource Board at Maxwell Air Force Base in Alabama, I made arrangements to travel to Rochester, New York to meet Dr. Margaret Sawin and to experience a Training Workshop in Family Clustering. It was 1975, and Family Clustering, Inc. was the only group training persons for leadership in family enrichment.

During the event, families joined the trainees in Rochester for two demonstrations. There were parents, grandparents, aunts and uncles and lots of little children. With warm and capable leadership, Jan Rugh molded this mixture into a supportive "extended-like" family. We sat on the floor, kicked off our shoes, played silly games, sang, learned, celebrated the goodness of God and prayed together. I recalled family therapist, Virginia Satir, saying in *Peoplemaking* that the generation gap was "an area of strangeness that had not yet been bridged." It was certainly being bridged on the carpet those days. Older people, little people and those of us in the middle were giving and receiving beautiful gifts from our various stations in life.

Potential Air Force Application

It seemed clear to me that Air Force families could use a model like this. They had left extended kin families in their hometowns. They were either single-parent families, nuclear families, or single persons who did not have the opportunity to enjoy or even endure the interaction of aunts, cousins, and grandparents. Clusters could be the framework for organizing simulated extended families.

I saw Family Clusters as a strategy for enlivening the total religious education program and supplementing the work of the chapel Sunday schools throughout the world. At the same time Family Clustering was not entirely different from some existing educational projects. Many of our chaplains were involved in values clairification, Christian growth groups, transactional analysis, and Parent Effectiveness Training.

I foresaw some of the problems for using Family Clusters in the Air Force as follows:

- the inevitable resistance to change
- lack of funds for training leadership
- inability to describe the process in non-threatening ways
- lack of trained directors of religious education who could become leaders
- negative reaction among the chaplains to anything that involved new skill training.

It also seemed to be, and proved to be, a very time-consuming activity, especially for the leadership.

Although we on the Chaplains' Resource Board could introduce the program through descriptions in direct mailings to the individual chaplains, I was convinced that senior chaplains must see the value of the program before it would ever be accepted. We introduced the concept to the individual chaplains through articles, the Chief of Chaplains' Newsletter, family resource and religious education publications, and in classes at the USAF Chaplains' School. We tested the program in several local chapel settings. Family Clusters worked on this small scale, but we still needed the vision and support of the senior chaplains for a wider exposure throughout the Air Force.

Introduction of Family Clusters at the Mars Hill Conference

It was Chaplain Richard Carr and his staff of chaplains at Tactical Air Command (TAC) who really gave Family Clusters their big chance in the Air Force. He was ably supported in this effort by Chaplain (Major) Dick Brown in the TAC Headquarters. The Board at Maxwell joined forces with the TAC office in designing and conducting Family Clusters at the 1976 Christian Encounter Conference, held at Mars Hill Baptist College in North Carolina. This proved to be the first big opportunity to look at the possibilities of Family Clustering for Air Force chaplains. Although conducted for a very short time (three mornings of the Conference), we hoped enough would happen to give a good sampling of this potential for ministry.

When the publicity packets for the Conference were sent to the participating bases, it was explained that the traditional program of age-graded Bible study, recreation and worship opportunities would be available. In addition, entire families could choose a learning experience with other families, which would focus on using an intergenerational approach. We were pleasantly surprised when the reservation requests filled up all slots allocated to the Family Clustering portion of the Conference, and four clusters were organized. This case study will focus on the one cluster led by my wife, Martha, and myself.

Advance Planning

To begin our planning, we roughly sketched objectives, basic assumptions, and the main components. As a result, we were prepared to provide growth experiences for the whole family, to teach and practice some basic communication skills, to increase awareness of the strengths and resources in each family, to help them set family goals for personal growth and family closeness and to model communication and nurturing ourselves.

We listed the following basic assumptions:

1 every family has potential for growth
2 values and behavior are learned in the family
3 persons develop best in a nurturing environment
4 families seldom structure time at home for affirmation, communication, strength and need assessment, and goal setting
5 each person learns at his or her own pace and choice.

While we did not know exactly what we would do each day, we listed the following possible components and took materials for them in case we wanted to use them:

1 family systems
2 "stroking" patterns
3 design patterns for communication, strength assessment, and goal setting
4 devotional readings, scriptural support for cluster activities, and theological reflections
5 other activities for family enrichment.

Cluster Leadership

As a couple, we had led a ten-week cluster for the Maxwell Air Force Base Chapel and several weekend cluster-like experiences. For several years we had conducted marriage enrichment retreats and had taught Parent Effectiveness Training and Couples Communication. We were trained in values clarification and group work. I had theological training, including a Doctor of Ministry degree in pastoral care and counseling. Martha is a registered nurse who had specialized in psychiatric nursing and had taken advanced training in transactional analysis. We were parents of six children, three of whom were with us at the Mars Hill Conference.

In a sense, the leadership of our Family Cluster at Mars Hill was shared by our twin daughters, Kimi and Keri who were 16, and our son, Kip, age 12. In addition to prior participation in several cluster events, they had experience talking about their family in public. On one occasion they had been with the family when we were interviewed by pastoral counselor, Howard Clinebell, in a graduate counseling class at the School of Theology of Claremont University in California. We were also the demonstration family for family therapist, Virginia Satir, in front of 700 helping professionals at the University of California in Los Angeles.

Martha and I had a companionship style of marriage based on our very similar personalities, interests, values, and goals. Because of this style of marriage we had been forced to develop effective communication. Since neither of us had to be a full time boss or subordinate, we invested a great deal of energy in dialogue and negotiations. At the time of the cluster we had just begun to discover the difficulties of having become too much alike, yet we did not know how to deal with our differences. Consequently, the children had not learned how to differ constructively from our marriage model. One of our family issues was to free them to be different from their older sisters and from ourselves as parents. This, too, required a new style of relating and some new communication skills. We were changing to a more open family style and a more loving way of being with each other. The change was not without a great deal of pain.

While many leaders may not want the distraction of their own children in the cluster, we found ours to be excellent models for the communication skills and other strategies we were introducing to families. It seemed to be a great source of permission for the other families to see ours struggling, rather than pretending to have "it all together."

The Other Cluster Families

Dick Jackson was a civilian employed by the Air Force. Mary, his wife, taught third graders in a private church school. Their son, Forrest, was thirteen and their daughter, Susan, was seven. Dick was rather serious and somewhat rigid in his attitudes. He had a need to know exactly what was expected of him and preferred structure. Mary went back to teaching when Susan started to school. It was none too soon for her, but she had understood why Dick had insisted that she wait at least until the children were in school. Mary had some resentment about all those years spent away from her beloved teaching, but another side of her was pleased that she did her "Christian duty" and stayed home. She had some guilt about being absent from home so much, but her excitement about work drove it away most of the time. Forrest was gregarious and self-confident, while Susan was shy and stayed close to her mother, at first.

Warren Lund was a Lieutenant Colonel in the Air Force and a pilot. He wanted to be boss around the house but in a benevolent kind of way. He tended to react from a rather chauvinistic position but frequently stopped himself and adjusted to fit what appeared to be a new self image with, perhaps, a new appreciation for others. Jean, his wife, was a full-time homemaker and had no noticeable desires to work outside her home. A college graduate, she was highly creative and did not appear to be the type that would ever experience boredom nor loneliness. This did not turn out to be the case, but clearly that was her public image. The Lunds have three daughters: Betty, age twelve; Marcia, age eight; and Dorothy who was six at the time. Betty was an independent young lady; Marcia was more unsure, and Betty didn't need to be bothered. All three were well dressed and minded their well-rehearsed manners!

Tim Logan was a Staff Sergeant in the Air Force. He was not highly polished socially but loved people, and his love was contagious. His family had caught his appreciation for people and nurtured one another naturally. His wife, Ruth, was a secretary for an insurance company. She had always worked outside her home but never found it particularly satisfying, yet never thought of pitying herself. She worked at the office, at home, and at the Base Chapel. They had stair-step sons: Tom, Lloyd, and Mark who were twelve, ten, and eight years old.

We had a cluster of 19 people ranging in age from six to 45 years. Immediately we were aware that we could plan the activities at a first-grade skill level so as to include all the children. We regretted that we had no grandparents in the group, but it is fairly typical of Air Force families that there are not older couples among them. All of the families were white, and all were organized around the fathers' occupations. They were all nuclear families with no history of divorce. All were Christian in faith and apparently in practice. Two families were Baptist, one was Methodist, and one Presbyterian. They had worshiped and served together in their respective chapels long enough to have become open and accepting of one another's uniqueness of faith. This produced a healthy Christian spirit and a diversity that was very stimulating on occasions. While in different stages of development as families and as individuals, all four families were functioning effectively which was helpful in light of the educational rather than the therapeutic nature of Family Clustering. The size of the group was sufficient, given the limited number of hours scheduled for the group.

The Lunds and the Logans were from the same base and knew each other as participants in the same chapel program. They were not particularly close, however. In fact, it was the Jacksons and the Logans who became close rather quickly, partly because sons Tony and Forrest hit it off so well. However, for the most part there was not much mixing at all until the program got underway officially. Each family came in and sat together as a unit. They were polite but clearly uncertain about that into which they had gotten themselves! They were understandably curious about the other families who had made the same decision. However, at first they were not asking—just looking. Some of the teenagers were worried about missing out on activities scheduled for the young people not in Family Clusters. We talked about this before the session and assured them that during the afternoons and evenings they could join their peers.

As the families entered we greeted them. We were immediately aware that there were other concerns they had from a lack of advance information. We were struck by how little information they had received in advance in spite of our attempt to describe the Family Cluster. To this day we still have difficulty with recruiting members for a cluster. Part of the difficulty is in the experiential nature of a good Family Cluster. One never knows what is going to happen with any given mix of families. We share our intentions and some of our expectations and leave off the promises. Families, who respond, do so in faith!

Since we had no previous contact with the families, we did contracting with them as they arrived and also during the organizational time of the first session and before each major activity. They were reminded repeatedly that they could choose to participate or even to suggest alternative activities at any point. The main problem in contracting was due to our not taking time to dialogue about needs and expectations to be met during the three days. With longer clusters we not only spend more time talking about our needs but also give family members much more responsibility in planning and in leading.

The First Day

We planned for the first day in detail. Our main task was to get acquainted and to begin building community. Martha and I had brainstormed the possible activities for the first session and came up with far more items than we would have time for in those three hours. From this list we developed the following agenda:

9:00	Opening prayer and reading of Matthew 18:3, "Unless you turn around and become like children, you will never enter the kingdom of heaven."
9:05	Wake up physical exercises—lots of stretching
9:10	Brief self introductions around the circle
9:15	Discussion of housekeeping items (i.e. rest rooms, breaks, use of facility, anxieties of any person) and contracting to work together
9:20	Making name tags and sharing information on them with a person unknown to you so the new acquaintance could introduce you to the group

Place where   *Favorite friend*
I'm happy

Name I want to be called this week

A thing that   Something I like
bugs me   about me

9:50	Singing "For health and strength and daily food we give our thanks, O Lord." Refreshment break and an outdoor game

10:15	Values clarification exercise of forced choice where everyone had to choose which they liked best: dog or cats, stateside or overseas living, watching sports or playing, etc.
10:20	Charades on theme, "What our family likes to do together"
10:55	Brief talk on rituals in society, church and family. Children and adults met in separate groups and created new "hello" and "goodbye" rituals which they then demonstrated
11:15	Each family drew a picture of their house on a large piece of newsprint, placed it on the wall, invited other families to come visit their house while each family member told what they liked best about the house
11:45	Brief talk about communication in terms of what had happened that morning Evaluation of the session in terms of expectations of each participant with suggestions of what they would like to do in the remaining two days.
11:50	Closing circle and sentence completion prayers Cleaning up room.

Leaders' Evaluation of the First Day

Our overall objective of getting acquainted and beginning to build community was very well accomplished. We were pleased with how quickly all participants seemed to relax and enjoy each other, although some were more resistant than others. Our overall agenda was too crowded, and we got behind schedule early in the session because the introductions took longer than we had planned. We did not need so many things to do! Fortunately neither Martha nor I are slaves to agendas, and we can be flexible; we preferred to have too much planned than too little. As leaders we needed to work on this problem, because I tend to prefer much less structure than Martha.

The name tags enabled each participant to begin self-examination and self-disclosure very early in the life of the group. This initially produced embarrassment, giggles and some stilted following of instructions. Most of the group wanted to do it "just right," rather than to relax and enjoy. We talked about that tendency and gave them permission to feel whatever they felt and to choose not to do anything they didn't want to do. We also talked about names and how they affect us. We discussed the family name that unites us and the individual name that identifies our uniqueness. Lloyd said he didn't like his name and wanted to be called "Frog." It stuck!

The values clarification polarity exercise helped us to see how cluster members organized themselves around their own interests and preferences. This gave permission for each to like what he or she liked regardless of what mom, dad, siblings, or peers happened to choose.

Charades turned out to be a humorous way to identify family strengths as well as preferences. As in all of the family exercises, the cluster leadership observed the process of decision-making within the families, the roles each family member assumed in group projects, how involved or uninvolved each member was, and learning styles of each family.

An unexpected "plus" of the morning took place during the break. As the Family Cluster members reassembled after getting their refreshments, we had them build a "people machine." One member started the machine by getting down on all fours, kicking one leg rhythmically and making a hissing sound. Another member took hold of the first part of the "machine," adding his or her own motion and sound. This continued as each person added to the growing machine. Naturally all of those sounds and this crazy "contraption" attracted the attention of the entire Conference. Suddenly everyone knew about Family Clusters and became increasingly curious about it throughout the week.

Another part of the experience that caught the attention of other conferees was the cluster ritual for saying "hello" and "good-bye," which was well liked by the group. We decided that anytime we saw each other on the campus during the week we would use the new rituals rather than the traditional ones. The motion of rotating our hands in front of us and pointing the right index finger skyward was our way of saying, "Go with God." The rest of the conferees may have thought it was a signal for having "flipped," and we had great fun with them over those rituals.

The house pictures revealed family strengths, preferences, and uniquenesses. The younger children became excited with showing off their pets, favorite rooms and hiding places. Visiting families became involved as if really visiting their homes, by asking questions and helping the family feel good about their place.

From the evaluation session with the cluster we learned that some needed and expected much more use of Scripture and specific expressions of how this all related to a Christian family life. We heard their concern in this manner and agreed to think about how we might make the cluster more explicitly Christian in experience. The hour immediately preceding the cluster time each morning was a Bible study for the entire Conference. We had assumed that this would start the day with a spiritual atmosphere and that this could be built on without further Bible study. A problem was that some families did not make it to the first session and missed the biblical imput.

Also, we learned that we could have used more time in visiting each other's house pictures. It was uncomfortable rushing through the meaningful sharing in order to finish before closing time. We cheated ourselves also on evaluation time at the end of the session. As leaders we value feedback from the participants before planning the next session. This required plenty of time to relax and recall the many events of the morning.

The Second Day

From the feedback and our own impressions we planned the second day around several perceived needs, one of which was low self-esteem. All families, including our own, could use some help with communication skills. Deepening of relationships was needed and would probably be enhanced by developing more skills in this area. We identified several strengths of the cluster before planning the second day's agenda. This group played well together, developed trust quickly, had a fairly common understanding of the Christian faith and seemed to like to be together.

Our second day of activities began with a brief study of Colossians 3:18 – 4:6 which discusses family responsibilities to each other and closes with the admonition to "study how best to talk with each person you meet." Then we loosened up with physical activity by doing the "Hokey Pokey," after which we revisited each other's house pictures to take care of growing interests in each other. It also allowed time to share as fully as they might have liked. This gave Martha and me an opportunity to interview some of the quieter members with questions like, "How does it feel to be the oldest child?" or, "Who made up that rule about picking up things in the bathroom?" or, "Who gets things going in your house every morning?"

Next, we showed a four-minute film, *The Gulf*, which reveals the frustration of two characters who cannot communicate well and have additional problems of not accepting each other when they do communicate. As the discussion indicated, we were reminded of the gulf that exists at times between individuals in families and between families in a cluster. The discussion led us to contract with each other for attempting to bridge gaps during the week and to try to learn skills and improve attitudes which would help us at home.

To begin immediately to practice sharing ourselves and paying attention to nonverbal communication, we played a fun game called "Guess My Feeling". Each person in turn made a face or used some bodily gesture to indicate what they were feeling. The person next to them simply tried to guess what feeling that nonverbal message was communicating. At the break we were ready to play another game outside. This time the teenagers took charge and led the rest of us in several new games.

The second half of the morning was spent with Virginia Satir's four characteristics of how people in families tend to function when self-esteem is low and pressure is on. Martha and I described and demonstrated the physical positions of the placater, the blamer, the computer and the distractor as Satir pictures them in *Peoplemaking* (See pages 59-79). Then we made up artificial families and asked each to take one of the four roles we had just described, planning a summer vacation while staying in those roles. They were predictably frustrated, but it was a fun way for all to experience and to remember the various roles. We then taught some simple communication skills such as using "I" messages and active listening. We had them try again to plan a vacation—this time with considerable success. It turned out to be a very helpful learning experience. However, once again in our excitement and involvement we ran out of time and did not allow a sufficient period for evaluation and closing.

The Third Day

On the last day we decided to work on self-esteem, family strengths, and goal setting. We wanted to end with positive feelings and with hope for the future. For self-esteem building we asked families to sit together and gave them slips of paper. One at a time members of the family left the room while the remaining family members wrote attributes of the missing member on the slips of paper and made a chain necklace out of the slips. When the member returned to the family, each person had an opportunity to tell what favorite characteristics he or she contributed to the chain. Additionally, the members told what they thought that person would be like in ten years if these strengths were fully developed and utilized.

We then moved from individual to family strengths. We asked each person in the family to list strengths present in their family. Those who wished were then permitted to share their lists with the entire cluster. We also asked them to comment, if they liked, as to how they felt while writing their lists.

To enable the families to talk about goals for the future we asked each member to list ten things they loved to do, indicating which ones they were able to do often enough. They discussed these in their families. The second part of the goal-setting exercise was that of imaging a perfect day for them as a family. We asked them to relax their minds and bodies and then led them in a guided fantasy of what they would do and feel with no limitations and all the resources needed for the best possible of family days. After discussing these fantasies we then led the families in writing out some long and short term goals. We asked them to establish who would be responsible for accomplishing any sub-goals or tasks required for reaching the goals. They were to give themselves completion dates, talk about money required for reaching the goals, and other preparations to be made before they returned home.

Cluster Evaluation

Before our closing celebration we asked for feedback on the entire three-day experience. Many in the group expressed a desire for more time and unanimously agreed to ask for a Family Cluster section in next year's Conference. Specific comments included:

"It was more than I expected."
"I liked the way the children were accepted as equals."
"It was helpful to have the family of the leaders with us. I liked their openness, non-pretending and way of communicating."
"I liked it when we used the Scriptures on feelings and communication."
"It was helpful to hear our son say he was happy."

Non-cluster conferees were intrigued with what they had observed and asked for a special meeting to talk about the experience and the model. We held this on the last evening of the Conference. Several cluster members helped the leaders describe the model, how it was experienced that week and how it could be used back home. It was a positive, spirited testimonial to the fun, learning and growth of the week.

Follow-up

The acid test and measure of the lasting value of the Family Cluster at Mars Hill surfaced a year later with the planning of the 1977 Mars Hill Christian Encounter Conference. At that time, Chaplain (Colonel) Walter R. Bauer, Chief of the USAF Chaplain Resource

Board, sent the following letter to all installation chaplains in the eastern United States:

> We are all aware of the current emphasis on the family and the growing national focus upon family life. This emphasis is a welcomed trend for Air Force chaplains who have long been ministering quietly to the needs of Air Force families.
>
> Therefore, you can understand our excitement when we discovered a model for family ministry which is both effective as a resource with others and as a means of personal family growth. One of the most promising family resources to emerge lately is family enrichment through Family Clusters! Clusters of three to five families work together in a supportive, relaxed and fun environment. All members of the family from first graders up are included. There is no probing nor interpretation of personal or private aspects of individual or family life. The experience is valuable to any family interested in growth and development.
>
> This model was successfully utilized with 15 families attending the TAC-sponsored Christian Encounter Conference at Mars Hill, N.C., July 1976. The response was so overwhelmingly positive that the Family Cluster part of the program for this year's CEC at Mars Hill will be expanded.
>
> (Bauer, Walter R. "Memorandum for Installation Chaplains in the Mars Hill Area," Correspondence, May 1977.)

The Mars Hill Conference paved the way for Air Force families to find strength and growth through the Family Cluster Model.

Resources

"Family Cluster Leader's Guide," an unpublished collection of leadership resources formerly available from Family Clustering, Inc.

Satir, Virginia. *Peoplemaking*. Palo Alto, CA: Science and Behavior Books, Inc., 1972.

Simon, Sidney, Howe, Leland and Kirschenbaum, Howard. *Values Clarification*. New York: Hart Publishing Company, 1972.

Film, "The Gulf," USAF Film Library. Available from Mass Media Ministries, 2116 N. Charles St., Baltimore, MD 21218 (301) 727-3270

Biographical Data

Charles B. Prewitt, D. Min., is Director of Family Life Education and Counseling in the Department of Religion at Baptist Memorial Hospital, San Antonio, Texas. A retired Air Force Chaplain, he is a clinical member of the American Association for Marriage and Family Therapy. He is married, and father of six children, with two grandchildren.

Address:

3006 Meadow Circle
San Antonio, TX 78231
(512) 492-3529

Responding to the Case Studies

The basic ingredients in a cluster are *individuals* within *families* who are part of a *group* process. The method used is that of experiential learning toward a growth/change process. Inherent in the philosophical underpinnings are the theological meanings within the process of clustering.

> **1** *Families as Systems: The System of the Family Cluster* by Ronald J. Hunsicker.
>
> **2** *Group Process of Family Clustering* by Lucinda Sangree.
>
> **3** *Theologizing: Inherent Ingredient in Family Clusters* by Robert P. Stamschror.

Families as Systems: The System of the Family Cluster
Ronald J. Hunsicker

Introduction

Many of the Scriptures use symbols and concepts related to family life, since those similarities best describe the nature of God and his work in the universe. The essence of God's spirit is in the relationship of family intimacies; therefore, the actual bonds of family life can best interpret the meaning of God. It is to this end that the Family Cluster was developed—to assist family units (no matter what type) in fostering the kinds of relationships which best interpret the nature of the Holy as found in love, care, nurturance, support, creativity, and reconciliation.

Adult members of families have learned how to relate from remembering their own families-of-origin. The patterns of past families are passed on to the offspring of new families. People have nowhere to go to learn how they might behave differently in families. The way the Family Cluster is structured within the system of the group helps to influence family life. Ron Hunsicker shares with us how the system of the cluster influences families, and how the systems of the participating families influence the cluster group. They are reciprocal and intertwined in complexity.

M.S.

In her previous book, *Family Enrichment With Family Clusters*, Dr. Sawin has joined the growing chorus of persons advancing the notion of enrichment as an approach to human development. She has eloquently established the fact that family growth groups—or Family Clusters—are educational in nature and do not address themselves specifically to pathological behavior. They deal with healthy families who want to learn to function in a more wholesome way.[4] The cluster is a process of intervention based on pre-arranged, program objectives which deal with interpersonal relationships between and among participants. The process emphasizes the active participation of "give and take" between an enricher (the leader) and participating family members in the experience. Through the confrontation of new tasks and new demands, it hopes to produce a certain degree of hopeful change and progress. The Family Cluster Model is but one of a host of models which attempt to introduce enrichment/growth into the lives of families.

The Notion of Systems

Over the years we have come to understand that there is a need to appreciate the holistic character of extremely complex life processes, and this has been facilitated by systems theory. General systems theory goes beyond the analytical method of traditional science and examines this holistic character.

Anatol Rapoport succinctly defines what is involved in such a theory:

> "A whole which functions as a whole by virtue of the inter-dependence of its parts is called a system, and the method which aims at discovering how this is brought about in the widest variety of systems has been called general systems theory."[1]

In considering systems, being, behaving, and becoming are fundamental aspects of all organized systems. In this sense, general systems theory is concerned with the nature of wholeness, believing that the nature of the parts alone is not basic but rather the way that they are inter-related. Furthermore, systems theory suggests that the parts (or family members) take on properties (or characteristics) that result from their being a part of a larger whole and in relationship to all other parts of this larger whole. In other words, the parts are more than what they contribute; they are also integrated into the larger totality.

Systems Theory in a Cluster

Sawin defines a Family Cluster as "a group of four or five complete family units which contract to meet together periodically over an extended period of time for shared educational experiences related to their living in relationship within the family. A Cluster provides mutual support, training in skills which facilitate the family living in relationship, and celebration of their life and beliefs together."[4]

Within the definition there are two very important systems at work. First, each one of the family units brings with it a developed family system. Once a system is started, it becomes an integral part of that family's characteristic way of behaving. Awareness of the family system's existence will go a long way in assisting this conglomerate group (the cluster) to consider the variety of systems brought together. The ideas from general systems theory have helped to inform family life immensely.

Second, the Family Cluster is a system in itself, created by persons coming together to perform specific tasks for a specific length of time. To some extent, this new system of the cluster is dependent on the systems brought to it by the four or five family units. It is important to note that the whole of the cluster system is greater than the sum of its family parts. Because of this, some of the individual family systems will need to accommodate or adapt themselves in order to be a part of the cluster system. Accommodation leads to re-structuring or changing. Consequently, one can hypothesize that, *as a result of participating in a Family Cluster, some family units may find themselves functioning differently as a result of adapting to the norms of the cluster system.*

Applications from the Case Studies

In an attempt to look at this phenomenon, we will examine how the cluster experience has an impact on the systems of various participating families.

Conflict

One of the important issues which has emerged out of the application of systems theory to family development has been in the field of communication. Virginia Satir has provided us with excellent writings in this arena.[2,3] One of the areas which is tested in communication is that of conflict. The manner in which systems resolve conflict becomes an indicator of the functioning of that system. The Unitarian Family Cluster provides an example of a conflictive situation not being addressed as an issue facing the entire group; though the group develops cohesion early in the cluster. While there was unclarity in terms of the relationship between a single woman and a single parent with her children, it can be assumed that this unclarity had some "spill-over effect" on the entire cluster system. The conflict was not simply one within the sub-system, but one which had its effects on the entire system. The resolution of conflict becomes a key issue in understanding how systems organize themselves, adapt, and change.

Rules

Each system tends to develop a set of rules which govern its functioning. Within family units these rules are usually more implicit than explicit. The Shalom Family Cluster illustrates well the difference between articulated and unarticulated rules within the example of a "visiting family" being introduced into the Family Cluster system. The reaction varied from infringement to embarrassement which are observable dynamics within any system. When change is introduced the entire system is changed. Therefore, any altering of the system will necessarily cause the system to further alter itself in response to this "invasion." An axiom which illustrates this is "any action will cause a reaction." Effective leadership of the Shalom Cluster assisted this system in re-establishing its equilibrium and forming some rules as to how to deal with guests. However, it is interesting to note that those rules were decided by adults in this particular case. An assumption might have been that this cluster decided that children were not considered to have been as affected by the guests; therefore, they did not help make the new rules. That assumption, of course, needs testing.

Intervening with a Sub-system

The systems perspective is helpful often in establishing a picture of an entire system and then asking the question: How does one enrich this system? In clustering, it means viewing the system, determining the most advantageous point of intervention, and designing goals which will assist the group to move in a particular direction. This activity is very common in family therapy which utilizes the systems approach. The notion is that intervention at any one given point in the system will automatically cause the entire system to reorganize. Family enrichment approaches build extensively on that theory also.

The Raleigh Cluster can be cited as an example of how an analysis of the system revealed both a core group and a fringe group. In a sense, this cluster system was composed of sub-systems which were or were not related to the family units. Educational strategies, which had enrichment as their goal, were developed in order to move the fringe family toward the core for greater involvement and enrichment. In this particular Family Cluster, it would have been helpful to have known if the family with irregular attendance had been asked to share their attendance difficulty with the entire group. It seems that one needs to pay attention to the way the action of sub-systems effects the entire system. For instance, non-verbal activity, such as irregular attendance, is a message to the larger system. Also this systems perspective might have allowed for an enrichment of the family with irregular attendance to look at its own understanding of commitment. An educational strategy might have helped the entire sub-system to examine its understanding and its participation in commitment.

Families Learning Anew

An amazing and intriguing cluster is presented in the case study of the mental health unit in Toronto. Drawing from a population which might not be defined as having healthy families in many circumstances, this case study presents material showing how the Family Cluster Model can set out specifically to impact individual family systems. At the same time, the case example illustrates well some of the problems using the model with these families. Just as systems theory helps one consider de-emphasizing the "identified client" (or the sick patient), so the Family Cluster Model can help de-emphasize the "problem families" within a cluster. The impact of this learning is that when a system is forced out of its normal way of functioning, it may learn some new ways to interrelate. The concept of people modeling or providing examples to each other is important. The Toronto Cluster exemplifies how clear determination of cluster rules often "unclogs" the communication process and allows for more openness.

Boundaries and Roles

In working with the families, issues of boundaries and roles occur often within their systems. The cluster model provides an excellent opportunity for boundaries to be explored and established and for roles to be viewed, experienced, and further developed. When the system is understood, then participants can ask "how" questions instead of "why" questions. Generally speaking, "how" questions produce information and understanding, and "why" produce defensiveness. The Australian Cluster designed an excellent activity building on the concept of boundaries and roles which allowed the cluster participants to ask more "how" questions than "why" questions. Using the systems theory as a background, they introduced role playing and family sculpting to help family members see and understand how typical roles in the family determine certain outcomes.

In these particular instances the Family Cluster became a way to teach families information about their own systems and to help them obtain new information. Helping persons to discover their part in the system at a given point in time and seeing the other parts of the system functioning in relationship to them is very exciting, though sometimes painful.

The Leaders' Understanding of Systems

In general, one can examine the various case studies and find the leaders' understandings of systems if not explicit then at least implicit, within the context of the cluster. Leadership within the Family Cluster Model ought always to be viewed as leadership within; therefore, the leaders join the system. Much like the family therapist who often joins the family system to effect any change, the leaders join the Family Cluster in order to bring about enrichment. A system can be changed by any one component taking a different position and sticking to it, and this is particularly true of leaders. Leaders can model values which are important to families which, in turn, are lived out before the group. Participants observe, are impacted by them, and values may be exchanged as if by osmosis. Introducing a new model of behavior is infiltrating a system, with the possibility for change. I believe that leadership has the capacity to achieve this goal in clustering. Therefore, it is valuable to include considerable training in system theory for potential leaders of clusters. Such training would allow persons to be able to plan strategies which would impact and restructure systems.

Conclusion

Understanding the characteristics of any given system offers a structured means of assessing what goes on in a system as well as providing a vehicle for understanding the meaning of behavior. Such an understanding provides the means by which one can define aspects of a system that tend toward a growth framework and those which tend to inhibit growth. From a systems standpoint, additional attention needs to be paid to the interactions within family systems. Research needs to be done to test the hypotheses that the creation of a Family Cluster system will alter, restructure, or change the individual families which are component parts. When attention is given to the interaction, one is able to define those aspects which inhibit or negate growth over against those which build and produce growth. The goal of an enrichment model would be to design strategies which strengthen those aspects which foster growth and to provide substitutes for those which inhibit growth within the family units.

From the case studies which we have examined it does seem that evidence is available to suggest that the Family Cluster Model is a viable model to help families work on understanding their systems, as well as developing and reinforcing those activities which strengthen family life. Additionally, the Family Cluster seems to be an excellent model within which a "learning center" can be developed so that family units can plan, discuss, debate and revise their own patterns of living in a world of rapid social change.

Footnotes and Bibliography

1 Rapoport, Anatol and Walter Buckley, (eds.). *Modern Systems Research for the Behavioral Scientist.* Chicago: Aldine Publishing Company, 1968, p. 17.

2 Satir, Virginia. *Conjoint Family Therapy.* Palo Alto, CA: Science and Behavior Books, Inc., 1967.

3 Satir, Virginia. *Peoplemaking.* Palo Alto, CA: Science and Behavior Books, Inc., 1972.

4 Sawin, Margaret M. *Family Enrichment With Family Clusters.* Valley Forge, PA: Judson Press, 1979, pages 20 and 27.

Biographical Data

Rev. Ronald J. Hunsicker is currently the Director of Pastoral Services for Memorial Hospital in South Bend, IN. He has had six years experience as pastor of a congregation, and for six years he served as Director of Pastoral Services in a community mental health center. As an ordained Mennonite minister, he has led many family and marriage enrichment events and published a number of articles on the subject as well.

Rev. Hunsicker has led Family Clusters in the congregation in which he worships, as well as providing leadership in Family Cluster Training Laboratories.

Address:

Memorial Hospital
615 N. Michigan Street
South Bend, IN 46601
(219) 234-9041

Group Process of Family Clustering
Lucinda Sangree

Introduction

The New Testament concept of Christian living includes that of relationships with others, particularly in a "koinonia"* type of caring community. Therefore, the nature of the group and behavior it manifests become important in understanding how to replicate the "koinonia" influence, so Christian nurturing can take place.

The Family Cluster is a group of

> individuals of all ages
> families representing various life styles
> males and females
> sub-groups, i.e. couples, teens, etc.
> persons in well-defined roles, i.e. parents, siblings, etc.

Therefore, the group process contains much complexity with strong, inbuilt factors. The nature of the group dynamics is of utmost importance to the functioning of the cluster in achieving its goals.

Knowledge and skills from the behavioral sciences contribute to our understanding of how cluster groups best operate, and Lucinda Sangree writes of this in the following discourse.

M.S.

---

*Koinonia the Greek word from the New Testament, meaning a mutual religious fellowship of giving and receiving which includes participation, impartation, and fellowship. (Kittel, Gerhard (ed.) *Theological Dictionary of the New Testament,* vol. III. Grand Rapids, MI.: William B. Eerdmans Publishers, p. 798.

The Family Cluster Experiment

The Family Cluster Model presents an interesting social experiment. The designer of this family enrichment process, Dr. Margaret Sawin, firmly believes in a view of social life that embraces the perspectives of cybernetics and analysis of family life from a systems approach. Probably cluster leaders have not read Norbert Weiner,[14] Gregory Bateson,[4] nor Walter Buckley,[7] who are significant contributors to modern systems theories; but they do become aware of the family functioning as a system within the cluster group, which in turn has its existence within the environment of the sponsoring institution or agency.

To obtain an understanding of the system, cluster leaders give attention to specific kinds of feedback from cluster participants. The concept of emergent design, which is fundamental to the cluster program, depends upon the ability of the leaders to assess areas of member satisfaction, levels of individual and group esteem, amount of fatigue, etc. In addition, the Family Cluster experience offers a unique opportunity for family systems to interpenetrate one another, thus offering family members valuable feedback about their own families via the contrasts and comparisons available from others in a non-competitive, non-threatening context.

In the early sessions of the cluster, activities such as contracting (which will be discussed at length later) encourage individuals to learn ways to bring about change within their own families. It is hoped that families and individuals within a cluster learn to distinguish the elements of systems, how to introduce change, and how to implement new agreements to make family life a recipient of behavioral science skills. This is the Family Cluster experiment.

Developing the Group Process

The cluster model contains guidelines that are based on insights about the development of the individual personality and about the functioning of individuals in groups. Great emphasis is placed upon building self-esteem and family-esteem. Individuals are encouraged to share positive attributes about themselves and their families; in this atmosphere of reward and appreciation the acceptance of individuals by one another flourishes. In addition, each family is affirmed in its present state, which is essential for building the trust and confidence that are necessary precursors to creating change within the family. The necessity of affirming the current state of family balance by not threatening its defenses as a basis for setting the stage for growth and change, has been elegantly demonstrated in the works of Mara Selvini Palozzoli,[10] as well as others. Several of the case descriptions refer to the anxiety that is present at the beginning of a cluster. It is likely that a good deal of this anxiety is the subconscious fear of change and loss of balance within the family system. It is the affirmation of each family, as frequently mentioned in the cluster descriptions, that allays this fear and paradoxically sets the stage for learning about the family system with possible avenues for change and growth.

Techniques, such as competition between factions or inducing fatigue in order to lower defenses of individuals, are carefully avoided by cluster leaders. The establishment of a sense of community is achieved by positive means.

The construction of a cluster contract, as a limited task in the early sessions, utilizes constructive group building processes in which all can participate; and it is usually completed successfully. As this task is achieved, questions are raised and answered both directly and indirectly. The spatial limits of the physical setting are explored. The safe limits of participation and intimacy are made explicit by the participants and by the modeling of the leaders via their interactions with each other and with group members. During the early sessions, a common language develops which may include "code" words, such as a name for the cluster. The contract is publicly signed and celebrated; thus, a declaration of commitment to the group and its norms is witnessed by the self and by others. This establishes the basis for individual internal dissonance and loss of self-esteem if the contract is broken. Equally important, the contract period is an opportunity for the cluster leaders to show by example how one may examine and share the elements of group life, including the power structure, the decision-making process, and possible alternative arrangements. This has a strong carry-over to family group life. The contract includes the possibility of re-negotiation which demonstrates the fact that groups can chart their own destinies, thus allowing for flexibility in a world of rapid social change.

Theories of Group Development

The phases, through which one conceives of a group moving, are part and parcel of the basic assumptions one holds about the nature of groups, i.e. about why groups are formed and how they are maintained. Some cluster leaders conceive of groups as moving through recurring cycles of inclusion/control/affection phases. These leaders are influenced by the theorist, Schutz,[12] who focuses upon the compatability and incompatability of the personal needs of individuals who make up the group. Such leaders hold that personal need profiles differ, but that persons can learn how to more effectively communicate their feelings of wanting to be close or to be less personal; wanting to control or to be controlled. They can learn to respond to parallel communication of others in a group, such as the family, in constructive ways. These leaders stress inclusion activities early in the program and at the beginning of each session. They are alert to indications from members that a person is feeling left out, powerless, or fearful of revealing feelings of affection. Observing leaders' responses to these personal needs is a vital learning experience for participants within their family groups, as there is likeness in a cluster with persons of different age groups who have strong emotional attachments.

There are other cluster leaders who conceive of groups as moving through phases of orientation/evaluation/control with the necessity of balancing individual expressions of feelings with group activity demand, i.e., an individual's bottled-up feelings should not be allowed to get in the way of cooperative problem-solving. Influential here are theorists, such as Bales[3] and Parsons.[9] The stress and problems of role performance, as well as inhibiting the expression of feelings, is important to these leaders.

The picture is even more complicated than that given above if the leaders conceive of the group as formed to perform tasks that are largely set by the external environment. Specific goals are set by the leaders or emerge in discussions facilitated by them. Some goals might be: learning to read non-verbal clues, discovering the role stereotypes that influence the behavior in the family, learning how to express values in the family, or studying aspects of society's impact on the family. In such task-oriented groups, either the model of inclusion/control-affection or that of orientation/evaluation/control is used as an interpretative frame by the leaders and guides their perception of feedback messages coming from the cluster participants. Some cluster leaders are inclined to be uneasy with the control phase of group movement, and some attempt to share leadership. If this sharing is done directly by assigning leadership tasks or by asking for volunteers to share in the planning, then the perspective of the group is retained as a task-oriented one. With this orientation, the experiential learning consists largely of finding ways to think about levels of family relations that all experience but rarely examine. People learn by watching other families, by pretending to be part of another family, by simulating a different family role, and by receiving feedback on their own family. They also learn by playing and working in new ways—the older generation with the younger, with new materials, with and without language, and with fantasy shared rather than kept private.

Training for Family Cluster Leadership

Pre-cluster interviews with families indicate a desire for structure; thus, cluster leaders are encouraged to perceive a cluster as primarily a task-oriented group. There is another way of thinking about groups that is not employed by leaders when they are leading clusters. However, it is an important perspective for those who are involved in the designing and leading of training laboratories for Family Cluster leadership. They find it useful to conceive of a group as meeting the needs and solving the problems which stem largely from the internal system of the training group as it forms. This is particularly true of the design skillshop and design teams part of the training. In this orientation the group interpretive framework is similar to the self-study or T-group, as described in the work of Bennis and Sheppard.[5]

In this type of group, the leader desires to extend experiential learning into the actual control of the group. In such an instance the leaders refuse to lead, and the group members take responsibility for their design teams and leadership planning. The tasks are largely internal to the system, i.e., to improve communication, to learn how to set and to revise group goals. The interpretative frame charts such a group as moving through phases of power struggle and affection. The training leader who was expected to minister to the dependency needs of the members is found wanting; the group members become angry as they move through the painful process of learning to understand and to guide themselves. Hopefully, the members reach a collegial relationship with the training "leader who wouldn't lead"; such can be a powerful growth experience.

The self-study group orientation is an appropriate one to persue in the training events for leaders of cluster. This approach encourages leadership responsibility that entails growth experiences of great value to the trainees. This is especially true if the trainers are able to make it clear to the participant trainees that the anger and confusion they may feel in learning to take responsibility for group direction are *not* appropriate for the Family Cluster experience itself.

The self-study of T-group orientation is not an advantageous one to use in a cluster, since families have hierarchies of authority within them which must be respected due to the greater experience and prescribed responsibilities of the parents. In fact, some problems which leaders of clusters encounter may be due in part to the fact that the two types of group life perspectives are not distinguished and employed appropriately. In the actual cluster experience, control may be delegated by the leader, but the leader should not "abandon" the cluster and leave the members to work out roles and relationships in a complex group consisting of many families. The cluster leader, when working and playing in a cluster, is advised to forego the T-group or self-study group orientation so useful in the leadership training experience.

Also, the leadership training for cluster leaders imparts skills needed to work as a co-leader back home with agencies important in sponsoring or financing cluster programs. The case descriptions contain many references to the time co-leaders spent working and playing with each other before the cluster sessions were held. It is likely that the leaders learned the value of such pre-cluster activities in a training situation which involved working through group phases of power and affection; thereby, becoming aware of their own usual manner of functioning in groups.

It is important to mention that Family Cluster Training Laboratories include the presence of families. Thus, trainees can be involved in a task-oriented group perspective with the Family Clusters while at the same time they are involved in self-study group perspective with other trainees and the staff. The new leaders help to facilitate learning for family participants about family roles, decision-making and rule-making, the sharing of feelings, and recognition of values held. This work with the families stands in an important contrast to work among the trainees with each other and the staff. As is usually the case, if the trainers are comfortable with extending experiential learning into the power dimension of the group, the trainee group may experience the struggle from dependency to collegiality among themselves, concurrent with learning the skills necessary to conduct Family Clusters.

Case Study Descriptions

It is worthwhile to note certain elements of particular clusters as described in the case studies included in this volume. As one reads them, the early remarks become specifically applicable. The language and reference frameworks of the social sciences are not meant to confuse but to enrich our understanding of group life by mapping out the ordered patterns that are present. It is my hope that these prefatory comments will make the cases more meaningful.

When a family does not contract. In a description of the Unitarian Church Cluster (Rochester, N.Y.), the authors are explicit about certain difficulties encountered, one of which is of special interest in the context of this discussion. One family was sporadic in its attendance at cluster meetings; because of this, the question was raised in the cluster of what to do about deviance. This family had not participated in drawing up the cluster contract nor was it present for the public signing. The cluster model relies strongly upon the contracting process to establish the basis for dissonance in individuals and in families who do not comply with the terms of the contract.[1] The leaders were correct in assessing a reluctance to attend as being a prelude to not joining the contracting process. However, we can go further and state that the lack of contract participation was the crucial element in the inability of the cluster members to exert any pressure of group norms upon the "deviant family." The members of the family in question did not experience dissonance when they neglected cluster responsibilities and suffered no loss of self-esteem nor strain due to inconsistency. Avoidance of dissonance and the related loss of self-esteem that may result from being inconsistent regarding publicly declared values and intentions are the principal bases for effective enforcement of cluster group norms. The importance placed by cluster leaders upon the completion of the cluster contract early in the group's life indicates an awareness that there is more to the contracting than a listing of ground rules and housekeeping duties. The contracting process iteslf is a basis for the enforcement of norm compliance. In addition, the contracting process is the model set forth by leaders as an alternative to the use of force. This has a carry-over to family life inasmuch as many families are searching for alternatives to punitive measures, i.e., physical punishment, as approaches to norm compliance within the family. Contracting skills is one way this can be done effectively.

Shared leadership assumptions. In the Sackville, Nova Scotia cluster the leaders explored with each other their respective points of view about child socialization and the way children learn. They did not need to probe specifics about theological beliefs, but they had to establish a common perspective on how children learn theological beliefs. The source of a person's beliefs and values comes from human experience. What matters most is what people do to and with children, not what they tell them. Without the ability to explore their assumptions about the nature of learning before the cluster was formed, these leaders would have probably presented a less coherent and less enjoyable cluster program to the families that joined.

Using the model flexibly. The Pullen Memorial Baptist Church Cluster (Raleigh, N.C.) offers a demonstration of the flexibility of the cluster model. The leaders had as their primary goal the increased involvement of the individual in the church community. They did not directly address issues of improved intra-family communication and increased understanding of the family as a small system with its own destiny. Instead they focused upon

1 offering families an opportunity for in-depth relationships across family and generational lines
2 increasing awareness that each family is a part of the family of God. (See page 69 of this volume.)

This cluster developed a curriculum with specific biblical content which did not focus upon family developmental issues. The leaders "hoped that family strengths and communication would develop as a byproduct of the process." (See page 73 of this volume.) The essential elements of the cluster model remained:

- contracting as a basis for building norm compliance and norm re-negotiation
- sharing specific and limited leadership
- examining and practising basic communication skills
- sharing meals
- playing together
- giving permission to express feelings in a safe and constructive context
- building self-esteem in one's self and in others through experiential learning.

The content of the curriculum gave short-term focus to the sessions which added to the group's sense of achievement. Completing these tasks helped integrate the participants into the larger church body, both because of this sense of achievement and because of the congruence of the lesson content with the religious education goals of the congregation.

Cluster goals interfacing with institutional goals. A similar and successful use of the cluster model occurred in the Public School Cluster Experience in Rochester, N.Y. Again, the goals of the cluster leaders were cross-family integration and better understanding of and involvement with the goals of the sponsoring institution. The cluster activities had positive results for both the particular individuals, the families, and the school institution itself.

Building self-esteem. An exciting example of the flexibility and usefulness of the Family Cluster Model is the description set forth from the Dellcrest Children's Centre in Toronto, Ontario. The experiences in these cluster sessions give witness to the central importance of building self-esteem. In this particular cluster environment, the aspect is emphasized more than any other.

> "Families who are identified by some community agency as 'families in need of help' tend to feel low self-esteem and low corporate esteem as they come to the Centre. The Family Cluster Model is an excellent way to create a normalizing effect or climate. At no time is any family or individual identified as 'the problem.' All of the activities of the cluster, in content and method, are designed to build the self-esteem of individuals and the family.
>
> Families, in which the common tendency of the parents is to suppress their children, present a major challenge to cluster leaders. This tendency works against the nurturant philosophy of clusters. However, by attending as much to the self-esteem needs of the adults as to those of the children, the tide soon turns. Our research has focused on self-esteem and use of power within the family with encouraging results that support the Family Cluster Model as not only an educational but a therapeutic resource." (See page 184 of this volume.)

Some of the reasons for the use of the Family Cluster in this environment and the excellent results of the program are briefly recounted by the author of the case description. This is an innovative and daring use of the cluster model, and a careful reading of the case description is informative.

Sharing of Power. Clear examples of all the points made in the early section of this discourse are present in the descriptions of clusters from the Rochester public schools and Melbourne, Australia. In the latter, the authors are quite explicit about the use of the con-

tracting process as a teaching model in the areas of conflict prevention and resolution.

> "The contracting process modelled for families a method
> of power-sharing within the family, and a conflict-resolu-
> tion method of setting clearly defined rules of access
> where sharing was a problem." (See page 156 of this vol-
> ume.)

In addition, these leaders recognized that the cluster guide faces a
power dilemma similar to that of parents. Regardless of how desirable shared decision-making is in theory, the leaders, in fact, are
responsible for certain agenda items, as they have the experience
and skills to facilitate learning in certain areas which participants
desire.

Evaluation

The cluster evaluation method most commonly followed was
the appraisal, written or spoken, at the end of the concluding cluster, followed by an interview at a later date. The most systematic
evaluation described in the studies was that of the Australian cluster. An interview guide was followed, which ensured that each
family was asked a minimum of the same questions; the interviews
were recorded, and then a summary constructed from the tapes.
This technique probably is more accurate in assessing behavior
changes, due to the program, than any battery of before and after
testing. My one criticism of the procedure is that the cluster leaders did the interviewing, which may have biased some of the
answers in a more positive direction than a less-involved inter-
viewer might have received. Specific behavior changes attributed to
the cluster experience recounted in the interviews are convincing,
however, and interviewer/interviewee bias is not likely to have been
a factor in these reported details.

Conclusion

Reading and thinking about these case studies has renewed my conviction that the Family Cluster Model is the most sophisticated and flexible model of family enrichment available in the area of family life education today. It also provides for a group which can facilitate family nurturing in a world of rapid social change.

Bibliography

1. Aronson, Elliot, "Dissonance Theory: Progress and Problems" in *Current Perspectives in Social Psychology*, (3rd ed.) Hollander and Hunt (eds.). New York: Oxford University Press, 1971, pp. 359-371.

2. Bales, R.F. *Interaction Process Analysis: A Method for the Study of Small Groups.* Reading, Ma.: Addison-Wesley, 1950.

3. Bales, R.F., and F. L. Stradtbeck, "Process in Group Problem Solving." *Journal of Abnormal and Social Psychology*, 46 (1951), pp. 485-495.

4. Bateson, Gregory. *Steps to an Ecology of the Mind.* New York: Ballantine Books, 1972.

5. Bennis, Warren G. and Herbert Shepard, "A Theory of Group Development" in *Analysis of Group* by Gebbard, Hartman and Nann (eds.) San Francisco: Jossey Boss, Publishers, 1974, pp. 127-153.

6. Bock, K.W. *Beyond Words.* New York: Russell Sage Foundation, 1972.

7. Buckley, Walter. *Sociology and Modern Systems Theory.* Englewood Cliffs, N.J.: Prentice-Hall, Inc., 1967.

8. Mills, T.M. *The Sociology of Small Groups.* Englewood Cliffs, N.J.: Prentice-Hall, Inc., 1967.

9. Parsons, Talcott and R.F. Bales, *Family Socialization and Interaction Process.* Glencoe, Il: The Free Press, 1955.

10. Palazzoli, Mara Selvini. Luigi Boscolo, Gianfrance Cecchin, and Guilana Prata, *Paradox and Counterparadox.* New York: Jacob Aronson, Inc., 1978.

11. Sawin, Margaret M. *Family Enrichment with Family Clusters.* Valley Forge, Pa.: Judson Press, 1979.
12. Schutz, W.C. FIRO: *A Three Dimensional Theory of Interpersonal Behavior.* New York: Holt, Rinehart, 1958.
13. Thibaut, J.W. and H.W. Riecker. "Some Determinants and Consequences of the Perception of Social Causality," *Journal of Personality,* 1955, (24), pp. 113-133.
14. Wiener, Norbert. *Cybernetics.* Cambridge, Ma.: M.I.T. Press, 1948, (2nd ed., 1961).

Biographical Data

Lucinda Sangree is a clinical instructor in the Department of Psychiatry at the University of Rochester Medical School. She also is a Mentor in the State University of New York's alternative college, Empire State College. Prior to her current appointments, she was an assistant professor at the State University of New York at Geneseo and a post-doctoral Fellow in Psychiatry at the University of Rochester Medical School.

She received her Ph.D in sociology in 1977 from the State University of New York at Buffalo and her M.A. in 1956 in the same field from the University of Chicago. Her research and teaching have focused on self-regulatory mechanisms in small systems with research specifically on the uses of laughter and humor. She has presented papers at professional meetings, one of which was with Walter V. Sangree on "The Family Cluster Movement in North America." She co-edited a book with Frederick Gearing, entitled *Toward A Cultural Theory of Education and Schooling.*

Dr. Sangree is an active member in The Society of Friends in Rochester, N.Y.

Address:

254 Highland Parkway
Rochester, N.Y. 14618
(716) 244-7291

Theologizing: Inherent Ingredient in Family Clusters   Robert P. Stamschror

Introduction

The act of reflection includes consideration of the experiences in light of a faith relationship with God. To persons in a faith setting this is an essential act, whether by word or deed.

Every person is a child of God's family; thus, every person can reflect on what it is like to live in relationship within that family. This is learned first in one's family-of-origin through the everyday behaviors between the persons in that family. During adolesence and young adulthood, the meaning of those relationships become articulated in words and expressed through symbols of faith affirmation. Christians are making theology all of the time by attempting to make sense or meaning out of their lived experiences. How one perceives this depends, in part, on how the family interactions are structured to facilitate human development or to hinder it.

The nature of the Family Cluster Model in building a faith community among families is an attempt to facilitate families within their intimate family systems so as to better the manner in which relationships are lived. This points families toward growth and health. Doing this together in a group allows for a natural extended family to be developed, which might be called a "faith family." The end result is assisting families to move toward holism and enrichment within the most intense arena of living—the family.

In this chapter Robert Stamschror helps us to reflect on the presence of God in the activities and interactions of the structure of Family Clusters. In so doing, he provides us with a grid which shows us the theologizing strength of Family Clusters within its own process. Thus, the cluster becomes a vital theological interpretation of God at work among people who live in initmate family systems.

M.S.

The Act of Theologizing

The act of theologizing is reflection by one who has a faith relationship with God in regard to the experience of this affiliation in all of the encounters of their human life. The field of theology is the articulation of this reflection in word. Together, the two constitute a hind-sighting, sorting-out, putting into words and deeds of what is going on in this relationship or what it is all about. Anyone who does this is theologizing and creating a personal system of theology. We are not used to recognizing it in this fundamental and individual way, with ourselves being the theologians. We are more inclined to see it only in its communal dimension and articulation, with formal and systematic theologians conducting the inquiry. If we do see ourselves as theologizing, it is usually only in terms of studying the common beliefs of the community already formulated by theologians. The theologizing and theology in Family Clusters, which is the subject of this essay, includes the fundamental and individual form, with the cluster participants being recognized as theologians wherever they are theologizing.

Organization of Theological Data

I developed a theological perspective which reflected personalistic and relational thinking from current theologians. This provided criteria for identifying references to theologizing in the case reports. The perspective, which follows a process stance, is as follows:

> God reveals self as one whose life is constituted by community. God exists in distinct persons in union with one another, which union gives life but also creates the distinctness and uniqueness of each person. God reveals self

as creator of human persons who are created in "the image of himself" and are destined to share and live in divine community forever. God became one with us in Jesus Christ so that "god persons" might be communicated to human persons who, in turn, might be enabled to respond in faith and come into the union with "god persons." The principle of life for both God and humans is that life comes from personal union which not only retains the distinctiveness and uniqueness of the individuals but creates and nurtures them. The mystery of human, life-giving relationships with God is intimately and inseparably joined by relationships with other individuals.

The kingdom of God consists of the human family living in God relationship as indicated in Christ's prayer: ". . . that all may be one as you, father, are in me, and I in you; I pray that they may be (one) in us" (John 17:21— *New American Bible*).

The kingdom of God in the human experience is recognized as a community, a fellowship, a family of mutual love, with respect, justice, and active concern for one another. The Church is identified as gatherings of believers who have received the revelation of God and have responded in faith. These are persons consciously in the process of becoming community with God who recognize a mission to witness and extend this community to all human beings. The means by which persons pattern the way of God and join in life-giving union, while at the same time grow in distinction and uniqueness, is called dialogue. This has identifiable characteristics and qualities. On the one hand, it includes mutual openness, trust, honesty, spontaneity, identity, self-worth, and self-esteem; on the other hand, mutual acceptance, affirmation, respect, reverence, commitment, and fidelity. Humans attempt to carry on dialogue within human limitation and sin. The attempt to communicate self can be and is met with rejection, ridicule, disrespect, irreverence, unfaithfulness and betrayal. The consequence of this is closedness, distrust, dishonesty, calculation, and manipulation. These can and do grow in individuals and become ingrained in the systems and sub-systems of human society. The consequence of human limitation and sin, its destruction of the individual, along with its life-destroying divisions, can be overcome only with God continuing to reveal his life and spirit in the form of mercy and forgiveness; the response of individuals is needed in renewed faith and reconciliation.

This theological perspective can be divided into three general areas:

1 God revealing Jesus Christ
2 Human faith response to God
3 Faith community or the Church.

There is no standard form for reporting these actions as written in the Family Cluster case studies; however, there are some common categories within which theologizing can be discerned, which I have selected:

Organization; Sponsorship; Cluster membership; General purposes; Specific learning objectives; Learning process; Content and Outcomes.

These categories provide a common base for analyzing and gaining a general profile. With the theological perspective (as an overlay) providing criteria, and the categories providing activities, I looked in the case studies for references to whatever theology or theologizing might be contained within them. The results are recorded on the grid at the conclusion of this essay.

I realized quickly that the reports contained few explicit references to God revealing himself, to human faith response or to church as a faith community. However, there were many references to behavioral involvement in what comprises the human reality of these mysteries that can rightly be classified as references to implicit theology and theologizing. It is my hope that this presentation will enable readers to recognize the theological richness which is contained in the Family Cluster Model.

Theologizing Results

Sponsorship. Organized church congregations sponsored nine of the (15) clusters reported. Two were initiated by interested families within a church setting, and another was sponsored by an agency with a church affiliation. Two clusters were devoid of a church context in its sponsorship. In most cases, the leaders of the clusters were either recognized ministers or persons active in church life. These references place the cluster experience within a church context; moreover, there is evidence in the majority of stories that the sponsoring groups and leaders considered this work an extension of their church ministry.

Membership. Families in the majority of case studies were clearly members of church congregations. This may explain partially why there is relatively little explicit reference to God, Faith and Church in the reports. It appears that conversion and initiation into a church community is presupposed and, therefore, is not a primary purpose of the cluster experience. The important point is that faith in God was clearly present in all but two cases, and belief in human community was present in all.

Purpose. The general purpose for having Family Clusters centered on building community within and among families. Again, none explicitly connected this purpose to building community with God (or building the community of the congregation), but the implication is that building community among member families is supporting community within the congregation, which is essentially a part of the congregation's faith response to God. This implication is explicit in several cases. In one, a sharing of the cluster experience with the entire congregation is part of the process. In two others the stated intent given is to create community within a Christian context. One further specifies this intent in terms of church characteristics such as worship, fellowship, education and ministry.

Objectives. The specific objectives of the clusters are those which the cluster model experience itself intends to bring about. The ones most frequently mentioned are: reflection, awareness, communication, sharing, affirmation, understanding, support, learning, decision-making, conflict resolution and acceptance of differences. These characteristics are recognized as being the substance of every personal relationship and are classified as references to implicit theology and theologizing. In two cases the specific objectives explicitly connected these with relationship with God, of which one states the intention to deepen awareness that each family is a part of the family of God; the other intends reflection on the God-like beliefs and values which are in family relationships. In both cases, the process and content dealt explicitly with the participants' relationships with God.

Process. The chart shows a large number of references to theologizing within the process of the cluster experience. This reflects the activity orientation of the process: it also shows that theology and theologizing can be present in activities. The activites identified as theological references are those that clearly involve the principle of a "God way of living." This principle as stated in the former theological perspective is that "life comes from persons being in union with other persons in such a manner that the uniqueness of each is created and nurtured." The process of every cluster reported is directed toward fostering identity and recognition for both individuals and families, while providing for the deepening of personal union at the same time.

The heart and foundation of the process is the contract which is part of every cluster. The extent to which it was carried out determined, in large measure, the success of the cluster as a whole. It established an agreement in and among families in terms of promise, commitment, and fidelity which is the very way God establishes personal relationships with human beings. Two clusters explicitly recognized the contracting as being like and part of God's covenant. Those clusters used Scripture to connect and deepen this belief.

The cluster activities were dominated by eating, singing, and playing which were all designed to build community; as such, they are classified as references to implicit theologizing. A number of the clusters included activities that explicitly included God and a faith response. These were designed into the process for the purpose of deepening faith with the motivation and inspiration which come from it. These activities were in the forms of worship services, blessings, prayers, Scripture readings, reflections, hymn singing and constructing religious symbols. Moreover, there is evidence that these kinds of activities were expected to continue to take place and to produce effect outside the cluster sessions.

There are two more references to the process which point out the model's theological character. One was its incorporated flexibility to accommodate the freedom and readiness levels of the participants, which existence is necessary for authentic faith response. The other is the references to the qualities that are seen as necessary in the leaders. Such qualities are described by one report as being: openness, willingness to learn, trust, facilitating the sharing of power, understanding, creativeness, and caring. These are recognizable as being desirable for those who minister in the name of God.

Content. The content of the clusters was primarily the lived experience of the participants which focused on the human experience of living as community rather than on the experiences of coming to initial faith in God and initiation into church community. This reflects the cluster pre-supposition of conversion and admittance into church community. It is the experiences of the participants that are shared, reflected, and discussed, especially in their relationship with one another. Much of this is done without explicit reference to God or faith and, as such, is classified as implicit on the chart. However, a number of clusters did incorporate explicit theological content in the forms of Scriptures, prayers, religious songs, study of the meaning of Christian feast days, the life of Jesus and the saints. This content had the role of providing insight and/ or inspiration for bettering the lived experience and, as such, was not usually the primary content of the cluster.

Outcomes. More than anywhere else it is in the outcomes of the cluster experience that theology and theologizing are revealed. Some outcomes can be classified as explicitly theological. These include the integration of daily experience with religious concepts/ beliefs, fellowship in a worshipping community, commitment to the church, deeper spirituality and relationship to God. Many outcomes are implicitly theological. All had to do with the enabling and facilitating of individual persons or families living in relationship. These outcomes were described in terms of self worth, self-esteem, identity, awareness, openness, care, trust and honesty; also, better communication, constructive problem resolution, deeper commitment, support, belonging, affirmation, and a deeper sense of community; furthermore, cooperation, enthusiasm, involvement, friendship and family bonding; and finally in all cases, the outcome of fun! Within a theological perspective, these outcomes clearly fit as being essential for community with God as well as for community with humans.

Conclusion

It appears to me that the primary purpose of the Family Cluster experience is to enable and nurture the personal and relational life of family members who belong to church communities, rather than enabling and nurturing new family members for participation in the church community. Family Clusters emphasize the response of individual men, women, and children to God, as God is present to and within each person. Clusters look to the uniqueness of the person, the growth and development of the person within nurturing relationships, the freedom and commitment needed for living personal relationships, the capacity and skills of personal communication, and the openness needed for change and growth. This can be contrasted to those types of family education or ministry approaches that are intended to encourage and nurture participation in the life of the larger church communities. These styles look more to the initiation into and sustenance in the common beliefs and practices of the church community and emphasize its sacraments, its history and traditions, its doctrines and its moral codes. The whole of faith life should include both, and a total program of family ministry would minister to both.

By responding to the personal/relational level, Family Clusters are responding to that level which is experiencing a dramatic increase in need. These days the cries from families are coming from hurts and stresses in their lives and relationships.

I hope that my assessment of the case studies, in terms of the inherent theologizing that takes place in them, will assure church leaders and pastors that the family needs being addressed in Family Clusters are solidly grounded in current theological perspective as legitimate faith life needs; and that the cluster approach can be a legitimate and effective church ministry activity. It presumes the existence of faith and belief and looks to enabling and facilitating faith living in the human community of the family.

Biographical Data

Robert P. Stamschror is a priest of the Diocese of Winona, MN. He has had extensive experience in religious education on parish, school, diocesan and national levels within the Roman Catholic Church.

He was representative for religious education in the Department of Education of the United States Catholic Conference of Bishops (USCC) and the Executive Secretary for the National Conference of Diocesan Directors of Religious Education—CCD (NCDD) from 1976-1979.

Currently he is a member of the pastoral team and faculty for Religious Studies at the College of Saint Teresa, as well as consultant to Saint Mary's Press in Winona, MN.

Address:

College of Saint Teresa
Winona, MN. 55987
(507) 454-2930

References to Theology and Theologizing in the Family Cluster Cases

*Cases with references in:		God revealing/Jesus Christ	Human Faith Response	Faith Community/Church
Church Sponsorship	explicitly			*****
That refer	to implicitly	*		******
Cluster Membership	explicitly	*	*	
That refer	to implicitly		*	*****
Cluster General Purposes	explicitly			*****
That refer	to implicitly	*		*****
Session Specific Objectives	explicitly	**	**	**
That refer	to implicitly		*	******
Learning Process	explicitly	******	***	*****
That refer	to implicitly	*********	********	*********
Cluster Content	explicitly	******	***	*
That refer	to implicitly	***	*****	********
Cluster Outcome	explicitly	*		*
That refer	to implicitly	***	*	******

INDEX of Books Used by Family Cluster Leaders

*Agard, Bonnie. *Family Cluster Resources*. Chicago: The Evangelical Covenant Church, 1978.

Anway, Carol Anderson and R. Daniel Fenn. *Family Enrichment Book*. Independence, MO: Herald Publishing House, 1979.

*Benson, Jeanette and Jack Hilyard. *Becoming Family*. Winona, MN: St. Mary's College Press, 1978.

Braga, Joseph and Laurie. *Children and Adults*. Englewood Cliffs, NJ: Prentice-Hall, 1976.

Briggs, Dorothy Corkville. *Your Child's Self Esteem*. Garden City, NY: Doubleday and Company, Inc., 1970.

Elkins, Dov Peretz. *Teaching People to Love Themselves*. Rochester, NY: Growth Associates, 1977.

Freed, Alvyn M. *TA for Teens*. Sacramento, CA: Jalmar Press, 1978.

Gordon, Thomas. *Parent Effectiveness Training*. New York: Wyden Books, 1970.

James, Muriel M. *Born to Love*. Reading, MA: Addison-Wesley Publishing Company, Inc., 1973.

Jenkins, Jeanne Kohl and Pam MacDonald. *Growing up Equal*. Englewood Cliffs, NJ: Prentice-Hall, 1979.

Johnson, David W. and Frank P. Johnson. *Joining Together*. Englewood Cliffs, NJ: Prentice-Hall, 1975.

Kantor, David and William Lehr. *Inside the Family*. San Francisco: Jossey Boss, 1975.

Larson, Roland S. and Doris E. Larson. *Value-Clarifying Exercises for Family and Church Groups*. Minneapolis: Winston Press, 1976.

Pfeiffer, J. William and John E. Jones. *A Handbook of Structured Experiences for Human Relations Training*. Vols. 1,2,3,4,5, San Diego, CA: University Associates, Inc., 1973-75.

*"The Purple Turtle" (A quarterly newsletter of Family Clustering, Inc.)

Satir, Virginia. *Peoplemaking*. Palo Alto, CA: Science and Behavior Books, Inc., 1972.

*Sawin, Margaret M. *Family Enrichment With Family Clusters.* Valley Forge, PA: Judson Press, 1979.

Simon, Sidney B., Leland W. Howe, Howard Kirschenbaum. *Values Clarification: A Handbook of Practical Strategies for Teachers and Students.* New York: Hart Publishing Co., 1972.

Simon, Sydney. B. *Meeting Yourself Halfway.* Niles, IL: Argus Communications, 1974.

Waschow, Louise *Experiential Exercises for Family Clusters.* Privately distributed from 416 Pine Street, Mill Valley, CA 94941.

*Items obtainable from Family Clustering, Inc.
P. O. Box 18074
Rochester, N.Y. 14618
(716) 244-0882 or
(716) 232-3530—(Ans. serv.)